THE CHINESE ARMY TODAY

D0140097

The Chinese Army Today is a unique and comprehensive study of all elements of Chinese military modernization, focusing on the ground forces to a degree not found in other contemporary work.

In 1999, the military modernization program of the Chinese People's Liberation Army that had been underway for 20 years increased in intensity and achieved a focus not seen in the previous two decades. Based primarily on Chinese sources, this book details the changes and key developments implemented since 1999 and puts them in the context of the many traditions that still remain.

Dennis Blasko uses first-hand observation of the Chinese military and three decades of military experience to weave many disparate threads from official Chinese statements, documents, and media reports into an integrated whole. This volume defines what forces make up the People's Liberation Army and examines in detail ground force organization and structure, personnel policies, doctrine and training, new equipment entering the force, and missions routinely undertaken in support of society.

This book will be essential reading for students of the Chinese military, Chinese politics, Asian regional security, and strategic studies in general.

Dennis J. Blasko served 23 years in the US Army as a military intelligence officer and foreign area officer specializing in China. He was an army attaché in Beijing and Hong Kong from 1992 to 1996, and previously served in infantry units in Germany, Italy, and Korea.

ASIAN SECURITY STUDIES
Series Editors:
Sumit Ganguly, Indiana University, Bloomington
and Andrew Scobell, US Army War College

Few regions of the world are fraught with as many security questions as Asia. Within this region it is possible to study great power rivalries, irredentist conflicts, nuclear and ballistic missile proliferation, secessionist movements, ethnoreligious conflicts and inter-state wars. This new book series will publish the best possible scholarship on the security issues affecting the region, and will include detailed empirical studies, theoretically oriented case studies and policy-relevant analyses as well as more general works.

CHINA AND INTERNATIONAL INSTITUTIONS
Alternate Paths to Global Power
Marc Lanteigne

CHINA'S RISING SEA POWER
The PLA Navy's Submarine Challenge
Peter Howarth

IF CHINA ATTACKS TAIWAN
Military Strategy, Politics and Economics
Edited by Steve Tsang

CHINESE CIVIL–MILITARY RELATIONS
The Transformation of the People's Liberation Army
Edited by Nan Li

THE CHINESE ARMY TODAY
Tradition and Transformation for the 21st Century
Dennis J. Blasko

TAIWAN'S SECURITY
History and Prospects
Bernard D. Cole

THE CHINESE ARMY TODAY

Tradition and transformation for the 21st century

Dennis J. Blasko

Routledge
Taylor & Francis Group

LONDON AND NEW YORK

First published 2006
by Routledge
2 Park Square, Milton Park, Abingdon, Oxon OX14 4RN

Simultaneously published in the USA and Canada
by Routledge
270 Madison Ave, New York, NY 10016

Reprinted 2006

Routledge is an imprint of the Taylor & Francis Group, an informa business

© 2006 Dennis J. Blasko

Typeset in Times New Roman by
Keystroke, Jacaranda Lodge, Wolverhampton
Printed and bound in Great Britain by
MPG Books Ltd, Bodmin

British Library Cataloguing in Publication Data
A catalogue record for this book is available from the British Library

Library of Congress Cataloging in Publication Data
A catalog record for this book has been requested

ISBN10 0–415–77002–5   ISBN13 9–780–415–77002–6 (hbk)
ISBN10 0–415–77003–3   ISBN13 9–780–415–77003–3 (pbk)

For my father,
Max J. Blasko

CONTENTS

ILLUSTRATIONS

Plates

(between pages 126 and 127)

Figures

TABLES

PREFACE

In March 2004, three colleagues suggested separately to me that I write a book on the Chinese People's Liberation Army (PLA). After much thought about how I could contribute to the field, reluctantly, I agreed. Because of important changes since 1999 and my focus on the PLA as it is today, I decided to write an introduction to the Chinese ground forces – something lacking in the recent literature.

This book is based primarily on Chinese sources. While Chinese government information on the PLA is often incomplete (and/or confusing), more data is now available through official and unofficial sources than could have been imagined 10 years ago. Though I nearly always ask for more, I credit the Chinese government for the efforts it has made in transparency over the past decade. May the Chinese leadership continue these trends as more information is likely to produce greater "mutual trust and understanding" than less information.

This book does not attempt to catalogue the many changes underway in non-Chinese forces throughout the region. Therefore, it is not a net assessment of military capabilities across the Taiwan Strait, nor is it a comparative study of the combat power of the PLA versus US forces or other militaries in Asia. This book also does not attempt to delve deeply into the political issues that could cause war in the region nor does it attempt to predict "red lines" one side or the other may cross that could lead to military action. Instead, it is intended to be a baseline for understanding the Chinese military and perhaps encourage future studies of issues only briefly mentioned here. I was able to incorporate data available through mid-July 2005. I am always willing to reassess my conclusions based on new information.

As I write, two generations of US Army China Foreign Area Officers are serving or have served in Afghanistan and Iraq. These superb soldiers understand the difficulty, complexity, danger, uncertainty, and sacrifice associated with modern war. Given the time, any one of them could have written this book better than I, but the opportunity fell to me while they performed their duty to their country elsewhere. Their experiences are always in my mind. My book is also intended to be a small contribution toward "mutual understanding" to avoid the misperceptions that could lead to an unnecessary armed conflict between the United States and China.

The Chinese Army Today does not answer all the questions about the Chinese military, rather it seeks to establish a foundation for future research as the PLA continues its "Long March" toward military modernization and transformation. I anxiously await others to build upon the groundwork presented in the following pages.

ACKNOWLEDGMENTS

I thank the many people who have read and commented on all or parts of the drafts of this book, among them are: Ken Allen, John F. Corbett, Jr., Dorothy Fontana, Harlan Jencks, Lonnie Henley, Cathy Johnston, Ron Montaperto, Ed O'Dowd, Susan M. Puska, Andrew Scobell, and David Shambaugh. In particular I thank Paul H.B. Godwin, Bud Cole, and Ellis Joffe for their encouragement, support, and guidance. Special thanks go to Ellis Melvin for his invaluable and unique support to this project. Susan Puska and Neal Sealock were especially helpful in sharing photographs. Any errors in the text, however, are my own.

ABBREVIATIONS

AAA	Anti-Aircraft Artillery
AMS	Academy of Military Sciences
AP	Associated Press
APC	Armored Personnel Carrier
ARF	Association of Southeast Asian Nations (ASEAN) Regional Forum
ATGM	Anti-Tank Guided Missile
AVIC-I	China Aviation Industry Corporation I
AVIC-II	China Aviation Industry Corporation II
CAS	Close Air Support
CASC	China Aerospace Science and Technology Corporation
CASIC	China Aerospace Science and Industry Corporation
CATIC	China National Aero-Technology Import and Export Corporation
CCP	Chinese Communist Party
CEIEC	China National Electronics Import and Export Corporation
CETC	China Electronic Technology Group Corporation
CGWIC	China Great Wall Industries Corporation
CMC	Central Military Commission
CNEC	China Nuclear Engineering and Construction Corporation
CNEIC	China Nuclear Energy Industry Corporation
CNGC	China North Industries Group Corporation
CNNC	China National Nuclear Corporation
COSTIND	Commission of Science, Technology and Industry for National Defense
CP	Command Post
CPMIEC	China Precision Machinery Import-Export Corporation
CRS	Congressional Research Service (US)
CSG	China South Industries Group Corporation
CSIC	China Shipbuilding Industry Corporation
CSSC	China State Shipbuilding Corporation
CSTC	China Shipbuilding Trading Company
DF	*Dong Feng* ("East Wind")

DZ	Drop Zone (for airborne operations)
ECM	Electronic Countermeasure
FBIS	Foreign Broadcast Information System
GA	Group Army
GAD	General Armaments Department (sometimes called the General Equipment Department, GED)
GLD	General Logistics Department
GLONASS	Global Navigation Satellite System (Russia)
GPD	General Political Department
GPS	Global Positioning Satellite system
GSD	General Staff Department
HJ	*Hongjian* ("Red Arrow")
HMMWV	High Mobility Multipurpose Wheeled Vehicle (or Humvee)
HN	*Hongying* (variously "Red Tassel" or "Red Cherry")
HQ	*Hongqi* ("Red Flag")
IFV	Infantry Fighting Vehicle
Il	Ilysuhin
IT	Information Technology (sometime followed by the word "application")
IW	Information Warfare
KMT	Kuomintang (Nationalist Party)
LSM	Medium Landing Ship
LST	Tank Landing Ship
LTD	Laser Target Designator
LZ	Landing Zone (for airmobile operations)
MD	Military District (also known as Provincial Military Command)
mm	millimeter
MND	Ministry of National Defense
MPS	Ministry of Public Security
MR	Military Region (also known as Military Area Command, MAC)
MRL	Multiple Rocket Launcher
MRO	Military Representative Office
MSD	Military Subdistrict
MSS	Ministry of State Security
MTEP	Military Training and Evaluation Program (also called the Outline for Military Training and Testing)
MUCD	Military Unit Code Designator
NCO	Noncommissioned Officer
NDMC	National Defense Mobilization Committee
NDU	National Defense University
NORINCO	China North Industries Corporation
NUDT	National Defense Science and Technology University (also known as the National University of Defense Technology)
PAFD	People's Armed Forces Departments

PAP	People's Armed Police
PGM	Precision-Guided Munitions
PKO	Peacekeeping Operation
PLA	People's Liberation Army
PLAAF	People's Liberation Army Air Force
PLAN	People's Liberation Army Navy
POL	Petroleum, Oil, and Lubricants
PRC	People's Republic of China
QW	*Qianwei* ("Vanguard")
RMA	Revolution in Military Affairs
RRU	Rapid Reaction (or Response) Unit
SAM	Surface-to-Air Missile
SARS	Severe Acute Respiratory Syndrome
SCO	Shanghai Cooperation Organization
SIPRI	Stockholm International Peace Research Institute
SOF	Special Operations Forces
SP	Self-Propelled
SRBM	Short-Range Ballistic Missile
Su	Sukhoi
SWAT	Special Weapons and Tactics
TO&E	Table of Organization and Equipment
UAV	Unmanned Aerial Vehicle
UI	Unidentified
UN	United Nations
US	United States
WWW	Worldwide Web (Internet)
WZ	*Wuzhuang* ("armed")

1

INTRODUCTION

Tiananmen Square. June 4th 1989. Lines of soldiers marching, firing in the dark. Burning armored personnel carriers. Civilians bleeding, dying, being carried away on carts. In the daylight after the assault, a lone civilian stops a column of tanks while the world watches on television.

Chicoms! Human wave attacks. Bugle calls in the night. Red flags waving. Peasant militia. Guerrillas swimming in a sea of the people. The largest army in the world.

These are the images of the Chinese army in the minds of many people throughout the world. While there is a kernel of truth in each image, the reality of the Chinese People's Liberation Army (PLA) today is quite different from the impressions of the past. Many traditions from the early days of the PLA remain, but just as many stereotypes are no longer valid as the PLA transforms itself into a smaller, more technologically advanced force. In numerous important ways, the Chinese army today is a vastly changed organization from a mere decade ago.

In the past several years, a number of books, studies, and articles have examined developments in the PLA Navy, PLA Air Force, and strategic missile forces, as well as addressed major themes in Chinese military modernization, such as strategic culture, civil–military relations, doctrine and strategy, information warfare, and the PLA's business empire.[1] The US government, through a series of annual reports to Congress from the Department of Defense and in congressional testimony and speeches by military, policy, and intelligence officials, also provides useful information about the PLA. The series of White Papers on National Defense issued by the Chinese government every two years since 1998 has become increasingly detailed and comprehensive.[2] However, compared to the other services and strategic issues, analysis of the Chinese army has been minimal.

This book attempts to fill that gap by focusing primarily on the Chinese ground forces, defined here as the Chinese "army" (active and reserve units), the People's Armed Police, militia, and airborne forces (though the airborne is actually part of the PLA Air Force), and placing these forces into the larger context of PLA transformation.[3] Many other texts describe in detail national-level organization, such as the Central Military Commission and four General Headquarters departments; this volume merely introduces these organizations and their general responsibilities in order to provide context for its examination of the ground forces.[4]

1

After an extremely short history of the "Red Army," the introductory chapter outlines traditional underpinnings of China's military transformation, identifies the components of the PLA's multifaceted, long-term modernization program, and briefly describes several themes which run through the book. Subsequent chapters answer the journalistic questions of what the PLA is (and what it is *not*), who makes up the PLA (conscripts, noncommissioned officers, officers, and civilians), where the PLA is located (order of battle) and what its missions are, how the PLA will fight (doctrine), what equipment it uses, how the PLA trains, and how it interacts with society. Information in the first six chapters builds the foundation for the discussion of PLA training and other activities found in the last chapters. The final chapter draws conclusions and addresses the legacy of Tiananmen. The text includes the *pinyin* for many important Chinese terms and alternative translations used mostly by the Chinese press in their English-language media (which often differ from the terminology used by foreign PLA-watchers). The book's journalistic "when" concentrates mainly on developments since 1998 and 1999, with the purpose to describe the Chinese army *as it is today* in the middle of the first decade of the twenty-first century.

This book does not dwell on history, either ancient or recent, nor does it analyze individual personalities to any extent. It also does not make judgments about many big questions, such as the military balance across the Taiwan Strait, the efficacies of foreign arms purchases or embargoes, etc., but should be useful to others in subsequent analysis of those topics. Though some professional PLA-watchers may find much of the information elementary, perhaps even long-time students of the Chinese military will discover something new. In brief, I have tried to write the type of book I would have liked to have read before becoming a US army attaché to China in 1992.

A short history of the "Red Army"

The "Red Army of Workers and Peasants" of the Chinese Communist Party (CCP) was established on 1 August 1927 during the Nanchang uprising led by Zhu De against the army of Nationalist Party (Kuomintang, KMT) led by Chiang Kai-shek. After a three-year period of cooperation with KMT to overcome warlord opposition throughout the country, beginning in 1924 and known as the "First United Front," the Chinese communists rose in revolt against the newly formed Nationalist government. The KMT suppressed this uprising and Zhu's small army retreated to the Jinggang mountains in Jiangxi province. There they were joined by other communist forces, including peasants and miners led by Mao Zedong, who had also been unsuccessful in his separate "Autumn Harvest Uprising." While in Jinggangshan, the communists formed "soviets" and began to exercise political control over the area. Not allowing the CCP any quarter, KMT forces initiated a series of "encirclement campaigns" to crush the guerrilla opposition. To escape the ever-tightening KMT noose, the communist forces broke out of the encirclement in October 1934 to begin their historic "Long March" that ended a year later in Yan'an in Shaanxi province.

Being the weaker military force at the time, guerrilla tactics predominated within the Red Army (with emphasis on speed, stealth, and stratagem), but there was always a number of professionally trained soldiers among the communists who advocated a shift to more conventional, regular-style military operations and organization. The vast majority of communist military leaders were also government leaders – a pattern that lasted for the four decades to follow.

The CCP continued its efforts to establish political control in Yan'an and nearby areas while under constant pressure from Chiang and KMT forces. The Japanese occupation of the northeastern provinces known as Manchuria, which had begun in 1931, created a new challenge to all of China. In 1937, the two Chinese forces joined once more, this time in opposition to Japan in a period that became known as the "Second United Front." After a shift to total war following the Marco Polo bridge incident of July 1937, the communists remained in their Yan'an stronghold where they persisted in exercising government functions while the KMT retreated to the city of Chongqing.

The Red Army established the "Eighth Route Army" and "New Fourth Army" to fight the Japanese. Through conscious decisions made by the communist leadership to obtain support of the Chinese populace, the Red Army's methods of operations among the common people of China were considerably different from the harsh policies of the warlord and the KMT armies. As the communists expanded their political control, Chiang once more began to exert military pressure to thwart their efforts. As a result, until the allied defeat of the Japanese in 1945, the KMT and CCP fought each other as much if not more than they fought the Japanese occupiers. Swift multipronged Soviet advances into Manchuria at the end of the war to defeat Japanese forces showed the vulnerability of that region of China, which soon became a communist stronghold.

By the middle of 1946 civil war had once again broken out in China. The Red Army had renamed itself the People's Liberation Army and took advantage of leftover Japanese weapons and equipment to rearm itself. With the communists controlling much of the countryside, the PLA initially waged a war of attrition against the KMT-held cities. Over the course of three years of fighting, the PLA employed not only guerrilla tactics but also conventional warfare to defeat the KMT, often in large-scale battles. After Chiang Kai-shek, the Nationalist government, and some two million followers fled to Taiwan, Mao Zedong declared that the Chinese people had stood up and established the communist People's Republic of China (PRC) on 1 October 1949.

A year later as American and South Korean forces approached the Yalu River, Mao committed "volunteers" from the PLA to enter North Korea to assist their communist brothers who had initiated a war on the peninsula in June 1950. Using infiltration and guerrilla tactics, the Chinese volunteers scored a number of striking successes against the United Nations forces, particularly those of the United States, from October to December. By July 1951, however, the situation had stabilized roughly along the 38th parallel, where the fighting had begun, and the war shifted to conventional, positional warfare waged for countless, bald hills across the peninsula. Over the next two years of fighting, the PLA was strengthened by an influx of modern weapons from the Soviet Union, and the newly formed Chinese navy and air force were integrated into the PLA. In the trenches of Korea the PLA learned the importance of firepower and combined arms operations to modern warfare. After the war and the volunteers' return to China, the PLA began its first attempt at military modernization along Soviet lines, but the domestic political upheavals of the Great Leap Forward at the end of the decade and the Cultural Revolution of the late 1960s and early 1970s derailed these efforts.

China's potential enemies also changed in this same time-frame as the KMT continued to persevere on Taiwan. Tensions in the worldwide communist movement arose after the death of Stalin. The Soviet Union withdrew its military and industrial advisers to China at the end of the 1950s. Friction increased to the point of nuclear threats and border skirmishes in the late 1960s. In the early 1970s China found itself facing a Soviet military buildup along its northern borders and in Mongolia. Previously, in 1962, it had clashed with India along its southern border in Tibet, and an area, the Aksai Chin, remained under contention. Also to China's south, as a result of the United States air campaign against North Vietnam, PLA air defense and engineer troops were dispatched to aid their communist neighbor. Beijing's strategic intention was to deter the United States from taking the war north to China. Furthermore, China conducted campaigns to regain islands from South Vietnam and maintained pressure against the KMT island strongholds off the Chinese coast. By the late 1970s, Beijing perceived the Soviet Union and its ally, Vietnam, as China's greatest strategic rivals, having reached political accommodation with the United States and mutual recognition in 1979.

In December 1978 at the Third Plenum meeting of the 11th Central Committee of the Chinese Communist Party, the Chinese government and CCP, now led by Deng Xiaoping, formally adopted a shift in national strategy to the development of the economy and discarded the "continuous revolution" of Mao's last years. China's commitment to achieving the "Four Modernizations" of "agriculture, industry, science and technology, and national defense" was the foundation for the period of reform to follow that continues to this day.[5]

On 17 February 1979, after a visit by Deng to the United States, the PLA initiated a "self-defense counterattack" to "teach Vietnam a lesson." In mid-March, Beijing announced it had achieved the objectives of its "punitive" invasion and withdrew PLA forces back to China. This brief campaign, fought using many of the tactics and methods from its Red Army and Korean War days, was the PLA's last large-scale operation against a foreign military in the twentieth century. The lackluster performance of the troops was a major impetus for pursuing a new round of military modernization, as advocated by Deng and other military leaders.[6] Artillery duels and small-scale operations along the China–Vietnamese border continued into the mid-1980s, and the PLA took advantage of the situation by rotating units and leaders into the region to give them a taste of combat.

The roots of military transformation

The Chinese military has been in the process of modernization and transformation for more than twenty-five years. Listed last among the "Four Modernizations," the subordination of military modernization to national economic development was a consistent theme throughout the 1980s and 1990s. This ranking was a rational strategic decision in a period of minimal external threat for a nation starting from a low economic base.

The prioritization of the elements of the "Four Modernizations" was central to the thinking of paramount leader Deng Xiaoping, who justified a long-term approach to military modernization by announcing the danger of major world war to be remote. In 1985, China's supreme military command organization, the Central Military Commission (CMC), led by Deng, declared the most likely military contingency China faced no longer was "early, major, and nuclear war" (as foreseen by Mao), but rather "local, limited war."[7] Because the threat of major war was low, a "bloated" PLA could take its time to reform, focusing first on downsizing its four million-plus force. But also, because a major threat was not imminent, it was not necessary for the Chinese government to sink vast sums of money and natural resources to modernize the PLA rapidly. In its early years PLA modernization, therefore, focused primarily on relatively inexpensive reforms such as personnel reductions, force restructuring, and doctrinal updates.

Moreover, for the first decade and a half of reform and military modernization in the PRC, Chinese leaders were content that the goal of peaceful reunification of Taiwan with the mainland could be accomplished sometime in the unspecified distant future. But by the fall of 1999, political developments on Taiwan had outrun Beijing's unchanging principles for reunification, and the Chinese leadership, then led by president of the PRC, general secretary of the CCP, and chairman of the Central Military Commission Jiang Zemin, determined China's military power needed to be perceived as more credible to prevent further steps toward Taiwan independence.[8] Thus, the decision was made to increase the pace and scope of military modernization in the 10th Five-year Plan (2001 to 2005) and beyond.

As part of the "Four Modernizations," the transformation underway in the PLA is part of the larger modernization process found in all of Chinese society. Many of the old methods of communist rule have been modified or discarded since 1979 to allow for market forces to take hold and raise the economic and technological level of the country. Yet, much of the *ancien régime* remains. Even while liberalizing economically and to a great extent socially, the Chinese Communist Party does not allow any challenge to its political control and has established an effective security apparatus to maintain its supremacy. Steeped in its traditions, the PLA remains the ultimate guarantor of the CCP. In many ways, the PLA's role in society is unchanged even while the army is in the midst of a major break from many practices of the past. Recognizing both the change and the continuity in the Chinese armed forces today is essential to understanding the strengths and weaknesses of the PLA at the beginning of the twenty-first century.

Elements of PLA modernization

From its beginning in the late 1970s and early 1980s, Chinese military modernization has been comprised of multiple component parts. A great deal of attention by the outside world over the past 15 years has focused on the equipment acquisition factor in Chinese military modernization. While the introduction of new equipment into the force is important, it is only one part of a much more complex modernization process, much of which focuses on the way the Chinese military mentally approaches war.

By the end of the last decade of the twentieth century, in addition to the obvious equipment acquisition component, other elements of Chinese military modernization included: (1) changes in force structure (for example, force reductions, changes to the way units are organized, and the creation of new units suited to the requirements of modern war); (2) changes in the personnel system (rebalancing numbers and roles of officers, noncommissioned officers, and enlisted personnel) and reduction of the period of conscription to two years for all soldiers; (3) doctrinal change to prepare the PLA to fight and win "Local Wars Under Modern High Technology Conditions"; (4) improvements in the frequency, content, and methods of military training; (5) transformation of the PLA logistics system to enable it to support "joint operations" (i.e., operations involving more than one service); (6) reorganization of the professional military education system in order to accommodate changes in force structure, personnel, and doctrine; (7) enhancing all soldiers' standard of living, pay, and life style; (8) reforming the structure and missions of the reserves and militia; and (9) modification to the PLA's interaction with society.[9] Following chapters address each of these elements and put them into the context of the themes summarized below.

The PLA and the party

Political loyalty has been the bedrock of the PLA since its founding in 1927. While in Yan'an in 1938, Mao Zedong wrote: "Every Communist must grasp the truth, 'Political power grows out of the barrel of a gun.' Our principle is that the Party commands the gun, and the gun must never be allowed to command the Party."[10] While party membership is not required of all members of the armed forces, to reach senior leadership positions officers must be party members. Many soldiers still join the PLA as a route to enter the party.

Political and ideological indoctrination has priority in training, and a complex system has been established down to the lowest levels of PLA units to maintain party fealty. In the 1990s, Jiang Zemin contributed his "Five Sentences on Army Building" to the development of the PLA: "Politically qualified, militarily competent, good work style, strict discipline, and adequate logistical support." Three of the "Five Sentences," which were prominently displayed on banners in military barracks all over China and repeated in the military media, address political reliability while the remaining two are concerned with purely military matters.

Later Jiang would add his theory of the "Three Represents" to party doctrine, and it, too, would become the topic of endless study, discussion, and reference in the military and all of Chinese society.[11] This formulation is the basis of political work at the beginning of the twenty-first century and is used to justify continuation of reforms in both the military and society as a whole.

The party–army relationship in the PLA is unlike the civil–military relationships found in most professional military organizations in other countries (where military personnel express loyalty to the state or constitution, not to a particular political party), yet the system that has evolved over the decades has proven to be effective for the Chinese situation. Civil–military relations are based on a close connection between the military and society that has been a hallmark of the PLA (with the glaring exception of the period from the Tiananmen massacre of 4 June 1989 until the end of martial law). In January 2004, the authoritative *People's Daily* newspaper carried a commentary stating: "The strong unity between the military and the civilian government and the strong unity between the military and civilian people have played an extremely important role in years of revolutions and construction in China, particularly over recent years."[12]

Military modernization and the national economy

One of the greatest examples of the PLA's loyalty to the party in the last 25 years has been the senior military leadership's acceptance of the relatively low priority afforded to military modernization in relation to other elements of the "Four Modernizations." At the turn of the new century, subordination of defense modernization to economic development was still a major principle in China's overall development program, but the emphasis had changed to *coordination* of economic development with military modernization. The Defense White Paper from 2000 reads:

> Developing the economy and strengthening national defense are two strategic tasks in China's modernization efforts. *The Chinese government insists that economic development be taken as the center, while defense work be subordinate to and in the service of the nation's overall economic construction.* Meanwhile, along with economic development, the state strives to enhance its national defense strength, to effectively support the armed forces in their efforts to improve their quality and to form a mechanism which enables national defense and economic development *to promote each other and develop in harmony.*[13]
>
> (emphasis added)

In February 2001, Jiang Zemin was quoted as saying:

> "We must persistently ensure unreserved coordination by building *a system of coordination* in the whole society to facilitate scientific or

7

technological development for national defense. We must combine military efforts with non-military efforts and build a structure full of vitality for developing science and technology for national defense" (emphasis added).[14]

The 2004 Defense White Paper did not include specific reference to "national economic development as the central task," but maintained the theme of "coordinated development of national defense and the economy, and to build modernized, regularized and revolutionary armed forces to keep the country safe" as a "major strategic task" of the Chinese Communist Party.[15] A *PLA Daily* editorial during the 2005 session of the National People's Congress, China's unicameral legislative body, echoed current PRC president, CCP general secretary, and Central Military Commission chairman Hu Jintao's reaffirmation of the central position of economic development in China's national strategy and the coordinated development of the national economy and military modernization:

> The army must rely on national economic and social development and integrate the national defense development into the national economic construction, attach importance to *the combined development* of national defense economy and social economy, military technology and civilian technology, and military talents and civilian talents, so as to create a fine situation in which national defense development and economic construction *would promote and coordinate* with each other. . . . The army must, *on the basis of national economic development*, speed up national defense development and its modernization drive, and strive to build itself into a force capable of ensuring China's security and protecting China's interests of development, effectively maintaining national security and unity, and safeguarding the smooth building of a well-off society in an all-round way.[16]
>
> (emphasis added)

Leadership organizations that combine the party, government, and military now exist from national to county level to coordinate economic and military development. At all echelons throughout the country, military and civilian sectors complement the development of each other; however, senior uniformed military leaders are primarily focused on military issues, while civilian leaders make political and economic decisions. For example, currently there are no uniformed members of the PLA on the CCP's highest policy-making organization, the nine-member Political Bureau Standing Committee of the Central Committee. The full Political Bureau has only two uniformed officers among its 24 members. The PLA does send some 250 to 275 delegates to the National People's Congress, which meets once a year in March for a full session of its approximately 3,000 members. While senior military officers inform their superiors of military needs, decisions on the size of the military budget are part of the larger governmental budgetary decision-making process.

The defense budget and the great unknown

Although there have been many requests for increased resources dedicated to the military, senior PLA leaders consistently have conformed to the party line on the issue of subordination of defense to national economic development. Partially as a result of their obedience to the party line, PLA generals have seen defense budgets increase significantly over the past decade as the Chinese economy continued to grow. In 1994, the officially announced defense budget amounted to about 52 billion *renminbi* (yuan) (about $6 billion in US dollars at the exchange rate of the time); in 1999, it had grown to 107.7 billion *renminbi* (about $13 billion); and in 2005 to about 248 billion *renminbi* (about $30 billion).[17] Chinese leaders and publications acknowledge these increases but frequently cite "improvements in soldiers' pay and living standards" as the main area toward which new funds are applied. Wages and subsidies for military members have indeed increased significantly over the past decade – from a very low start point – amounting to an 84 percent increase for officers and 92 percent for enlisted men.[18] Moreover, the nationwide emphasis on barracks construction and facility upgrades is readily apparent even to visitors to the country. These efforts have helped maintain morale among the troops, but they do not explain fully where all the additional money available to the PLA has gone. Nor does the Chinese government officially disclose the *total* amount of money used to fund all military-related activities.

Chinese spokesmen usually do not acknowledge sources of extrabudgetary income, for example, from other central government allotments or from local governments, that add significantly to the amount of money available to the PLA. The impact of "relative buying power" of less expensive Chinese-produced goods is also not factored into Chinese government figures. Therefore, foreign analysts often project an estimated range for the size of actual Chinese defense expenditures varying on the conservative side from two to three times the size of the officially announced budget to much larger (and less credible) estimates of up to ten or more times the officially announced numbers.[19] Whatever the true numbers may be, the Chinese military has a much larger pot of cash to spend on fewer troops than it did ten years ago. At the same time, personnel, equipment, and training costs for a more modern, technologically advanced military are also significantly higher than in previous decades.

Compared to other militaries, and particularly because of its size, the PLA is still relatively constrained in what it can do because of funds available. Therefore, a common theme for Chinese military leaders is *saving money* and finding innovative ways to conserve or better spend available funds.[20] A key to understanding many developments in the military modernization program is to look for how any specific policy saves the PLA, and thus the Chinese government and society, money.

Consensus, connections, and communications

Over many years, Chinese political and military leaders have reached a consensus concerning the need to fund the PLA adequately while not adversely affecting the growth of the civilian economy. Acceptance by the PLA leadership of the limited defense budget highlights another fundamental found in Chinese society applicable to the military: the need for consensus building in the decision-making process. The concept of consensus building is found throughout the military from the highest levels of command to grass-roots units.

Though an established line of command exists from chairman of the Central Military Commission down to company and squad level, except in tactical or emergency situations leaders prefer to discuss important decisions before they are made within small groups of commanders, political officers, and their deputies. Unit-level party committees are the focal points for the consensus-building process. These small leadership groups are formalized structures that meet on a regular basis to discuss a variety of issues appropriate for their level of authority. Using an iterative process of study and discussion, strategies are developed and specific actions are agreed upon by the group. The details and length of this process may vary at the different levels of command, but the objective is to reach common ground through active participation by all members of the group.

Another important group dynamic of special relevance to the PLA can be found in the Chinese concept of *guanxi*, or connections. *Guanxi* has been defined as a web of an individual's blood and/or social connections which define who he or she is and what he or she is capable of accomplishing without accounting for other resources available (such as money, access to technology, etc.).[21] For members of the military, both family and social *guanxi* may be important to a person's status, influence, promotion, and assignments.

Social *guanxi* in the military is formed among members of units, schools they have attended, hometowns, or provinces. The classic study of traditional PLA social *guanxi* was written by William Whitson, who, along with Chen-hsia Huang, outlined in exquisite detail the relationships among senior Chinese military leaders in five field armies from 1926 to 1968.[22] The personal connections among members of the field armies influenced the PLA for decades, causing both cooperation and conflict. Most observers believe the web of field-army connections became tenuous in the 1990s as many elder leaders died, and posit that military academy ties or hometown/provincial connections have risen in importance in the contemporary PLA. Naturally, *guanxi* also exists among members of large units, especially because the vast majority of officers and soldiers spend long periods, if not their entire terms of service, in just one unit. As in other militaries, PLA professional connections result in the formation of mentor–protégé relationships between senior officers and capable, trusted subordinates. *Guanxi* is a reality in the PLA, just as it is in all of Chinese society.

Another form of connections of value to understanding the PLA is the relationship of members of a particular organizational *xitong*, or system. These systems, sometimes called "stovepipes," are vertically integrated associations in government, industry, and other areas of society. Information is passed up and down the line within systems and generally not horizontally to other systems. Many *xitong* exist in the military, such as command, intelligence, logistics, education, each of which could further be broken down into smaller subsystems. The proliferation of modern communications and computer capabilities in the PLA has helped to break through the walls of some of these systems, but control of information remains an important consideration among members of individual *xitong*.

One of the most important systems in the PLA is the political system, which controls the propaganda or "publicity" (*xuanchuan*) subsystem. Many outsiders may be surprised by the degree the information revolution in China has been extended into the Chinese military. Although much specific data are still considered secret, and many books and journals are still categorized as for "internal use" (*neibu faxing*) or for "internal military use" (*junnei faxing*), more books, magazines, and electronic media are available than might be expected in an authoritarian regime, including websites for many military and defense industry newspapers and magazines. A growing number of independent, non-government-controlled publications of varying reliability are also available. Accordingly, care must be taken in discerning what is accurate, timely, and trustworthy. While the PLA propaganda system will repeat the "Big Lies" required of it by the party, many small details can be used to piece together a relatively accurate portrait of the PLA. Some speeches and essays also include criticism and realistic evaluations of the current state of affairs in some units. While generally maintaining positive attitudes, such criticism often provides insight into the actual conditions within the force.

Though they may bluster as the political situation requires, certain portions of the writings and speeches of many senior PLA leaders reflect a realism about the PLA that can easily be lost in a sea of meaningless, unverifiable statistics and seemingly endless political boilerplate. Often confusing are Chinese slogans and forms of shorthand, which commonly use catchy word combinations and numbers, to describe political campaigns and areas of leadership emphasis prevalent throughout Chinese society. New slogans arise as conditions and leaders change. Some slogans are discarded over time, others maintain their viability. For example, in the 1990s the term "People's War" no longer seemed relevant to many observers as Chinese military modernization was directed toward fighting future Local War(s).

People's War and Local War

For decades, the foundation of China's military thinking was based upon Mao's military thought (*junshi sixiang*) formulated in the 1930s and 1940s, which included the concept of People's War (*renmin zhanzheng*). Fundamentally People's War was intended to defend the Chinese mainland (i.e., a continental defense focused on ground forces) from a more advanced enemy by taking advantage of China's inherent strengths (a large population and vast land mass) while at the same time employing traditional Chinese fighting skills of speed, surprise, deception, and stratagem. In particular, Mao emphasized the role of man over weapons, mobilization of the population, and use of guerrilla tactics until enough combat power could be accumulated for a transition to conventional operations. As China's actual and potential enemies changed and its technological base improved, People's War

11

was modified to adapt to new circumstances. This process began in the 1950s with the change in terminology to "People's War Under Modern Conditions," and continued into the twenty-first century when the term "People's War Under Information Conditions" began to be used. In the Chinese military mind, this new construction reflects both the continuing applicability of People's War concepts to the conflicts China considers most likely and the recent advances in the world's communications and computer technologies.

A common misperception is that People's War *is* guerrilla war; however, guerrilla *tactics* are only a small component of People's War. Far more important is the role of the Chinese population, and the country's natural and industrial resources which are *mobilized* in times of emergency to support the Chinese armed forces. The concept of People's War still has a major impact on the thinking of Chinese military leaders today as they prepare for the most likely *condition for* conflict that China expects to encounter: Local War (*jubu zhanzheng*).

Local War was envisioned as a short, mid- to high-intensity conflict on China's borders or not far from the border region. The idea of "Local War" was modified to "Local War Under Modern High Technology Conditions" (*gaojishu tiaojianxia jubu zhanzheng*) as conditions changed in the late 1980s and 1990s, and then to "Local War Under the Conditions of Informationalization" (*xinxihua tiaojianxia jubu zhanzheng*) in the early twenty-first century.[23] In their efforts to "prepare for military struggle," Chinese strategists primarily focus on training to fight wars within a few hundred miles of their borders.

A related theme, still prevalent in PLA modernization, is China's portrayal of itself as the "weaker" military force in future conflicts. The PLA leadership unremittingly encourages its troops to develop new ways for the "weak to defeat the strong." Considering itself the less technologically advanced force, the PLA stresses using "existing equipment to defeat a high technology enemy." Even as large quantities of new equipment enter the force, constant emphasis remains on traditional PLA operational methods incorporating speed, mobility, stealth, deception, and use of stratagem to confuse or mislead the enemy. These methods depend more on Chinese ingenuity than expensive technology, though PLA planners also seek to exploit modern technologies to enhance their traditional operational methods.

Transformations – man and machine

In recent years, Chinese military leaders have summarized the main direction of PLA modernization with several slogans and descriptive phrases. Much has been written about the "two transformations" (*liangge zhuanbian*): transforming from a manpower-intensive, technologically backward force into a quantitatively smaller, qualitatively better, technologically advanced force; and transforming from preparing to fight a major defensive war in China to preparing to fight and win local wars on or near China's periphery.[24] Frequently "two historic tasks" are cited as underway to accomplish these transformations: "Mechanization" (*jixiehua*, changing from an army based on manpower and manual labor to one which uses vehicles and machines to improve its combat effectiveness) and "Information Technology (IT) application" (*xinxihua*, integrating modern communications, computers, software, training simulators, and command and control techniques into all levels of the force to make it more efficient, flexible, and responsive).[25] Though there may be debate about whether mechanization or information technology application should receive priority, in reality both objectives are being pursued in tandem, with some units moving faster in some aspects than others.

In 2003 and throughout 2004, the PLA officially endorsed the concept of promoting "military transformation with Chinese characteristics" or "Chinese-style military change" (*zhongguo tese junshi biange*) to build an "informationalized army" capable of fighting and winning an Information War.[26] This formula takes the concept of the Revolution in Military Affairs (RMA) and applies it to the Chinese situation *as the method by which China will build its new military force*. In fact, the Chinese terminology *zhongguo tese junshi biange* is sometimes translated by both Chinese and foreign sources as "the RMA with Chinese characteristics." This use of this terminology was codified by the Chinese government's official 2004 White Paper on National Defense, which has an entire chapter on the "Revolution in Military Affairs with Chinese Characteristics" that describes how the PLA is being transformed through structural, training, and logistics reform and political work.[27]

The PLA recognizes, however, that due to its relatively low technological base what is understood to be the RMA in other armies is not the same as what is happening in the PLA's military transformation.[28] In many ways, "advancing the RMA with Chinese characteristics" is the logical continuation of the PLA's multifaceted military modernization program that has been underway for 25 years, enhanced by a large dose of electronics, computers, and advanced communications technologies made available by advances in China's economic development. In a Chinese-style blending of the old with the new, there is no contradiction in the PLA's collective mind today about employing advanced weapons developed as part of the Revolution in Military Affairs to prosecute a Local War using principles of People's War.

The role of man in war

The Chinese military leadership understands the importance of properly training its soldiers to operate, maintain, and employ its newly acquired weapons and equipment. In the 1990s Jiang Zemin observed: "Though we're unable to develop all high-technology weapons and equipment within a short period of time, we must train qualified personnel first, *for we would rather let our qualified personnel wait for equipment than the other way round*" (emphasis added).[29] This principle has long been a fundamental component of PLA modernization and has been expressed by many senior officers in the period of reform. For many years it was easy to repeat these words as the PLA saw little new equipment enter the force; however, since 1999, when much more new equipment has been distributed to units, Jiang's emphasis – and its repetition by PLA leaders – indicates that the concept remains essential to the PLA modernization process.

"The role of man in war" has been a traditional point of emphasis and contention in the PLA. From the PLA's earliest days to the 1990s, debates raged over the relationship of man to weapons and which should have priority. As military technologies advanced through the twentieth century, Chinese leaders argued over the optimum balance between "Red" (being politically reliable, often using simple, guerrilla-style tactics and weapons) and "Expert" (taking a professional approach that employs regularized tactics and integrates technology into the force). After careful examination of the 1991 Persian Gulf War, the PLA leadership concluded its soldiers must now be *both* "Red" and "Expert."

Disruptions due to change and ground force leadership

A transformation as complex as this – one that also has been adjusted repeatedly to fit the domestic and external environment – cannot be accomplished in a short period of time. Moreover, along this protracted course of change, life in the forces can be extremely disruptive, resulting in periodic or localized drops in troop morale. Indeed, there have been indicators of morale problems in some units and resultant action to ameliorate such problems.[30]

If the Chinese military leadership had its way, the modernization process would likely continue for at least another decade or two before they would feel fully confident in the PLA's combat abilities. However, should the situation require it and the PLA be ordered by proper authority, the Chinese military will make use of whatever progress it has made to date and devise plans appropriate to its current conditions to accomplish the missions assigned. Likelihood of success will be dependent upon many factors, a large portion of which will be beyond the control of the PLA. But the PLA leadership is unlikely to tell its civilian leaders the PLA is not ready for battle.

The Chinese penchant for secrecy has resulted in much speculation by foreigners about the exact nature, extent, and objectives of Chinese military modernization. Since the late 1990s, the Chinese army has undergone as much change as the other service arms of the PLA. The changes to the largest segment of the PLA are important because ground force officers still dominate the senior levels of the uniformed Chinese military leadership, though this situation is gradually beginning to change. Many high-ranking army officers, whose formative years were spent in strictly ground force operations, bring with them a way of thinking that until recently may not have been exposed to some of the intricacies of modern, joint warfare involving land, air, sea, space, and electromagnetic components. This ground force-oriented approach to war is also colored by the PLA's last military campaign against a foreign foe, the Vietnamese in 1979, and sporadically through the early and mid-1980s along China's southern border. However, doctrinal changes since 1999 make single-service, land-based operations an exception to the general rules envisioned for future conflicts. And even conservative ground force leaders now accept this fact.

The remainder of this book examines the developments in Chinese army modernization and transformation since 1999. Though much has been accomplished, many hurdles remain. For interested observers, the first step in the Long March to understanding the PLA is to define exactly what the People's Liberation Army is, and what it is not.

2
WHAT IS THE PLA?

Visitors to China may rightly be confused by the number of people they see on the streets wearing military-looking uniforms. People in various shades of green, blue, beige, and camouflage are everywhere. A possible conclusion is that these uniforms are all part of the Chinese army – after all, it's the largest army in the world. In fact, in addition to military personnel who wear uniforms both on and off duty, as in most countries, police and paramilitary forces wear uniforms. Unlike some other countries, however, many government officials who have non-military or security functions, such as in the legal, transportation, and health and sanitation systems, also may wear military-appearing dress. Moreover, parts of military uniforms, which are relatively cheap and sturdy, are available for sale to civilians, although purchase of military insignia requires presentation of proper identification. Green military overcoats in particular are popular among the poor. The problem of identifying who is who wearing the many different uniforms underlies an important question – just what exactly is the People's Liberation Army? In order to understand the role of the PLA in contemporary Chinese society, it is just as important to understand what the PLA is *not*.

The Chinese security apparatus

A variety of Chinese government entities are tasked with domestic security and external defense missions. An overarching term for the entire spectrum of the official Chinese civilian police, government security forces, and military forces is the Chinese security apparatus.[1] These forces include the Ministry of Public Security (MPS), the Ministry of State Security (MSS), and the Chinese armed forces consisting of the PLA, People's Armed Police (PAP), and militia. While some of the functions of the individual entities in the security apparatus overlap, their primary and secondary missions and chains of command are different. The forces that make up the official government security apparatus may be categorized as civilian, paramilitary, or military organizations.[2]

Furthermore, an offshoot of China's economic success and rising crime rates has been the creation of *private* security companies to guard construction sites, businesses, residential areas, and especially banks and armored cars transferring cash. These private security companies often recruit demobilized soldiers as guards, or transient peasants who have come to the city to earn money. Because of the availability of military uniform parts, personnel in many security companies may wear bits and pieces of uniforms to present an official-looking appearance. They may also practice marching and other military drills, but basically stand static guard duty on perimeters and entry points, and must call for the police in emergencies. Some private security forces, such as bank and armored car guards, may be armed. But they are not part of China's official security structure.

The Ministry of Public Security and the Ministry of State Security

Civilian police and security forces responsible to the Chinese government's State Council include the Ministry of Public Security (*gong'an bu*) and the Ministry of State Security (*guojia anquan bu*). The MPS, as its name implies, is "in charge of public security in the country"; i.e., domestic law enforcement operations. A main function of the MPS is to "coordinate the action against serious cases and turmoil and major public security incidences . . ."[3] Approximately 1.7 million MPS police officers (*renmin jingcha*) are found throughout China.[4] Chinese police have many functions including domestic patrol, traffic control, detective, anti-crime, anti-riot, and anti-terrorism. In 2001, the MPS issued an order for major cities to establish an anti-riot force of no less than 300 personnel, or 200 for capitals of provinces.[5] Police anti-riot units often are equipped with armored cars or armored personnel carriers and sophisticated small arms. These special units, often dressed in black, look and operate like SWAT teams in police forces throughout the world.

The majority of civilian police wear blue uniforms – a fairly recent change from the drab olive-green uniforms of previous years, which made them look even more like soldiers than they do today. Some MPS officers wear civilian clothes when in undercover roles. The civilian police force has its own system of schools for training, a unique set of ranks and insignia, and a chain of command that goes from neighborhood stations (*paichusuo*) up through local government and provincial levels to Beijing. While other elements of the security apparatus may assist the police, MPS officers have arrest authority and generally take the lead in domestic and criminal operations.

The Ministry of State Security is the Chinese government's main domestic and international intelligence organization. Officially, the MSS is responsible for

counter-espionage work, preventing, holding in check and combating illegal criminal activities endangering China's state security and interests in accordance with law, defending state security, maintaining social and political stability, guaranteeing socialist construction, publicizing and educating Chinese citizens to be loyal to the motherland, maintaining state secrets, state security and interests.[6]

MSS officers routinely do not wear uniforms in the performance of their duties, which often require stealthy activities such as surveillance of Chinese citizens as well as foreigners. The MSS system extends from the national level down to offices subordinate to provincial and local governments. MSS officers are basically "secret police" for internal matters and spies and counterintelligence agents for external purposes.

The Ministry of Public Security and Ministry of State Security are civilian systems which report to the State Council headed by the premier.[7] Uniformed military officers *are not* involved in this chain of command. Military units, as well as the paramilitary People's Armed Police and militia (see next section), may cooperate with the police under certain circumstances, but will do so after collective decisions are made by government, military, and party authorities.

The Chinese armed forces

The Chinese armed forces (*wuzhuang liliang*) are responsible to a different chain of command than the MPS and MSS that culminates in the national level Central Military Commission (CMC, *zhongyang junshi weiyuanhui*). According to the PRC Law on National Defense adopted on 14 March 1997, the Chinese armed forces have three major components, two of which are considered paramilitary forces:

- Active and reserve units of the Chinese People's Liberation Army (*zhongguo renmin jiefangjun*)
- Chinese People's Armed Police Force (*zhongguo renmin wuzhuang jingcha budui*)
- People's militia (*renmin minbing*)

The PLA is a military force composed of both active duty (*xianyi budui*) and reserve units (*yubeiyi budui*) primarily responsible to defend China from external threats, while the PAP and militia are paramilitary organizations. By law and definition, the PAP is *not* part of the PLA. The PAP is further different from the PLA in that it has a dual command structure that includes both the CMC and the State Council through the Ministry of Public Security. Likewise, the State Council is also in the militia's chain of command (through local government bodies).[8]

The three individual components of the armed forces each wear similar, but distinct uniforms, and have similar organizational and rank structures; they undergo similar basic training, but have separate systems for promotion, education, and training. Nevertheless, there is cooperation among the systems. For example, basic regulations apply to both the PLA and PAP; often senior PLA leaders are assigned to top positions in the PAP. Moreover, the PLA may assist in training the militia. Missions for the three components overlap, but different priorities are assigned to each force.

According to the National Defense Law, the missions for the Chinese armed forces are defined as:

- The active units of the Chinese People's Liberation Army are a standing army, which is mainly charged with the defensive fighting mission. The standing army, when necessary, may assist in maintaining public order in accordance with the law. Reserve units shall take training according to regulations in peacetime, may assist in maintaining public order according to the law when necessary, and shall change to active units in wartime according to mobilization orders issued by the state.
- Under the leadership and command of the State Council and the Central Military Commission, the Chinese People's Armed Police force is charged by the state with the mission of safeguarding security and maintaining public order.
- Under the command of military organs, militia units shall perform combat-readiness duty, carry out defensive fighting tasks, and assist in maintaining the public order.[9]

Thus, the PLA, both active and reserve units, is primarily responsible for the external defense of China, but has the secondary mission of domestic security *in accordance with the law.* By including the terminology "in accordance with the law," the National Defense Law implies that the civilian government can call on the PLA to assist in domestic security operations in exceptional circumstances, but the PLA itself does not have the authority to decide unilaterally to perform the functions of an internal security organization.

In contrast, the primary mission for the PAP is domestic security, but it, too, has a secondary mission of local defense in wartime. The militia, like the PLA, also has the primary duty of external defense and also may *assist* in maintaining domestic security. It is possible, depending on the local conditions, to see civilian police forces operating in conjunction with PLA, PAP, or militia forces. In such instances of domestic law enforcement activity, the local police forces have primary responsibility for arrests and detainment, while the PLA, PAP, and militia provide

Table 2.1 China's security apparatus[10]

Force	Type	Primary mission	Secondary mission	Chain of command
MPS	Civilian	Law enforcement/ domestic security		State Council
MSS	Civilian	Counter-espionage/ intelligence	Domestic security	State Council
PLA	Military	External defense	Domestic security	CMC
PAP	Paramilitary	Domestic security	External defense	CMC and State Council
Militia	Paramilitary	External defense	Domestic security	CMC and State Council

backup support. A summary of the components of the Chinese security apparatus and their missions is found in Table 2.1.

The People's Liberation Army

The name "People's Liberation Army" reflects the ground-force orientation of the modern Chinese military from its earliest days, beginning in 1927. The PLA includes the Chinese army (or ground forces), PLA Navy (PLAN), PLA Air Force (PLAAF), strategic missile forces (known as the Second Artillery), and reserve units for each component. The exact number of personnel estimated in the PLA varies according to sources. For example, the Chinese 2004 White Paper on National Defense states the total size of the PLA to be 2.3 million, while the International Institute of Strategic Studies estimates "some 2,255,000."[11] Official public Chinese documents do not specify the numbers of personnel in the army, navy, air force, or Second Artillery. The International Institute of Strategic Studies estimates the army to number about 1,600,000 personnel, the PLA Navy approximately 255,000, the PLA Air Force about 400,000, and the Second Artillery roughly 100,000. In addition to the active duty numbers, reserve forces are estimated to number around 800,000.[12]

An unknown number of uniformed PLA civilians (*wenzhi ganbu*) is included on the rosters of active duty units, a practice which China acknowledges is different from the method of counting active duty forces in other countries.[13] Uniformed PLA civilians perform a variety of non-combat functions, similar to civilians working for other militaries. (See Chapter 3 for additional detail about PLA civilians.)

The PLA ground force (or army) is composed of numerous branches or arms (*bingzhong*) and support units:

- Infantry, divided into motorized (using trucks), mechanized (using wheeled or tracked armored personnel carriers and includes some amphibious mechanized units), and mountain units.
- Armored, with both tank and mechanized infantry units.
- Artillery, using both towed and self-propelled artillery, multiple rocket launchers, anti-tank guns and missiles, and conventionally armed surface-to-surface missile units.
- Air defense, including anti-aircraft artillery (AAA) and surface-to-air missile (SAM) units (army formations with a combination of AAA guns and SAMs are called "air defense" units; the PLA Air Force also has air defense troops armed with large caliber AAA guns and SAMs that reach to longer ranges and higher altitudes than those found in the army).
- Army aviation, primarily using helicopters, but also with a few small fixed-wing aircraft.
- Engineers, including combat and construction, pontoon bridge, camouflage, and water supply units.

- Chemical defense, including flame thrower and smoke generating units.
- Communications, both mobile and fixed.
- Electronic warfare, including electronic countermeasure (ECM) units.[14]
- Logistics, including supply (quartermaster), petroleum, oil, and lubricants (POL), medical, and transportation units including both truck and ship units.
- Armaments units, responsible for equipment maintenance, repair, and ammunition storage.

In the 1990s, special operations forces (SOF) were created to add new capabilities and augment existing reconnaissance units. SOF units are small, highly trained, specially equipped elite units tasked with accomplishing difficult and sensitive tasks, such as long-range infiltration, reconnaissance, intelligence collection, and strike missions including anti-terrorist actions. The majority of Chinese SOF units likely have capabilities similar to commando or US Army Ranger units, but not US "Green Beret" or Special Forces. (In addition to army SOF units, special operations units are also found in the PLA Air Force airborne and PLA Navy marine forces.) Other new "high technology" units have also been formed (such as electronic warfare and information warfare units), as well as psychological warfare units.

Forces are further categorized as "main force units" that may be dispatched throughout the country and local forces responsible for defense of the areas in which they are stationed. Local forces include combat units (infantry, armor, artillery, or AAA), border (frontier) and coastal defense units, reserve and militia units, as well as supporting logistics and armaments units. The PLA ground forces are structured in formations known as group army (*jituan jun*, usually considered equivalent to a western corps level organization), division (*shi*), brigade (*lu*), regiment (*tuan*), battalion (*ying*), company (*lian*), platoon (*pai*), and squad (*ban*). Units from squad to battalion size are sometimes called *fendui* or elements, while the term *dadui* refers to groups or regimental-size organizations. The term *budui* can apply to units ranging in size from regiment to group army.[15]

PLA force reductions

In September 2003, chairman of the CMC Jiang Zemin announced a reduction of 200,000 personnel in the size of the PLA to be completed by 2005. The majority of personnel reductions are expected to be felt by officers and headquarters units, with the army, as the largest service, likely to bear the brunt of the impact. Thus, by the middle of the first decade of the twenty-first century, the PLA should have roughly 2,300,000 personnel or less in its active duty ranks (with the ground forces around 1,500,000). The size of the reserve force may grow slightly while the active force is reduced. If the PLA did not use the unusual practice of including its civilian personnel on its active rolls, by creating a separate accounting category for civilians outside the active force, the nominal size of the PLA could undergo a further significant reduction without any effect on its combat capabilities.

Previously, in September 1997, Jiang announced a 500,000-man cut that was conducted over a three-year period ending in 2000. In that round of reductions, the army was cut by about 19 percent (or about 418,000 personnel), while the navy and air force were both reduced by about 11 percent, which due to their smaller sizes amounted to far fewer people.[16] To achieve these cuts, the army eliminated three group army headquarters, deactivated over a dozen divisions, downsized about 30 divisions to brigades, transferred 14 divisions to the PAP, and transformed a division in Guangzhou province into a marine brigade in the PLA Navy.[17] Some units, which had belonged to headquarters that were eliminated but were not themselves deactivated, were transferred to other headquarters. Variations of some of these themes have been repeated in the 200,000-man reduction of the first decade of this century.

PLA reserve units

The PLA reserve unit force as known today was established in 1983.[18] The majority of personnel in reserve unit are civilians, many of whom have been demobilized from military service. Technical specialists, who have not previously served on active duty, may be specifically recruited into the reserves as unit needs dictate. All reserve units also have a backbone of active duty military cadre. After 1996, military ranks were given to reserve officers for the first time and more officers were recruited from active service.[19] Reservists range in age from 18 to 35 and are categorized as Category One or Two based on their age and "military qualities" (*junshi sushi*).[20] Military qualities presumably include education levels, prior military service, military training received, and technical skills.

Like the active duty ground forces, reserve units have undergone significant restructuring in the years following 1998. Reserve units are organized into divisions or brigades based in single provinces, autonomous regions, or centrally administered cities, with subordinate regiments, battalions, companies, and platoons. Reserve divisions and brigades are classified as infantry, artillery, and AAA. Unlike the active PLA, the reserves have no organizational level above division, i.e., no reserve group armies exist. Several reserve chemical defense, engineer, and communications regiments also are found in its order of battle. Since 1999, each Military Region has formed a reserve logistics support brigade capable of providing logistics support in the field to both active and other reserve units. Some reservists, particularly in the PLAN, PLAAF, and Second Artillery, are tasked to act as individual replacements for personnel in active duty units.

In peacetime, reserve units come under the command of provincial Military District headquarters or the garrison commands found in the four municipalities under the State Council, Beijing, Tianjin, Shanghai, and Chongqing. In war, reserve units may be assigned to and commanded by active units or operate independently. Over the past five years, reserve units have begun training with active duty forces, something that had not been attempted previously. Coordinated training among active forces, reserve units, and militia forces is slowly taking hold throughout the country. PLA active and reserve units and militia forces also commonly cooperate with units from the People's Armed Police to conduct disaster relief operations in all parts of China.

The People's Armed Police

The People's Armed Police was formed in 1983 from elements of the PLA's border patrol and internal security units, as well as units from the Ministry of Public Security. The total PAP force currently is estimated to be as large as 1.5 million.[21] It is composed of several different types of units, each with specific tasks. Internal security units (*neiwei budui*) comprise the largest portion of the PAP and are organized in division-size elements (known as *zongdui*, or "contingents") in each province, autonomous region, and centrally controlled city (Beijing, Tianjin, Shanghai, and Chongqing).[22] The 14 PLA divisions transferred to the PAP during the 500,000-man reduction of the PLA in the late 1990s perform internal security functions, and as a result some provinces have more than one internal security *zongdui* present. In time of war, internal security units can function as light infantry in local defense missions in conjunction with the PLA. PAP internal security forces are estimated to number about 800,000, or over half the total PAP strength.[23] The PAP also has border security forces (*bianfang budui*) found throughout the country at ports and airports and on China's land and sea frontiers. Other PAP units guard China's forests (*senlin jingcha budui*), hydropower facilities (*shuidian budui*), gold mines (*huangjin budui*), and perform fire-fighting (*xiaofang budui*) and road transportation construction (*jiaotong budui*) functions. PAP units also perform guard duty in China's civilian prison system and provide personal protection services for some senior government officials.

PAP forces wear different uniforms and insignia from the PLA, but have a similar rank structure and obey PLA general regulations. The PAP also has its own system of education and training institutions separate from the PLA. New soldiers for the PAP are conscripted at the same time, from the same civilian population pool, using the same procedures as PLA conscripts, though they are trained in PAP, not PLA, basic training units.[24]

Some sources, both foreign and Chinese, sometimes incorrectly and inaccurately call PAP personnel or units "military police." The term "military police" implies that these forces are part of the PLA, which, by Chinese law, the PAP is not. A better term would be "paramilitary police." Many observers, both foreign and Chinese, cannot distinguish the difference between PLA and PAP units and do not understand the difference between each organization's missions. Photographs are often published that misidentify PLA personnel as PAP, or PAP as PLA. Confusion in identification can result in misperceptions about the actual responsibilities of these separate forces. PLA soldiers performing "military police" functions wear PLA uniforms and have authority only over members of the PLA. (See discussion of garrison commands in "Local commands" section, pp. 34–35.)

The militia

The militia is "an armed mass organization not released from production,"[25] which basically means that the militia is composed of civilians who work in civilian jobs and are organized into military formations. According to the Military Service Law, "male citizens from 18 to 35 years of age who are fit for military service, excluding those enlisted for active service, shall be regimented into militia units to perform reserve service." The militia is divided into two categories, the primary (*jigan minbing*) and the ordinary militia (*putong minbing*):

- The primary militia is defined as "a selected group of militiamen under the age of 28, including soldiers discharged from active service and other persons who have received or are selected for military training." The primary militia receives training "in militia military training bases of administrative areas at the county level" for 30 to 40 days.[26] Additionally, "the primary militia may recruit female citizens when necessary."
- The ordinary militia is composed of "other male citizens belonging to the age group of 18 to 35, who are qualified for reserve service."

Militia units are found in "rural towns and townships, administrative villages, urban sub-districts, and enterprises and institutions of a certain scale." Personnel to man militia units are drawn from rural areas, factories, research institutes, and commercial enterprises; militia personnel may have served in the PLA or PAP and have been demobilized, but prior service is not required. Some Chinese workers in foreign-owned enterprises may be members of the militia, and militia units may be found in some foreign-owned companies.[27]

By definition, the militia is a vast organization. The 2004 Defense White Paper acknowledged 10 million primary militia members, but did not estimate the number of ordinary militia members.[28] In prior years, in some places militia rosters were simply lists of names and any actual training conducted was problematic. Currently, the emphasis is on adjusting the size, in particular reducing the size of the ordinary militia, and modifying the roles of the militia so it can better support the PLA in time of war.

The militia assists the PLA by performing security and logistics functions in war. Militia units are organized into infantry, anti-aircraft artillery, anti-aircraft machine-gun, man-portable air defense missile, artillery, communications, chemical defense, engineering, and reconnaissance units. Militia units are especially important to mobilize land, sea (or river), and air assets to augment the PLA's transportation capacity in times of emergency. The militia has also been assigned the task of repairing civilian infrastructure, such as roads, bridges, railroads, electric power plants, or communications facilities, damaged during attacks on China. To accomplish its new missions the militia has formed many thousands of "emergency" or "high technology" units, including some that have been organized to provide information warfare support. In 2002, Chinese leaders began emphasizing the role of the "Urban Militia" in the defense of China. Rapid mobilization and response are stressed in organization and training utilizing all forms of China's modernized communication system.

Like the PLA, the militia may also be used in domestic security roles. In December 2003, the Ministry of Public Security Central Committee for Comprehensive Management and the PLA General Staff Department's Mobilization Department issued a joint circular on the militia's role in "safeguarding the public order." *In accordance with the law*, and under the command of the People's Armed Forces Departments (see p. 35), the militia is tasked to:

- organize and carry out joint defense and protection of roads, to safeguard factories, mines, villages, waterways, and power facilities, and to handle regional guard duties;
- help the public security departments strike at all kinds of criminal offenses, to restore peace and order in chaotic areas and places, and to maintain public order;
- guard important targets, and to defend the country and protect the people's life and properties; to participate in dealing with sudden group incidents (i.e., demonstrations and riots); and to coordinate with the troops and public security departments to strengthen administration of the border regions and protect the security of the frontiers.[29]

In performing the missions indicated above, the militia would act in support of local public security forces and would assume such roles only if requested by local authorities in conjunction with the military chain of command.

Reserve forces versus reserve units

Before concluding the discussion on the components of the Chinese armed forces, a definition of the term "reserve force" may be helpful to reduce the confusion it sometimes engenders. The terms *yubei liliang* or *houbei liliang*, translated as "reserve force(s)," are often used at the macro-level to describe China's entire part-time civilian, uniformed force, including *both* PLA reserve units (*yubeiyi budui*) and militia units (*minbing*). For example, in the 1990s, as described above, *the reserve force* (both reserve units and the militia) underwent a series of adjustments and reforms. In particular, "size control" was identified as a major topic with the goal of making the reserves "more scientific and rational in scale and more commensurate with quality building as well."[30]

At the tactical, operational, and strategic levels of war, the terms *yubei* or *houbei* may also be used as an adjective to describe reserve, alternate, or emergency forces, locations, or equipment that are not committed to the current battle, but are being held by a commander for employment when necessary. In this case, PLA reserve units or militia units, as well as active PLA units, could act as reserve forces.

National level command authority

The national level command structure for the PLA consists of approximately a dozen major organizations, divided roughly into three levels (see Figure 2.1), most with headquarters located in Beijing.

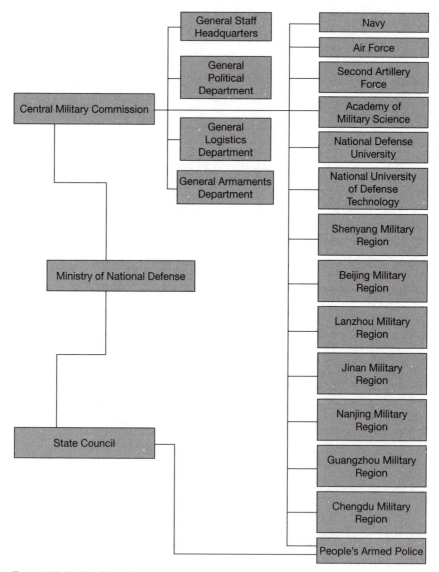

Figure 2.1 National-level organizations

Source: *PLA Daily* online at http://english.pladaily.com.cn/special/strength/content/index.htm

The supreme command and leadership organization for the Chinese armed forces is the Central Military Commission.[31] The CMC is both a Chinese Communist Party and a government organization – technically it is two separate entities, established by both the state and party constitutions, which in practice are identical.[32] The size and composition of the CMC have varied over time and there are no formal parameters for inclusion on this body; only the names of the positions of "chairman, vice chairmen, and members" are identified in Article 93 of the PRC constitution. Earlier articles (62, 67, and 80) give the state president and National People's Congress power to proclaim martial law or a state of war and to issue mobilization orders, so it would seem likely that the PRC president should always be on the CMC. Article 22 of the party constitution requires the party Central Committee to select members of the CMC, thus giving the CCP's highest decision-making organ control of the CMC and enforcing "party control of the gun."

In reality, the CMC is the formal organization composed of China's highest civilian leader(s) and most senior uniformed military officers, all of whom are party members. It exercises command of the Chinese armed forces and determines national defense policies (such as the size and composition of the armed forces, planning priorities, sources for major foreign equipment purchases, etc.). The ranking member of the CMC is the chairman, currently PRC president and party general secretary Hu Jintao, who assumed this position in September 2004. Hu's predecessor, Jiang Zemin, held on to this position for two years after he retired from his other government and party positions, while Hu was senior vice-chairman. (Before Jiang was promoted to chairman of the CMC in 1989, Deng Xiaoping likewise had held this position for several years after giving up other official duties.) Neither Jiang nor Hu had any experience in the uniformed military before assuming their positions on the CMC.

The CMC chairman is assisted by several vice-chairmen. Three of the most senior PLA officers now serve as vice-chairmen, generals Guo Boxiong, Cao Gangchuan, and Xu Caihou, but the number of vice chairmen is not permanent. A secretariat position is sometimes created between the vice-chairmen and members. The number of members of the CMC may vary, but usually includes at least the heads of the four General Headquarters Departments (see pp. 28–30). Also in September 2004, when Hu became CMC chairman, the commanders of the PLA Navy, Air Force, and Second Artillery were added to the CMC as members. The expansion of the CMC to include the service chiefs was generally regarded as a move to increase "jointness" in the PLA (i.e., to enhance the ability of the four services to operate together), and also as a result of the importance of preparing military options for the Taiwan scenario. Most campaigns directed toward Taiwan would likely see navy, air, or missile forces in dominant roles, especially in the early stages of an operation.

The CMC vice-chairmen sit on the State National Defense Mobilization Committee (*guojia guofang dongyuan weiyuanhui*), a party–army–government leadership system that extends down to county level to coordinate mobilization of personnel and resources in times of emergency, to integrate military and civilian economic development, and to oversee civil air defense and national defense education for the civilian population. The CMC also directs the work of the People's Armed Forces Committee (*renmin wuzhuang weiyuanhui*) system, which supervises conscription/recruitment and demobilization of personnel for the armed forces. The CMC has a small staff to assist in holding meetings, managing projects, and conducting research. It holds formal meetings of its membership and may invite other military or government leaders to attend "expanded meetings." A normal function of the chairman of the CMC is to promote senior PLA officers.

The four General Headquarters Departments

The CMC sets policies and directions which are executed by the four General Headquarters Departments: the General Staff Department (GSD, *zongcanmou bu*), General Political Department (GPD, *zongzhengzhi bu*), General Logistics Department (GLD, *zonghouqin bu*), and General Armaments (or Equipment) Department (GAD, *zongzhuangbei bu*). The GSD is led by the chief of the General Staff (*zongcanmou zhang*), while the senior officers in the other general departments are known in English as "directors," with variations in their Chinese titles (*zongzhengzhi zhuren* for director of the GPD; *zonghouqin bu buzhang* for director of the GLD, and *zongzhuangbei bu buzhang* for director of the GAD). All have a number of deputies who oversee various portfolios from their department's functions, along with political commissars and their deputies in each department (except for the GPD, where everyone is a political officer). In July 2004, in a major step toward "jointness" that foreshadowed the expansion of the CMC in September, an air force general and navy admiral were assigned as deputy chiefs of the General Staff. Formerly, the deputy chief positions were nearly always filled by ground-force officers.

When officers hold multiple posts, such as vice-chairman of the CMC and chief of the General Staff, officially both positions are identified with the higher post listed first. Similarly, when multiple officers are mentioned in speeches or writings, they are listed in protocol order according to seniority and duty position. Protocol order for the PLA services (*junzhong*) is army, navy, air force, Second Artillery (based on the dates of their creation); similarly listings of staff functions follow the precedence of GSD, GPD, GLD, and GAD.

According to regulations, members of the PLA address each other (1) by their duty position, or (2) by their position plus surname, or (3) by their position plus the title "comrade" (*tongzhi*). When the duty position of the other person is not known, one service member may address the other by military rank plus the word "comrade" or only as "comrade."[33] (These customs differ from other militaries where the person's rank and surname are the most common form of address. This system stems back to the various periods in PLA history when a formal rank structure was not used, prior to 1952 and then again from 1965 to 1988.[34])

The General Staff Department is responsible for operations, intelligence, electronic warfare, communications, military affairs, training, mobilization, meteorological and survey, cartographic functions, and foreign affairs for the entire PLA. The GSD also acts as the service headquarters for the army (the GPD, GLD, and GAD perform similar functions within their areas of responsibilities). The GSD Service Arms Department (*bingzhong bu*) directly oversees the development of the army's armored, aviation (helicopter), artillery and air defense, chemical defense, electronic warfare, and engineer forces. Officers and NCOs who perform command and staff duties from the GSD down to the grass-roots units are considered to be part of the "military" system. (See Chapter 3 for a description of the various duty systems in the PLA.)

The General Political Department is responsible for political and ideological reliability and training in the PLA, which includes many aspects of morale building (often referred to as cultural affairs) and propaganda (publicity) functions, such as song and dance troupes, sports teams, museums, and a wide array of media – newspapers, magazines, television, film, and the Internet. Perhaps most importantly the GPD system is also responsible for personnel matters, including party discipline, internal security, legal affairs, management of dossiers, and promotions. GPD functions are performed by officers known as political commissars (*zhengzhi weiyuan* or *zhengwei*) or political instructors (*zhengzhi jiaodao yuan*) in units and staffs throughout the army. At all levels of the PLA, principal commanders (or primary staff officers) and their respective political officers usually share the same rank just as they share responsibility for the performance of their units. (Ranks may vary between commanders and political officers due to promotions or reassignments, and it is possible for a political officer to outrank his commander.)

In addition to personnel who are part of the political officer system, all units have party committees to help guide ideological training and participate in collective or consensus decision making. The party committee is formed of principal commanders and political officers, their deputies, and other senior officers within the unit. The political commissar/instructor acts as secretary of the party committee and the commander as deputy secretary. Party committees at all levels are very active in all aspects of military training as well as political training. Guidance from national level headquarters is passed down the chain of command through a series of party committee meetings extending from Beijing to the grass-roots unit level. After disseminating information to party committees, unit leaders hold training sessions with all soldiers to ensure understanding and compliance.

The General Logistics Department is responsible for finances, military supplies (also known as quartermaster functions), health services, military transportation, POL, barracks (capital) construction, and auditing for the PLA. It provides supplies and services common to all services of the PLA. The GLD also supervises production in the factories and farms operated by the PLA and controls several national level logistics bases consisting of supply and POL depots and transportation units.[35] Under GLD oversight, units below brigade and regimental level run farms to produce vegetables and raise livestock (especially fish, pigs, and chickens) to supplement unit mess funds, while higher level agricultural and sideline production bases focus on production of grain.[36] The GLD also runs about 50 numbered factories that produce quartermaster items for the PLA, such as uniforms, helmets, field and bivouac gear (called "camping gear" by the Chinese), and food and beverage items; however, these factories *do not* produce weapons used by the forces.[37] The GLD sponsors several military research institutes, manned by military personnel, dedicated to improving the PLA's equipment. In contrast to the GLD's responsibility for common-use items, specialized supply and services are provided by the General Armaments Department system.

The GAD is responsible for the weapons and equipment of the PLA, including maintenance, repair, ammunition, and research, development, testing, and acquisition, including the procurement of major weapons, equipment, and ammunition. Many of the GAD's functions are considered logistics functions in other armies, and were incorporated into this new national level General Headquarters Department formed in April 1998. The GAD maintains numerous research institutes and weapons test centers, including the nuclear test base at Lop Nor and China's satellite launch and tracking network. It also oversees the production of nuclear weapons. The GAD assigns personnel to Military Representative Offices (MRO) in many Chinese civilian factories that produce weapons. Military Representative Bureaux in selected industrial cities perform liaison work with the defense industrial sector.

Both the GLD and GAD supervise a major element of logistics reform instituted since 1998: the "socialization" or "out-sourcing" of services by contracting with local civilian entities to perform functions previously undertaken by soldiers or units. These tasks range from food storage to running mess halls to purchase of spare parts and vehicle/equipment repair. For example, instead of the PLA and local civilian governments each maintaining separate grain storage facilities, the PLA is experimenting with civilian-managed joint storage facilities to replace or supplement PLA warehouses. In peacetime or emergency conditions, PLA units can draw rations from these civilian warehouses and pay for them using modern "smart card" technology. Likewise, the PLA has established contractual relations with many civilian vehicle repair and auto supply shops throughout the country so vehicles may receive maintenance or repair when away from their home base. A primary purpose of out-sourcing is to save money by having the civilian community augment the PLA's existing facilities. Reportedly, "out-sourcing" has allowed many logistics support personnel slots to be eliminated or reallocated to other purposes.[38]

Senior level professional military education institutes

One organizational level below the four General Headquarters Departments are the Academy of Military Sciences (AMS, *junshi kexue yuan*), the National Defense University (NDU, *guofang daxue*), and the National Defense Science and Technology University (*guofang keji jishu daxue*, also known as the National University of Defense Technology, NUDT), which are directly subordinate to the CMC. The AMS in northwest Beijing is primarily a research center for the study of military strategy, operations, and tactics; military systems; military history; and foreign militaries. The AMS does not focus on student education, but rather is the premier doctrinal research and development institute for the entire PLA.

Differing from the AMS, both the NDU (also in northwest Beijing) and NUDT in Changsha form the pinnacle of the PLA professional military education system, offering a number of courses to senior PLA, PAP, and a few civilian officers. Students at the NDU are senior commanders, staff officers, and researchers and civilians from government organizations above provincial level. NUDT students are senior scientists, engineers, and commanders of technical units (such as maintenance and repair units or military run scientific or technical research institutes) and cadets who will enter the PLA to serve in technical units. (See Chapter 3 for a complete description of the PLA professional military education system.)

Service headquarters and the Ministry of National Defense

The CMC exercises command of the PLA through the four General Headquarters Departments to the PLA Navy, PLA Air Force, Second Artillery, and the seven Military Regions, all of which are at the same organizational level as the AMS, NDU, and NUDT. The army, navy, and air force are characterized as separate "services," while the Second Artillery technically is an "independent arm" or "branch" (*bingzhong*). The PLAN, PLAAF, and Second Artillery each have their own commanders and separate national level headquarters and staffs in Beijing. As mentioned earlier, the army has no separate service headquarters. Instead, the four General Headquarters act as the national level army headquarters with direct links to the Military Regions. The national PAP headquarters is also found at this organizational level, but with a line of command to the State Council through the Ministry of Public Security, as well as to the CMC. The PAP national headquarters building is located separately in Beijing from PLA headquarters facilities.

The Ministry of National Defense (MND, *guofang bu*) is a government body responsible both to the State Council and the Central Military Commission. The Minister of National Defense (*guofang bu buzhang*) is usually a senior military officer. The Minister of National Defense is *not* in the operational chain of command running from the CMC through the General Headquarters to the various military commands and services. The minister's power comes primarily from his seat on the CMC and his personal relationships with other senior leaders. The ministry itself is composed of very few people and is mostly concerned with the conduct of defense and military relations with other countries. In particular, the MND oversees military attachés assigned to Chinese embassies throughout the world, with the GSD Second Department (Intelligence) responsible for their daily operations. Most staff work for the ministry is performed by the General Headquarters Departments.

The Central Military Commission and Ministry of National Defense Foreign Affairs Office (*waishi bangongshi*) plans, executes, and coordinates interactions with foreign militaries, both in China and outside its borders. Personnel from this one office perform these functions for the GSD, Defense Ministry, and CMC. Smaller Foreign Affairs Offices are found in the other General Headquarters Departments and lower level headquarters, such as the PLA Air Force, Navy, and Military Regions.

Military Regions

The Chinese mainland is divided into seven large Military Regions (MR, *da junqu*, Chinese sources usually translate this term as "Military Area Commands"), each covering several provinces, autonomous regions, or centrally administered cities, and are named after the city in which their headquarters is located. In 2005, the seven MRs were structured as follows (listed in the protocol order assigned by the PLA[39]):

- Shenyang MR, consisting of the Liaoning, Jilin, and Heilongjiang Military Districts
- Beijing MR, consisting of the Beijing and Tianjin Garrisons and the Hebei, Shanxi, and Neimenggu (Inner Mongolia) Military Districts
- Lanzhou MR, consisting of the Shaanxi, Gansu, Qinghai, Ningxia, and Xinjiang Military Districts
- Jinan MR, consisting of the Shandong and Henan Military Districts
- Nanjing MR, consisting of the Shanghai Garrison and the Jiangsu, Zhejiang, Anhui, Fujian, and Jiangxi Military Districts
- Guangzhou MR, consisting of the Hunan, Guangdong, Guangxi, Hainan, and Hubei Military Districts[40]
- Chengdu MR, consisting of the Chongqing Garrison and the Sichuan, Xizang (Tibet), Guizhou, and Yunnan Military Districts.

Subordinate to MR headquarters are (1) army, navy, and air force units in the region; army units may be either main force units organized into group armies or independent units of division, brigade, or regimental size that report directly to MR headquarters; (2) logistics and armaments support units organized into logistics subdepartments (*houqin fenbu*); and (3) provincial Military Districts (MD, *sheng junqu*, also called "Provincial Military Commands") and Garrison Commands of the four centrally administered cities of Beijing, Tianjin, Shanghai, and Chongqing (using the terminology *weishuqu* for the Beijing Garrison Command and *jingbeiqu* for the other three cities). Military Districts and Garrison Commands control local forces that may include both active and reserve combat and logistics/armament units as well as border and coastal defense units.

Each Military Region commander (*siling yuan*) is assisted by a political commissar; several deputy commanders (*fu siling yuan*), including the regional air force commander and naval commander (for the Nanjing, Jinan, and Guangzhou MRs); and a number of deputy political commissars (*fu zhengwei*).[41] These personnel form

Figure 2.2 Military Regions

the nucleus of the MR level party committee. MR staffs parallel, but are smaller than, the organization of the four General Headquarters Departments and are overseen by an MR chief of staff (*canmou zhang*). Each MR has a headquarters element (consisting of operations, intelligence, communications, etc.), political department, joint logistics department (*lianhoubu*), and armaments department. Joint logistics departments were formed in 2000 in order to better provide support to all services located in the MR. To date all MR commanders have been ground force officers. Another major move toward "jointness" would be assigning a navy or air force officer as an MR commander.

During peacetime, MR headquarters are administrative organizations charged to prepare the forces in their regions to accomplish the missions assigned. Depending on their location and geographical situation, various MRs have differing orientations and force composition. In time of emergency, MR headquarters are likely to be formed into temporary operational War Zone headquarters (*zhanqu*) to conduct military operations. These *ad hoc* wartime headquarters would be formed around the structure of an MR headquarters, but could be augmented, and perhaps commanded, by officers from higher headquarters in Beijing. The boundaries of

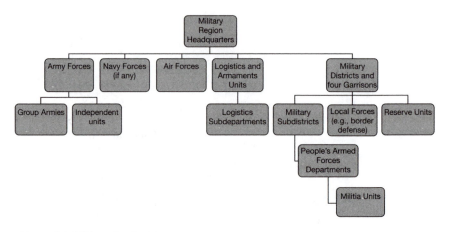

Figure 2.3 Military Region structure

a War Zone will not necessarily correspond directly with the pre-existing MR boundaries, but will vary according to the operational objectives assigned to the War Zone.

Local commands

Each Military District headquarters is responsible for a single province or autonomous region and bears its province's or region's name. MD commanders (*siling yuan*) are responsible for the local and reserve forces (both reserve units and militia units) in their province and for mobilization preparations. Active duty local forces may include coastal defense and border defense regiments, as well as infantry, armor, or artillery units. Reserve units in each province fall under the command of the Military District (or the Beijing, Tianjin, Shanghai, and Chongqing garrisons commands) in peacetime and may operate independently in wartime or be assigned to augment main force units. MD headquarters also oversee logistics depots and bases and armaments units, such as repair and maintenance depots, in their province. MD commanders are assisted by political commissars, deputy commanders, deputy political commissars, and staffs similar to, but smaller than, MR headquarters. MD commanders coordinate closely with local government leaders and PAP forces in their area.

In addition to the garrison headquarters in Beijing, Tianjin, Shanghai, and Chongqing, within the Military Districts are local garrison commands in most Chinese cities, which also use the Chinese term *jingbeiqu*. Garrison duties are frequently assigned to operational PLA units or other headquarters units stationed in the area as an additional duty of the local commander. The primary duty of garrison units is to guard military facilities and maintain order among the troops when they are outside of their military barracks on pass, leave, or official duties, similar to

Military Police functions in other armies. According to the 1998 Defense White Paper, garrison units in large and medium sized cities are responsible to "check, inspect and handle cases of infringements of military discipline by military personnel as well as cases of violations of relevant rules by military vehicles."[42] Soldiers performing garrison duty are often seen patrolling the streets on foot or in vehicles, or setting up "military vehicle checkpoints." These soldiers have authority only over members of the PLA and are not involved in the law enforcement activities of the local public security apparatus.

Each Military District is divided into numerous Military Subdistricts (MSD, *junfenqu*, also called Military Sub-Commands). MSD are found in prefectures or cities and counties and take the name of their prefecture, city, or county. Like MR and MD commanders, MSD commanders are also known as *siling yuan* and have small staffs. MSD headquarters are responsible for formulating mobilization plans, organizing conscription, supporting reserve and militia training, and supervising the activities of People's Armed Forces Departments in their areas.

People's Armed Forces Departments (PAFD, *renmin wuzhuang bu*) are found at county, city, district, and sometimes work unit level, such as in large factories. PAFD are primarily responsible for meeting local conscription quotas for the active force and the militia as determined by MSD and MD headquarters. In addition to providing manpower to the military, they also assist in obtaining local material resources for the units in their area (logistics support) and are involved with supporting demobilized soldiers and organizing reserve and militia training. PAFD officers wear PLA uniforms but have distinctive epaulets of rank. Local PAFDs provide peacetime command for militia units in their areas of responsibility.

The National Defense Mobilization Committee system

Each level of PLA regional and local command is part of the National Defense Mobilization Committee (NDMC) system, which originates in Beijing and extends down to county level. The NDMC system was created in 1994 and refined over the subsequent years. At the national level, the premier of the State Council is the chairman of the State NDMC with the vice-premiers of the State Council and vice-chairmen of the CMC serving as vice-chairmen. Other members include heads of government ministries and commissions and senior leaders from the PLA General Headquarters Departments.[43] A deputy chief of the General Staff is assigned the position of secretary-general of the State NDMC and is primarily responsible for overseeing mobilization work in the PLA.

Moving down the government structure at each level – provincial, prefecture/city, and county – the chairman of local NDMC is the principal leader of the local government (governor, mayor, etc), and is assisted by several vice-chairmen. Local NDMC vice-chairmen are deputy leaders of the local government and the principal leaders (commanders and political commissars) of military units at the same level (such as MR, MD, and MSD). All Military Regions have intermediary level National Defense Mobilization Committees formed by the NDMCs in each province of the region. The NDMC system is linked by various means of modern communications made widely available in the 1990s and can form "Joint Military–Civilian Command Centers" integrating military, government, and party leaders in times of emergency.

The primary function of the NDMC system is to "organize and implement" national defense mobilization by coordinating "relations between economic and military affairs, the armed forces and the government, and manpower and materials support in defense mobilization" so that the shift from peacetime to war can be made efficiently.[44] During peacetime, the NDMC system allows for military and civilian leaders to meet regularly to plan the coordinated development of the economy and military and to make preparations to transform resources (such as personnel, vehicles, ships, planes, and material) and economic production to support wartime operational needs. Local NDMCs and military headquarters have conducted detailed surveys of civilian personnel and equipment that can be used to support military operations. Each NDMC is organized according to the functions of:

- manpower mobilization (reserves, militia, and civilians);
- economic (industry, agriculture, science and technology, material supply and storage, commerce and trade, and finance) and transportation (transportation, communications and postal services, repair, and construction) war readiness;
- civil air defense;
- national defense education for the general civilian population.[45]

The level of activity over the past decade in NDMCs at all levels indicates that the PRC has not abandoned its traditional emphasis on the role of "the masses" in defense of the mainland. Material and political support of the Chinese public is considered essential for success in any military campaign the PLA undertakes in the twenty-first century. The NDMC system's mission is to ensure that the proper level of civilian support is always available to the PLA.

Tactical organizations: squads to battalions

The basic organizational building blocks of the ground forces are squads, platoons, companies, battalions, and regiments. Few, if any, official Chinese sources available to the public discuss the composition of these units at a level of detail to allow the construction of an accurate and timely Table of Organization and Equipment (TO&E), which spells out the number of personnel and equipment for each type of unit at every level. PLA regulations, however, provide insight into the duties of a number of leaders, staff officers, and specialists at regimental/brigade level and below.[46]

Squads of about 10–12 personnel are found in a variety of types of units: infantry, engineers, communications, headquarters, and logistics units, etc. Specific personnel numbers will vary according to the type of squad and its mission. Infantry squads are led by a noncommissioned officer squad leader (*banzhang*), who is assisted by a deputy or assistant squad leader, a radio operator, vehicle driver (if a vehicle is assigned to the squad), and possibly a rifleman who also carries a portable anti-tank weapon. The squad leader is responsible for the combat readiness, military and political training, equipment maintenance and employment, and discipline of all members of the squad. The remainder of the squad is likely divided into two sections of roughly equal size (three to four people) armed with an assortment of individual or crew-served weapons. In tactical situations, squad leaders use hand signals and small flags to control their unit's actions. In units equipped with larger weapons systems, such as tanks, artillery, air defense artillery, or missiles, the equivalent to the squad is the crew for a tank, artillery piece, surface-to-air missile system, etc. Depending on the specific type of equipment, these weapons systems require from three to about ten personnel to operate; each crew is also led by an NCO (unless the vehicle is commanded by a platoon leader or other commanding officer). Usually three or four squads or crews form a platoon.

The platoon is the first organizational level commanded by an officer, usually a first or second lieutenant, known as platoon leader or commander (*paizhang*). This junior officer is required by regulations to live in the barracks with his platoon. Platoon leaders are responsible for their unit's combat readiness, military and political training, equipment maintenance and employment, and discipline. The platoon chain of command goes from the platoon leader to squad leaders. Current regulations do not mention a deputy platoon leader, either officer or NCO, but it is likely, as the PLA NCO corps increases in size and responsibilities, that "platoon sergeants" will be assigned to assist platoon leaders in their duties. Like the squad leader, a platoon leader is assisted by a radio operator to maintain communications with subordinate squads and company headquarters above. An infantry platoon will likely have three infantry squads and an additional weapons squad with machine-guns and anti-tank weapons. Tank platoons traditionally consisted of three tanks each, but may have expanded to four tanks per platoon in some units. Platoons in other arms will likely be composed of three or four squads based on the mission of the type unit. As a rule of thumb, platoons have about 40 personnel assigned (but could be larger or smaller depending on the type of equipment assigned).

A company usually is composed of a headquarters section, mess squad, and three or four platoons. A company commander (*lianzhang*), usually a captain, has a small headquarters section with a political instructor (and possibly a deputy political instructor), deputy commander, mess officer (*siwuzhang*, now being changed to NCO[47]), and a few enlisted personnel who serve as armorer-clerks, medical orderlies, communications personnel, and technicians. By regulations, the company commander and the company political instructor jointly are responsible for the work of the entire company. The political instructor concentrates primarily on the company's political indoctrination and loyalty and performs many duties related to the morale of the troops. Deputies to the commander and political instructor assist their principal officers and assume their duties when they are away from the company. The mess officer or NCO is responsible for company supply and equipment (such as bedding and company furniture) as well as supervising a mess squad of about ten people that prepares the unit's meals. The mess squad is overseen by a separate mess squad leader. The duties of the mess officer or NCO are similar to company supply sergeants in other militaries. The armorer-clerk is responsible for maintaining and securing the company's weapons and keeping the company's records and other required forms. Medical orderlies perform first aid and evacuate sick or wounded personnel to higher headquarters and also work with the mess squad to ensure sanitation. Specially trained "technicians," who are responsible for the service, maintenance, and training in the care of equipment, may be assigned to various positions in the company (and higher units). Farms and sideline production (raising pigs, ducks, fish, etc.), where soldiers work part time to help provide basic sustenance, are found at company level and are the responsibility of the commander.

Subordinate to the company are three or four platoons depending on the type unit. In infantry and armored units, in addition to three infantry or tank platoons, a weapons platoon with mortars and anti-tank weapons (such as recoilless rifles, anti-tank guided missiles) is found.[48] In total, a company may have from about 120–150 personnel depending on its type, with armored and mechanized companies having approximately ten armored vehicles plus additional trucks and jeeps for support. Regulations require a series of meetings within the company to be held to review past work and plan for the future. Squads hold weekly meetings, platoons once or twice a month. Squad leaders and above attend a monthly "company affairs meeting," while all members of the company take part in a separate "company soldier's conference" held monthly or at the end of major work (or exercise) periods.[49] A party cell is also present in the company, made up of members of the party and Communist Youth League. This party organization includes both officers and enlisted personnel who discuss political work and assist in maintaining party discipline.

Three to five companies generally make up a battalion led by a lieutenant-colonel battalion commander (*yingzhang*). The battalion commander has only a small staff consisting of a political instructor, deputy battalion commander, and director of the battalion medical clinic. The battalion commander and political instructor jointly share responsibility for the work of the entire battalion, with the battalion commander having primary responsibility for the military work and the political instructor, political work and morale. The battalion has a small clinic responsible for medical training, disease prevention, rescue, care, and evacuation of sick and wounded. The small staff found at battalion level indicates that many command and staff functions move primarily from regiment (or brigade) headquarters directly to subordinate companies. Infantry and likely armored battalions have three companies and a heavy weapons company. Total number of personnel in a battalion will vary according to unit type, but will probably range from some 200 to around 700 officers, NCOs, and conscripts. Armored and mechanized battalions will likely have over 30 armored vehicles with a significant amount of trucks and jeeps in supporting units.

Tactical organizations: regiments and brigades

Regiments and brigades are important organizational levels where true combined arms formations are first found (integrating elements from more than one arm, such as infantry, armor, artillery, AAA, engineer, chemical defense, and logistics, etc., into an organic unit). Therefore, regiment and brigade headquarters are staffed by significant numbers of personnel. Since 1998, the brigade level has become more prominent in the PLA as many divisions have been reduced in size and new brigades formed.

Regiments usually are composed of numbered companies (identified by numbers one through nine) of their basic type (infantry, armored, etc.), which are assigned under the command of three battalion headquarters. In addition to maneuver battalions, combat regiments will likely have an artillery battalion and AAA unit permanently assigned. Regimental headquarters may also command engineer, chemical defense, and logistics and armament support units, usually of company size. Depending on the type of unit, regiments may have from about 1,000 to over 2,500 personnel and over 100 armored vehicles in armored and mechanized units.

Maneuver (infantry and armored) and artillery brigade headquarters exercise direct command over a number of subordinate battalions. Some older brigade headquarters may have regimental headquarters below brigade level, but such a command structure appears less common than it may have been in the past. Brigades are probably manned by 2,000 to 6,000 personnel depending on type and organizational structure, with numbers and types of vehicles assigned varying greatly. Within brigades, combat units (infantry and armor) will be organized into approximately three to five battalions; artillery, AAA, or air defense units may be of battalion or company size; and logistics and armaments support units likely of company size. Logistics and equipment support capabilities in brigades are greater than found in regiments. It is likely that experimentation is still underway for the optimal brigade structure for the various types of brigades that have been formed during and after the 500,000-man reduction of the late 1990s.

Current regulations treat the regiment and brigade staff as being at an equivalent level with similar functional structures (though staff "offices" within regimental headquarters are called "departments" in brigades). Regimental commanders usually are colonels, while senior colonels usually command brigades. The regimental commander (*tuanzhang*) or brigade commander (*luzhang*) is assisted by a political commissar (*zhengzhi weiyuan*), deputy commander, deputy political commissar, and chief of staff. The commander and political commissar are jointly responsible for all the work of the regiment or brigade, with the commander focusing on military work. The director of the headquarters political department/ office reports to both the commander and political commissar and is assisted by a deputy director in the performance of political work for the entire unit. The chief of staff is the senior officer of the headquarters department who oversees the work of several staff officers and their subordinates. Reporting directly to the chief of staff is at least one deputy chief of staff, the director of the logistics department/office,

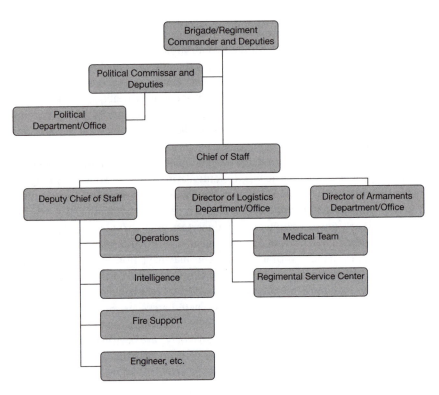

Figure 2.4 Brigade/regimental headquarters structure

and the director of the armaments or equipment department/office. All of these officers have specialized staff personnel to perform the functions of the various systems for which they are responsible. The deputy chief of staff probably is responsible for planning operations and has several assistants who perform other operations-related functions such as intelligence, fire support, and engineer planning. Answering to the director of logistics is the chief of the regimental medical team and the director of the regimental service center. The regimental service center works directly with subordinate companies to ensure proper supply and preparation of food for all units.

The number of personnel present for duty often differs from the number authorized to be in any unit. Units may be short of personnel because of (1) sickness, injury, or death, (2) discipline problems resulting in the removal of offenders, (3) absence for training in a separate location, (4) temporary duty assignments outside of the unit, (5) authorized leave or pass, and (6) insufficient numbers of properly trained personnel or insufficient personnel of appropriate seniority or rank. It is not known whether or how the PLA takes these factors into account when determining the number of personnel assigned to each type and level of unit.

Tactical organization: divisions

The organizational level immediately above regiment and brigade is division, though *operationally* brigades appear to have become equivalent to divisions now that many former divisions have been downsized into brigades. (See pp. 42–44 for discussion of group armies.) In addition to maneuver (infantry and armored) divisions and brigades, the PLA also has artillery and AAA divisions and brigades. Air defense units, i.e., units with both AAA guns and SAMs, are organized as brigades. PLA divisions are structured with regiments as their next lower organizational level; unlike some other militaries, PLA division headquarters *do not* control brigades.

Beginning in the 1950s, PLA maneuver divisions were usually organized along the Soviet model. Most Soviet maneuver divisions (either tank or infantry, which was also known as "motorized rifle") were composed of three regiments of the "type" unit that identified the division. For example, a motorized rifle (i.e., infantry) division had three subordinate infantry regiments and a fourth tank regiment; a tank division had three tank regiments and a fourth regiment of infantry. Full-strength PLA infantry and tank divisions followed that structure until the late 1990s. (In the late 1990s, the PLA stopped using the term "tank" (*tanke*) to designate unit type and substituted the word "armored" (*zhuangjia*) to better indicate the combined arms nature of the unit.)

Likewise, according to Soviet organizational structure, each full-strength PLA division had a subordinate artillery regiment, an AAA regiment, and an assortment of reconnaissance, chemical defense, engineer, communications, and logistics (medical, supply, maintenance, repair, etc.) battalions or companies and a few additional units to perform guard or headquarters functions. It is likely that PLA divisions also have been assigned organic transportation regiments consisting of various large cargo trucks, POL tankers, and heavy equipment transport trailers (for carrying heavy armored vehicles to spare them wear and tear during long movements).

Depending on their state of readiness (or readiness category), not all divisions were manned and equipped at the same levels. For example, instead of tank regiments, lower readiness category infantry divisions might have had tank battalions or no tanks at all, with similar decreases in unit size for other support elements. The time required for mobilization and movement out of barracks varied according to readiness category. Previously readiness levels were known in English as Category "One, Two, or Three," or "A, B, or C," and used the Chinese characters of *jia, yi, or bing* with the addition of the word *lei* for "class."

Force restructuring continued after the completion of the 500,000-man reduction in 2000 into the 200,000-man reduction period that began in 2003. More divisions have been downsized to brigades or transformed into different type units (such as changing from motorized to mechanized infantry or armored units). Some infantry divisions that previously had three infantry regiments have been downsized to consist of only two infantry regiments, while the third infantry regiment was transformed to an armored regiment. Thus, the pre-reduction number of 12,000 to

13,000 personnel in a division may now be reduced by 2,000 to 2,500 combat soldiers in some divisions, though it is likely logistics or armament units, such as maintenance/repair and transportation units, have been expanded to better support the more mechanized force.

In the late 1990s, many, but not all, divisions received priority for new equipment entering the ground forces. At the same time, brigades were told to find new ways of fighting to use their "existing equipment to defeat a high-technology enemy." However, by about 2002 some brigades, too, began the process of upgrading to newly produced Chinese weapons and equipment.[50]

In Chinese military writing, a formula frequently used to depict a division is "10,000 men and 1,000 vehicles." This formulation is still generally accurate. A brigade may be said to have "several thousand personnel and hundreds of vehicles," which, too, is more or less accurate (see Table 2.2).

Table 2.2 Estimated personnel numbers (all numbers are approximate)[51]

Type unit	Division	Brigade	Regiment	Battalion
Infantry	10,000–12,000	5,000–6,000	2,800	700
Armor	10,000	2,000	1,200	175
Artillery	5,000–6,000	2,200	1,100	275
AAA	5,000	2,000	1,000	250

A division commander (*shizhang*) usually is a senior colonel and is assisted by a political commissar, at least one deputy commander and deputy political commissar, a chief of staff, and a larger staff organization than found in brigades and regiments. The staff is responsible for military (operations, intelligence, and communications), political, logistics, and armaments functions. When deployed to the field, the division staff must have enough personnel to man a series of field command posts (CP), including the division main CP (*jiben zhihuisuo*), division rear CP (*houqin zhihuisuo*, primarily responsible for logistics, armaments, and administrative functions), forward CP (*qianjin zhihuisuo*), and alternate CP (*yubei zhihuisuo*). Mobile satellite communications equipment is becoming prevalent in field headquarters for formations down to division/brigade level.

Tactical/operational organization: group armies

Group armies are composed of combinations of divisions, brigades, and regiments. After the reductions of the late 1990s, the variation in group army composition has increased considerably from previous years. A few group armies have only divisions as their main maneuver elements; a few others are composed of all maneuver brigades. The majority of group armies contain a mix of both maneuver divisions and brigades ranging from three to five in number. (These variations are clearly evident in Tables 4.1–4.7.) The structure of the various group armies is likely to

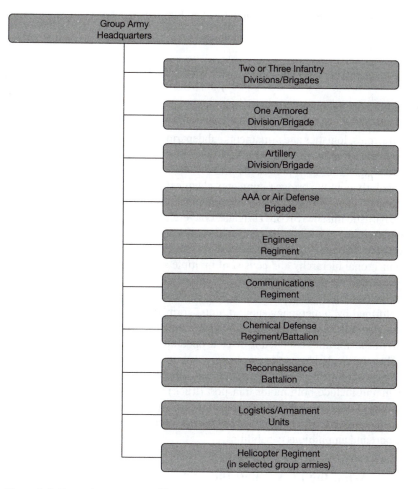

Figure 2.5 Group Army structure[52]

continue to evolve during the 200,000-man reduction and beyond. Most group armies have a combination of units similar to that found in Figure 2.5, with an army aviation (helicopter) regiment assigned to a few selected formations.

Total personnel assigned to group armies probably varies from roughly 30,000 to about 50,000, depending on the number of divisions and brigades. Group army commanders (*junzhang*) usually are major generals and are assisted by a similar, but larger, assortment of political commissars, deputy commanders and deputy political commissars, and staff elements as found in divisions. Additional capabilities, such as army aviation and electronic warfare, that may be assigned to the group army also require staff representation at group army headquarters. When deployed from garrison locations, group armies also will be capable of setting up multiple command posts with increasing numbers of mobile command and communications vans and vehicles.

Tactical organizations: independent units and logistics subdepartments

Each Military Region headquarters has an assortment of combat and support units reporting directly to it that are not part of group armies. In addition to its subordinate group armies, logistics and armaments subdepartments, and local forces (reporting through the MD chain of command), Military Regions may command independent infantry, armored, reconnaissance and/or SOF, aviation (helicopter), engineer (particularly pontoon bridge regiments), chemical defense, electronic warfare, and psychological warfare units, often at regimental or group (*dadui*) level. One short-range ballistic missile (SRBM) brigade, converted from a traditional artillery unit, is present in the Nanjing Military Region opposite Taiwan.

Military Region logistics subdepartments are equivalent to divisions in the PLA's organizational hierarchy and consist of multiple storage and repair depots, bases, hospitals, and the units that man these facilities. Logistics subdepartments provide both fixed and mobile support to forces in the region. Forward and mobile support is performed by "emergency support units" formed on a case-by-case basis from subordinate elements of logistics subdepartments to satisfy the logistics requirements of specific units conducting discrete operations. Logistics subdepartments are usually commanded by senior colonels.

Transportation regiments are major components of the MR logistics support system and include both motor transport (truck) units and army ship *dadui* in at least three MRs for coastal and river operations. Army ship units include a variety of small ships and vessels, operated by ground force soldiers, that augment PLAN transport and amphibious capabilities.

What the PLA is not: the civilian defense industries

Before examining who makes up the PLA, it is necessary to define one final example of what the PLA is not.

The PLA also *does not* include the large number of Chinese civilians who work within the civilian-managed defense industrial sector. The Chinese defense industries are divided into six sectors – nuclear, aerospace, aviation, shipbuilding, ordnance, and electronics – and produce the majority of weapons and equipment used by the PLA. The six sectors together employ a total of approximately two million civilian workers, scientists, staff, and managers.[53] The corporations, factories, research institutes, schools, trading companies, and other associated entities which make up the six sectors are organized into 11 large enterprise groups:

- China National Nuclear Corporation (CNNC)
- China Nuclear Engineering and Construction Corporation (CNEC)
- China Aerospace Science and Technology Corporation (CASC)

- China Aerospace Science and Industry Corporation (CASIC)
- China Aviation Industry Corporation I (AVIC I)
- China Aviation Industry Corporation II (AVIC II)
- China State Shipbuilding Corporation (CSSC)
- China Shipbuilding Industry Corporation (CSIC)
- China North Industries Group Corporation (CNGC)
- China South Industries Group Corporation (CSG)
- China Electronic Technology Group Corporation (CETC)

Each sector of the Chinese defense industries also has at least one import-export company responsible for representing the companies and factories in the sector overseas and for buying and selling equipment and technology from abroad. Perhaps the best known, or most infamous, of the import-export companies is NORINCO (China North Industries Corporation) that services the ordnance sector (China North and South Industries Groups). Several others also remain operational, such as the China Nuclear Energy Industry Corporation (CNEIC); China Great Wall Industries Corporation (CGWIC), and China Precision Machinery Import-Export Corporation (CPMIEC) for the aerospace industries; China National Aero-Technology Import and Export Corporation (CATIC) for the aviation sector; China Shipbuilding Trading Company (CSTC); and China National Electronics Import and Export Corporation (CEIEC). In addition to specifically designated import-export companies, individual entities within the defense industries, such as factories and research institutes themselves, are increasingly being authorized to conduct sales to foreign countries and purchase foreign supplies and technology.

The system of defense industry enterprises is supervised by the ministerial-level State Commission of Science, Technology and Industry for National Defense (COSTIND), under the State Council, which is now completely separate organizationally from the PLA. Within the defense industrial sector, however, are PLA officers *who perform liaison functions* between the military and industries. These officers are organized into a system of Military Representative Offices in factories and Military Representative Bureaux in selected industrial cities overseen by the General Armaments Department or service headquarters.

Prior to 1998, COSTIND was part of the PLA general headquarters structure and led by uniformed military generals, as well as civilian managers and technicians. In April 1998, the old COSTIND was abolished, reformed, and given the same name as in the past, but completely separated from PLA headquarters. All uniformed military left COSTIND and were reassigned within the PLA, mostly in the GAD. The new COSTIND is now staffed only by civilians and performs policy-making and government regulatory functions for the defense industrial sector. Though COSTIND may help market products and services, it is not directly responsible for production, a responsibility which has devolved to civilian corporation and factory managers over the period of economic reform.

Fifty years ago the relationship between the PLA and defense industries was much different. But during the period of reform the two systems have evolved separately so that the relationship that now exists is primarily one of PLA "buyer" to civilian defense industries "seller." Though both systems seek to defend China's national security, the defense industries operate under a "for-profit" motivation, while few members of the military serve in order to get rich. (In 1998, the PLA was ordered to divest itself of the *commercial* enterprises, such as hotels, real estate companies, etc., that had proliferated throughout the PLA. Originally these entities were tasked to make money for the units they represented to supplement official funds available to units, but greed, corruption, and illegal activities marred their activities. While many sideline production enterprises are still subordinate to PLA headquarters and units, thousands of commercial enterprises have cut their formal ties with military units. Along with them, some officers, who were responsible for these activities, also left the PLA. A close, but unofficial, relationship between many of these enterprises and their former units likely remains.)

Like the defense industries, the PLA is trying to attract and retain highly educated and trained personnel, but must compete with the civilian business sector where the money is better and the life easier. The people who make up the PLA and how they are trained and educated are vital elements of the military transformation in progress.

3

WHO IS THE PLA?

Highly educated, properly trained, and motivated personnel are the heart of a modern army. Since the late 1990s, the PLA has made great efforts to attract and retain the kind of people needed to operate and maintain its more technologically advanced weapons and equipment as well as plan and execute its new military doctrine. In the process, the Chinese military has made changes to its personnel system and the training and education systems for conscripts, NCOs, and officers. In particular, the force is in the process of rebalancing the number of conscripts with NCOs, and NCOs with officers. In both cases NCOs are assuming more duties and responsibilities than in previous years.

Often Chinese terminology and practices not found in other armies make it difficult for outsiders to fully understand many of the details of the PLA's personnel system. For example, the term *ganbu*, or cadre, refers to leaders in general and is often used in reference to officers and PLA civilians, and does not include enlisted soldiers (*shibing*), meaning both conscripts and NCOs. (As noncommissioned officers assume greater leadership responsibilities, it will be interesting to see if NCOs are included in future uses of the term "cadre.") The PLA also makes a distinction between personnel responsible for various aspects of military, political, logistics, and armament affairs, and technicians or technical personnel, who are principally responsible for equipment maintenance, repair, research, development, and testing.

As new equipment has entered the PLA, the role of technicians has risen in importance. Bureaucratically, the creation of the GAD in 1998 is an example of the increased attention given to how equipment is handled and personnel are trained to maintain and operate it. Technical personnel are identified by special insignia on their collars consisting of a red star (thinly outlined in gold) with the Chinese characters 8–1 (*bayi*, which commemorate the founding of the Red Army on 1 August 1927) superimposed over the elongated orbits of two electrons on a white background. For all members of the PLA, it is important to distinguish among the various services, military ranks, duty positions, and specialties.

PLA ground, naval, and air forces, as well as the PAP, can all be identified by their uniforms and insignia. In total, the PLA uses some 29 different types and styles of uniforms, including dress, spring/autumn service, summer, winter, and field

PLA ground force collar insignia   PAP collar insignia

Figure 3.1 Collar insignia

Figure 3.2 PLA cap insignia

uniforms.[1] PLA ground force personnel (other than technicians and PLA civilians) wear collar insignia consisting of the *bayi* insignia on a red star (superimposed over a second, underlying five-pointed gold star protruding between the points of the red star).[2] Ground force personnel also are recognized by a red band on their service hat (a black brimmed, peaked saucer hat), with officers, PLA civilians, and NCOs having a thick (or wide) red band and conscripts a much thinner red band. The red star *bayi* cap insignia is affixed over the brim of the peak hat and field caps, on the beret introduced in recent years, and sometimes on helmets. PLA ground forces wear matching green jackets and trousers with dress, spring/autumn service, and winter uniforms. The dress and spring/autumn service uniforms are four-button, open-neck jackets worn over a shirt and tie (black tie for men, red tie for women), while the winter uniform jacket is the traditional Mao-style jacket that buttons to the top with a closed collar (the women's winter dress jacket is double-breasted). In December 2004, the PLA announced the quality of winter uniforms for enlisted soldiers would be improved in material and color. The Mao-style did not change. Summer uniforms consist of short- and long-sleeved shirts of lighter green worn over dark green trousers. PLA ground forces use both camouflage battle dress uniforms and/or solid green fatigue uniforms, both of which can be worn with soft-brimmed field caps (with red star *bayi* insignia) or helmets (either "Kevlar" style or older Japanese-style steel pots). Ceremonial dress uniforms and insignia for ground forces differ considerably from uniforms worn on a daily basis and may cause confusion with PAP forces' uniforms. The PLA guard of honor, which greets senior foreign dignitaries, routinely wears the ceremonial uniform.

Ranks are indicated by epaulets worn on the shoulder, with hard epaulets (with gold background for officers) for dress, service, and winter uniforms and soft epaulets (with dark green-black background) for summer and camouflage or fatigue uniforms. Ground force enlisted ceremonial epaulets are red, like the daily use PAP epaulets. PLA soldiers performing "courtesy patrol" duties may also wear ceremonial epaulets while on the street. PLAN and PLAAF personnel are easily distinguished from the ground forces by different color uniforms, hats, and insignia.

This chapter will look at who makes up the modern PLA ground forces, the manner by which their ranks and duty positions are classified, and how the soldiers are individually trained and educated, starting first with the conscript force, moving on to noncommissioned officers, the officer corps, PLA civilians, and finally the personnel who make up reserve units.

The conscript force

The enlisted ranks within the PLA are divided into (1) conscripts (*yiwu bing*), soldiers who are recruited according to quotas levied upon local governments and serve for two years, and (2) volunteers (*zhiyuan bing*), who are selected from the conscript pool to voluntarily extend their period of service to become non-commissioned officers (*shiguan*). Prior to 1999, the period of conscription for ground troops was three years (with four years for the navy and air force), but partly because of the hardships placed on some families who had only one son (as a result of the nation's "one child policy"), the decision was made to reduce the time of conscripted service in order to allow the youth to return to their families quicker. At the same time, a complementary decision was made to readjust the ratio of conscripts to NCOs, with the NCO corps becoming larger in size as the number of conscripts fell. The period of adjustment would take several years to reach the proper mix of conscripts, NCOs, and officers. The number of officers in the force is also being adjusted as noncommissioned officers assume many responsibilities previously assigned to officers.

According to China's "Conscription Work Regulations," males aged 18 to 22 may be drafted to serve in the PLA (or PAP) if qualified physically and politically. Females may be recruited depending on the "needs of the military." Students in that age range attending full-time schools may be deferred from service.[3] Persons who are the sole supporter of their family may also be deferred from service.[4] There are no official education requirements for service, but graduation from lower middle school (nine years of education) or higher is preferred. Conscription quotas are based as much as possible on the distribution of the population – about 70 percent from rural areas and 30 percent from the cities in the first decade of the new century. These percentages will shift as China's population distribution changes, but inherent in these numbers are differing levels of education and technological sophistication found among those from the countryside and those from urban areas. City youth, who often are more highly educated and have greater economic opportunities available to them, may be less inclined to serve in the PLA than peasants from the country-side. Urban youth often are not as physically fit and accustomed to hardship as their cousins from the farms. However, the hearty peasant is less likely to be prepared to operate and maintain advanced weapons and equipment than the better-educated city dwellers. Stories abound concerning various ways young men have tried to avoid conscription. Accordingly, the tasks of enlisting, training, and retaining new recruits from such varied backgrounds have become increasingly challenging.

The conscription process and basic training[5]

In September each year, the General Staff's Mobilization Department and General Political Department decide how many conscripts are needed to be inducted that year.[6] The Central Military Commission and State Council then jointly issue a "conscription order" which is sent to each of the seven Military Regions. Quotas are passed to the provincial Military Districts, which then send specific require-ments for new soldiers to Military Subdistricts and local People's Armed Forces Departments. The local PAFDs are responsible for enlisting the number of recruits necessary from their district. Quota numbers include both PLA and People's Armed Police recruits. The PAFD also decides which new soldiers go into the PLA (army, navy, air force, Second Artillery) or into the PAP. As a general rule, new recruits from a single district are sent at most to three separate division or brigade level units. Some recruits are assigned to units in their province, but others are dispatched outside their home province so every PLA and PAP unit is composed of soldiers from many parts of the country.

Personnel selected as conscripts are notified in early November by their local PAFDs. The potential conscripts then undergo physical and political tests admin-istered by the Military Subdistrict. If the recruits pass the screening process, in early December they are issued uniforms and bedding and travel to induction training units (usually by train). Units receiving new soldiers establish reception committees to meet the incoming recruits and help them settle into their training units.

Division and brigades establish temporary recruit basic training units called "training regiments" that operate out of a "training center," which is in or near their garrison areas. Division and brigade commanders and political officers are responsible for basic training to be conducted according to standards set by the GSD and supervise closely the activity at each training center. NCOs and junior officers are selected from the unit to be training cadre and conduct most of the actual training instruction. One or two NCOs are responsible for a squad of about 12 new soldiers. Squads are organized into platoons and companies; each training regiment may have up to nine training companies. In addition to the training cadre, many members from the permanent unit support basic training, such as cooks, supply personnel, clerks, and armorers. Basic training lasts for about three months until approximately February and the Chinese New Year.

All new soldiers go through the same basic training course of instruction, which includes how to wear the uniform, saluting, marching, physical conditioning training, how to shoot and maintain a rifle, and especially the history of the PLA and how to be a good soldier and citizen. Instilling discipline and accustoming recruits to obey orders are fundamental to recruit training. During this period, new soldiers do not wear rank or insignia. At the end of training, the new soldiers are given insignia of rank and take the "Soldier's Oath" that says,

> "I am a member of the People's Liberation Army. I promise that I will follow the leadership of the Communist Party of China, serve the people wholeheartedly, obey orders, strictly observe discipline, fight heroically, fear no sacrifice, loyally discharge my duties, work hard, practice hard to master combat skills, and resolutely fulfill my missions. Under no circumstances will I betray the motherland or desert the Army."[7]

Conscripts in units

After basic training soldiers are assigned to permanent companies in larger units where they receive additional training. There they learn how to function in squads and platoons within the company. Specific functions, such as driving, operating radios, how to be a member of a tank or artillery crew, or fire machine guns and grenade launchers, will be taught in special training facilities/instructional units within permanent units. Some new soldiers are sent to specialty training at facilities outside of their permanent units, such as mechanics, supply, specialized communications, engineers, chemical defense, etc. This specialty (technical) training may last several months. Later, some soldiers are selected to serve as squad leaders and receive additional training of three months or longer. (The process to select and train soldiers to be squad leaders is being revised as volunteer NCOs are given that responsibility.) By about April, companies have integrated new soldiers into their positions and are ready to begin training at higher organizational levels. Individual and small unit skills are practiced and expanded throughout the year. Physical fitness is emphasized constantly in unit training.

First-year soldiers are called "private" or "private second class" (*lie bing*) and have a single chevron of rank on their shoulder epaulets. In their second year, conscripts are called "private first class" (*shangdeng bing*) and receive a second chevron on their epaulets. Pay is based on rank and years in service, with subsidies given for being stationed in "difficult living conditions." Privates are not allowed to marry, must live in the barracks, and are discouraged from having their family visit. Privates are not authorized vacation leave, but may be granted passes for a day on Sundays or holidays and are encouraged to travel in groups of two or more with one person in charge.

At the end of their second year, in November, conscripts may be allowed to volunteer to become NCOs and remain on active duty or they may be demobilized and returned to their homes. If demobilized, soldiers receive a small stipend for their service and are transported back to their original residence. Some demobilized soldiers may join reserve units in their local areas depending on the needs of the reserve unit. If allowed to extend their time on active duty, the volunteers will enter the ranks of the noncommissioned officer corps.

The noncommissioned officer corps

The PLA's noncommissioned officer corps has undergone substantial change since 1999. During the 20 years of reform from 1979 to 1999, many PLA delegations had observed the roles of NCOs in other armies and the functions of the professional NCO had been studied carefully in PLA academic and research institutes. The decision to cut conscription time to two years was accompanied by a concurrent decision to increase the number of NCOs and give them greater responsibilities. Most NCOs are selected from conscripts at the end of their two-year enlistment, but others may be brought into the service directly from the civilian world, provided they have professional/technical qualifications needed by the army. These civilians-turned-NCOs receive introductory basic training to prepare them for military life and are spared the hardships of the first two years of conscription. Policies for NCO recruitment continue to evolve and are likely to change according to the needs of the army and the success of experiments undertaken since the turn of the century.

In 2003 only 630 NCOs were recruited directly from local civilian schools; in 2004 that number was raised to 1,064 NCOs, including some 300 female NCOs.[8] An article in the Jinan Military Region newspaper in 2002 reported that after just a few days of training, the first group of 40 new NCOs to be recruited directly from civilian technical schools were said to have abilities comparable to soldiers who had been in the army for five years.[9] If accurate, this report indicates the relatively low level of technical sophistication among PLA enlisted troops in the late 1990s. Reforms in the NCO corps are intended to overcome such shortcomings.

The NCO corps is divided among professional and technical NCOs as well as non-professional and non-technical NCOs.[10] NCOs are divided into six grades and may stay on active duty for 30 or more years up to the age of 55. NCO ranks and lengths of service for each grade are categorized in Table 3.1.

NCOs who are recruited initially from conscript ranks must be graduates from lower middle school (nine years of education) or higher and have received training at or above regimental level or from a military academy or institute during the period of their two-year conscription. They must also have demonstrated technical proficiency and preferably served as a squad leader (having previously received squad leader training), deputy squad leader, or equivalent of squad leader (such as tank commander). In late 2004, the General Staff Department announced the goal for 2005 of recruiting 2,000 company level mess NCOs from conscripts who entered the PLA in 2002 and 2003 and another 9,000 "short-term training" NCOs, who

Table 3.1 NCO categories and ranks

Category	Rank/grade	Term of service in grade
Junior sergeant (*chuji shiguan*)	NCO Grade 1 or Class 1 NCO (*yiji shiguan*)	3 years
Junior sergeant	NCO Grade 2 or Class 2 NCO (*erji shiguan*)	3 years
Intermediate sergeant (*zhongji shiguan*)	NCO Grade 3 or Class 3 NCO (*sanji shiguan*)	4 years
Intermediate sergeant	NCO Grade 4 or Class 4 NCO (*siji shiguan*)	4 years
Senior sergeant (*gaoji shiguan*)	NCO Grade 5 or Class 5 NCO (*wuji shiguan*)	5 years
Senior sergeant	NCO Grade 6 or Class 6 NCO (*liuji shiguan*)	9 years

were currently serving in units as squad leaders, from NCOs who entered service from 1998 to 2001. Newly selected NCO candidates take an exam in January and those accepted report to PLA schools on 1 March for two or more years of training. Upon graduation, NCOs are obligated to serve for 12 years or longer.[11]

An NCO candidate must submit a formal, written application and be recommended by his grass-roots unit (company), including an evaluation by the party branch within the unit. NCOs Grade 1 and 2 are approved at the regimental or brigade level after review of the candidate's application and physical checkup. At the end of each term of service, NCOs undergo similar processes of volunteering to extend their duty, including recommendations by personnel in the unit. Promotions are approved at division or brigade level for NCO Grades 3 and 4, and at army level for Grades 5 and 6. NCOs are encouraged to continue their professional education either through correspondence courses or attendance at military or civilian institutions of higher learning. NCOs who earn merit citations may be promoted ahead of schedule and given a pay raise.

Regimental and higher headquarters are tasked with developing, recruiting, selecting, and training noncommissioned officers. Battalion commanders assign soldiers to be squad leaders or deputy squad leaders.[12] According to regulations, first priority is assigned to filling NCO slots in emergency and mobile combat units, especially those involved in high-technology operations and at the grass-roots level. In other words, headquarters staffs should not rob tactical units of their NCOs. In general, NCOs are prohibited from serving as acting officers, though exceptions can be made with the approval of higher headquarters, and they are not allowed to transfer to other units. Nor are professional and technical NCOs allowed to change their specialties at will.[13] Units establish methods by which NCOs brief their senior officers of their activities and by which they are evaluated by "the masses," i.e., the soldiers in their unit. NCOs receive annual formal evaluations by their companies when units prepare their year-end reports. Those who perform below standards may be placed on probation.

NCOs may marry, though they are required to live in the troop barracks in grass-roots units (exceptions may be made for NCO families to live in garrison areas when conditions permit). NCO spouses are allowed to visit the barracks once a year, staying at quarters inside the garrison for up to 45 days. Senior NCO families are authorized to live in the barracks when approved. NCOs are also authorized vacation leave according to time in service. Noncommissioned officers are paid according to their rank and duty position and may receive food subsidies, housing allowance, child-care and child-education allowances, one-child parent bonus, and subsidies for professional and hazardous duties. They also receive insurance, free medical care, and a discharge allowance when demobilized.

NCO ranks are distinguished by their shoulder epaulets, which have an increasingly complex insignia of a star, crossed rifles, and a wreath centered on the epaulet, as well as a series of thick and thin chevrons at the edge nearest the shoulder. In contrast, conscripts do not have any insignia in the center of their epaulets.

The number of noncommissioned officers in the force is understood to have increased substantially since 1999, but specific figures are not available to the public. NCOs have also been given greater leadership, training, and maintenance responsibilities including squad leader, deputy squad leader, and repairman. The trend to replace company mess officers with NCOs reflects a new degree of confidence in the modern NCO corps in an area of great importance to troop morale. If all company level mess officers were replaced by noncommissioned officers, this would lead to the reduction of many thousands of officer billets and a similar increase in the rolls of the NCO corps. Such a transformation will likely take several years to implement fully as enough properly trained and experienced NCOs gradually become available. NCOs with tactical experience in field units are also being assigned to teach within the military's system of professional education academies and institutes.[14] According to the *PLA Daily*, "tens of thousands" of officer positions are being converted to NCO billets.[15]

The PLA now expects its noncommissioned officers to be capable of commanding operations, organizing training, and managing subordinates (known as the "Three Abilities," *sanzhong nengli*) and to "speak, do, teach, and perform political work" (known as the "Four Can Do's," *si hui*). To acquire these abilities, NCOs are required to receive training throughout their careers at professional military education schools and colleges, as well as through correspondence courses while at their units. Accordingly, the PLA has established six NCO schools; 28 officer academies and schools have assumed NCO training responsibilities. In the three years from 2000 to 2003, more than 20,000 NCOs received training at these schools.[16] According to the *People's Daily*, the PLA intends to enroll "a record number of 15,000" students for NCO training in "about 35 Chinese military academies" in the fall of 2005.[17]

As the number and quality of NCOs expand, the number of officers can be reduced. Nevertheless, in an army well over a million strong (even after the completion of the 200,000-man reduction), a large number of personnel must be recruited, educated, trained, and integrated into the officer corps every year.

The officer corps

The PLA officer corps is categorized according to (1) the nature of their duties (*zhiwu xingzhi*, referred to below as "categories"), (2) grade level and military rank (*dengji*), and (3) duty position grade (*zhiwu dengji*, also translated as "post").[18] PLA officers are assigned duties in five categories: military (or operational) officers (*junshi junguan*), political officers (*zhengzhi junguan*), logistics officers (*houqin junguan*), armaments officers (*zhuangbei junguan*), and specialist technical officers (*zhuanye jishu junguan*). These categories correspond to the four systems established by the four General Headquarters Departments (GSD, GPD, GLD, and GAD) with the addition of technical officers directly responsible for equipment maintenance, repair, research, development, and testing. For the most part, officers are inducted into one of these systems, are trained and educated throughout their career in the system, serve in units and headquarters within that system, and do not routinely transfer from one system to another until relatively late in their careers, if at all.[19]

Officers are further categorized into three grade levels and ten ranks (*sandeng shiji*). The lowest grade level consists of company grade or junior officers (*weiguan*) with the ranks of second lieutenant (*shaowei*), first lieutenant (*zhongwei*), and captain (*shangwei*). Company grade officers are recognized by a single thin stripe running lengthwise centered on their epaulets with one, two, or three stars, according to rank, centered on the single stripe.[20] Above company grade are field grade officers (*xiaoguan*) consisting of four ranks: major (*shaoxiao*), lieutenant colonel (*zhongxiao*), colonel (*shangxiao*), and senior colonel (*daxiao*). Field grade officers are identified by two parallel stripes running lengthwise in the middle of their epaulets with one, two, three, or four stars centered between the two stripes. The highest grade level is for general officers (*jiangguan*) with three ranks, major general (*shaojiang*), lieutenant general (*zhongjiang*), and general (*shangjiang*). General officer epaulets have no stripes, but instead have a wreath at the shoulder edge of the epaulet with one, two, or three stars in the center as appropriate. On average, an officer is promoted from one military rank to the next higher rank approximately every four years, except when he or she is assigned to a higher duty position grade.

The officer duty position grade (or post) system is essential for understanding protocol order and seniority among officers. Duty position grades are divided into 15 levels from platoon to chairman of the Central Military Commission. For the most part, two military ranks are associated with each level, as is a mandatory retirement age for officers serving at that level. Retirement ages, or maximum age limits, vary among officers, with officers in combat units required to retire a few years earlier than those in non-combat units. The duty position grade (from platoon to CMC) takes precedence over military rank (lieutenant through general). If an officer is assigned to a higher duty position grade than his current military rank, the officer will be promoted to the proper military rank for the duty position assigned. (Thus, it is now apparent why PLA regulations first require service members to address each other using their duty position title and not military rank. See Chapter 2 for a discussion of preferred forms of address.) An officer may be promoted to a higher duty position grade after three years of service at the current duty position. Duty position grade levels apply to commanders and political officers; officers serving on staffs will have lower grade levels than principal commanders and commissars at that same level. For example, a staff officer in the operations department of a division is likely to have a grade level equivalent to regiment, deputy regiment, or lower level. The 15 duty position grades, associated military ranks, retirement ages, and equivalent unit organization levels are listed in Table 3.2.[21]

Officers below the regiment level (levels 10–15) are promoted by the political department at army/corps level (group army) headquarters; officers at the regiment to division levels (levels 7–9) are promoted by authority of the political department at Military Region headquarters; and officers above deputy army level (levels 2–6) are promoted by the General Political Department.[22] Officers routinely serve three to four years in a single assignment as commander, political officer, deputy, or staff officer, and change jobs, moving laterally or up the chain, within an army level/group army structure for the majority of their career. Officer transfers outside of a group army usually do not occur until reaching higher level duty positions (above division level) and ranks (senior colonel and above). Commanders and senior officers at Military District and higher levels are rotated periodically, usually every few years, so they do not form "unhealthy" relationships that could lead to corruption or misplaced loyalties (as occurred in previous decades when it was called "mountain-topism" or "warlordism"[23]). Senior officer rotations also broaden their professional experience base through service in different units in different regions of the country.

Technical officers are divided into three duty position categories: senior technical officers (*gaoji zhuanye jishu zhiwu*) with military ranks from lieutenant general to major; intermediate technical officers (*zhongji zhuanye jishu zhiwu*) from senior colonel to captain; and junior technical officers (*chuji zhuanye jishu zhiwu*) from lieutenant colonel to second lieutenant.[24]

Like conscripts and NCOs, PLA officer pay is calculated on a variety of factors. Since taxes in China make distinctions between salaries and what are called subsidies (*butie*), bonuses, and allowances, additional pay is often called a "subsidy, bonus, or allowance" in order to minimize the tax burden on soldiers. All officers receive a base salary, with increases based on duty position grade, military rank, and time in service.[25] Officers also receive housing allowances and have been encouraged to purchase their own houses. Additional money (subsidies) is paid for specialties and living conditions. For example, subsidies for officers stationed in Tibet can almost triple the amount they would receive if assigned to other areas in China.[26]

Table 3.2 PLA officer duty position grades and military ranks

Duty position grade or post (zhiwu dengji)	Military rank (junxian)	Retirement age (Combat unit/ non-combat unit)	Equivalent unit level
1 CMC chairman	None	None	
2 CMC Vice-chairman or member	General		General Headquarters Departments
3 Military region (dajunqu zhengzhi)	General/lieutenant general	65	
4 Deputy Military Region (dajunqu fuzhi)	Lieutenant general/major general	63	
5 Army/corps (zhengjunzhi)	Major general/lieutenant general	55/60	Group Army/Military District
6 Deputy army/corps (fujunzhi)	Major general/senior colonel	53/58	
7 Division (zhengshizhi)	Senior colonel/major general	50/55	Division
8 Deputy division (fushizhi)	Colonel/senior colonel	48	Brigade
9 Regiment (zhengtuanzhi)	Colonel/lieutenant colonel	45/50	Regiment/group
10 Deputy regiment (futuanzhi)	Lieutenant colonel/major	43/45	
11 Battalion (zhengyingzhi)	Major/lieutenant colonel	40	Battalion
12 Deputy battalion (fuyingzhi)	Captain/major	38	
13 Company (zhenglianzhi)	Captain/first lieutenant	35	Company
14 Deputy company (fulianzhi)	First lieutenant/captain	33	
15 Platoon (paizhi)	Second lieutenant/first lieutenant	30	Platoon

Sources of new officers

New officers for the PLA come from four sources: graduates from civilian colleges and universities; "national defense students" (*guofang sheng*) from civilian colleges; cadets graduating from PLA military universities (*daxue*), academies, and institutes (*xueyuan*); and personnel selected from the enlisted ranks to become officers. (Military universities are made up of several smaller, related colleges or academies, not necessarily all in the same location.) The last category of "up from the ranks" is a traditional source of leadership for the PLA and reflects the kind of upward mobility, both in the social and political sense, the Chinese army has afforded its personnel. Currently the practice is still in effect, but the number of enlisted soldiers who become officers annually is not known.

New officers who attend civilian schools include both those who decide to join the PLA upon graduation without previously having made a commitment to the army and those who attend civilian institutions on military scholarships having made a commitment to join the PLA after graduation – the latter group is known as "national defense students" and is managed by "Reserve Officers Selection and Training Offices" in the various universities. Students are motivated to join the PLA by a variety of reasons, such as patriotism, financial assistance offered, and guaranteed employment after graduation. In 2002, the PLA was reported to accept more than 10,000 graduates annually from civilian colleges and universities.[27] At that time, the "national defense" scholarship program was only in its second year of operation.

After a short period of experimentation in a limited number of schools in the late 1990s, the PLA officially established the national defense student system in May 2000. The program grants a scholarship of 5,000 yuan annually (with cost of living adjustments) in exchange for a promise to serve in the PLA after graduation. High school and junior college students who apply must pass physical, political, and cultural examinations to be accepted. While in school, national defense students are treated like other college students except they also receive basic military training. Most students study engineering and information technology; some national defense students may pursue advanced degrees immediately after graduation if an agreement is made with the unit to which they will be posted.

By the fall of 2005, the PLA planned for a total of some 35,000 students in all years of schooling to be distributed among about 110 civilian institutions participating in the program, which supports both the PLA and PAP.[28] In 2005, the PLA planned to enroll more than 12,000 national defense students, up from some 8,000 freshmen who entered colleges under the program in 2004.[29] In 2003, more than a thousand national defense students graduated from about 30 institutions in the program and entered the PLA; in 2004, that number rose to 1,800.[30] The rapid expansion of the program indicates that it is fulfilling both the increase in military requirements for college graduates and social needs for upward mobility through access to tuition-assisted college education.

In contrast to the 8,000 national defense students who entered college in 2004, some 20,000 high school graduates entered PLA and PAP military universities, academies, and institutions in that same year.[31] The 20,000 goal for new military cadets remained constant in 2005.[32] The numbers for national defense students and cadets entering military academies are the result of a joint planning effort conducted by the Ministry of Education and the General Political Department. Applicants for military academies must be under 20 years old, unmarried, and physically and politically qualified. Tuition is provided by the government, and cadets (*xueyuan*) are paid modest sums progressing from 110 yuan in the first year up to 230 yuan in their last year. Cadets are recognized by solid red epaulets with gold stripes on the edges but no stars or chevrons.

Students attending military institutions are at the bottom level of the PLA professional military education pyramid composed of induction or basic level institutes or academies, intermediate level command academies, and senior level universities. The most recent reform and reorganization of the professional military education system was initiated in 1999, resulting in the streamlining and consolidation of what previously numbered about a hundred academies, institutes, and universities. In 2004, two basic level PLA institutions were changed to intermediate level command academies and several basic level colleges and universities were transferred to civilian control. During the summer of 2004, the former First Military Medical University, the Quartermaster University in Changchun, the Jilin Medical College of the Fourth Military Medical University, and the Chengdu Medical Institute of the Third Military Medical University began their transformation from the PLA's GLD supervision to local government control.[33]

Basic-level PLA academies

Approximately 35 four-year schools for personnel initially entering the PLA ground force comprise the largest group of institutions within the PLA professional military education system. Many of these academies and institutes have also developed shorter-length courses for noncommissioned officers as the NCO corps has expanded. "Distance learning" courses are also being set up for officers and NCOs in units to continue their education without having to be transferred to an academy.

Cadets graduating from basic academies' four-year courses receive bachelor's degrees and are commissioned as second lieutenants. These institutes provide both university level education *and* basic military training to prepare cadets for assignments to operational units immediately after graduation. Basic PLA army-related academies or institutes are subordinate to the various systems overseen by the four General Headquarters Departments, the GSD, GPD, GLD, and GAD. These relationships are identified in Table 3.3.

As can be seen, the functional areas of responsibility found within the four General Headquarters Department systems are represented in the schools each department oversees. For example, the GSD-supervised academies educate officers who enter the military system, including infantry, armored, artillery, aviation, engineer, etc. The large number of schools under the GSD accounts for the majority

Table 3.3 Basic level PLA ground force academies or institutes and locations[34]

General Staff Department	General Political Department	General Logistics Department	General Armaments Department
• Armored Force Academy, Bengbu • Army Academy, Dalian • Army Academy, Jinan • Army Academy, Kunming • Army Academy, Nanchang • Army Academy (Mechanized Infantry), Shijiazhuang • Army Academy, Xi'an • Army Academy (Military Medicine), Urumqi • Army Aviation Corps Academy, Beijing • Artillery Academy, Hefei (with Nanjing Branch) • Artillery Academy, Shenyang • Communications Academy, Chongqing • Communications Academy, Xi'an • Electronic Engineering Academy, Hefei • Foreign Languages Academy, Luoyang • Information Engineering University, Zhengzhou (with four campuses) • International Relations Academy, Nanjing • Physical Culture (Sports) Academy, Guangzhou • Science and Engineering Technology University, Nanjing (with Engineer Corps School)	• Art Academy (or College) • Political Academy, Nanjing (with Shanghai branch) • Political Academy, Xi'an	• Logistics Engineering Academy, Chongqing • Military Communications (Transportation) Academy, Tianjin • Vehicle Management Academy, Bengbu • Military Economics Academy, Hubei • Military Medical Sciences Academy, Beijing • Second Military Medical University, Shanghai • Third Military Medical University, Chongqing • Fourth Military Medical University, Xi'an • Beijing Military Medical Academy, Fengtai, Beijing	• Armored Force Engineering Academy, Changxindian, Beijing • Armored Force Technical Academy, Changchun • Ordnance Engineering Academy, Shijiazhuang

of junior officers needed to enter the force each year as platoon leaders and low level staff officers. The GLD functions of transportation, economics, and medical support are readily apparent in the academies within that system, as are the political specialization of the GPD schools and the technical specialties of the GAD academies. Each academy or institute graduates several hundred cadets each year, some of whom may stay on for graduate education or return at a later date in their service to pursue advanced degrees.

The seven "army academies" indicate the prevalence of infantry officers in the force. Some infantry cadets also receive several months of specialized combined arms training at Military Region training bases in preparation for their assignment to mechanized units. In February 2005, the former Army Academy in Guilin, which up to that time had been an eighth army academy, was transformed into Guangzhou Military Region Integrated (or Comprehensive) Training Base (*Guangzhou junqu zonghe xunlian jidi*). The former academy merged with a communications training group to form the new training facility.[35] In addition to the Army Academy in Xi'an, the Lanzhou Military Region has a second army academy in Urumqi specializing in military medicine. The recent emphasis on building Special Operations Forces has resulted in the establishment of a unique course within the Physical Culture Academy in Guangzhou that includes anti-terrorist, peacekeeping, and information technology operations.[36] The Nanjing International Relations Academy also has a reconnaissance and SOF leaders course in addition to its role in training future Chinese military attachés.

Many PLA institutions at all levels offer advanced degrees. As of 2002, 36 institutes within the professional military education system offered doctorates, and 55 were authorized to grant master's degrees. Additionally, the PLA sends officers to civilian universities, both in China and in foreign countries, to receive advanced degrees. In 2003, about 3,000 officers studying for advanced degrees were enrolled in some 29 civilian institutions in China. The "Program of Strengthening the Army by having More High-Caliber Talents" was started in 2001, with participating schools setting aside about 60 billets each for PLA students, allowing for nearly 1,800 officers to be enrolled annually. The program is funded by the Ministry of Education, not the PLA.[37]

According to the 2004 Defense White Paper, induction level academies "offer basic courses in joint operations."[38] In order to further promote "jointness," some academies have begun exchange programs with academies from other services. Such programs provide students with an opportunity to expand their professional horizons by participating in another service's training and having extended personal contact with officers outside of their normal duty category. It is unclear how extensive this program has become, but is another example of the PLA's intention to better prepare its officers for modern combat.

Intermediate level academies

A much smaller number of intermediate level academies, referred to as "command academies or institutes" (*zhihui xueyuan*), train serving mid-level officers from battalion to division level, including commanders, political officers, and staff officers. Command academies "offer courses on service campaigns and combined operations."[39] In addition to field grade students, many, if not all, intermediate level academies also educate cadets out of high school before they become junior officers. Furthermore, command academies provide postgraduate education in which graduate students often research specific operational and equipment-related subjects directly applicable to their field experience. The Nanjing Army Command Academy also has a Foreign Training Department which is attended by officers from many different countries.[40]

Ground force command academies include the:

- Air Defense Command Academy in Zhengzhou
- Army Command Academy in Nanjing
- Army Command Academy in Shijiazhuang
- Armament Command and Technology Academy, Huairou, Beijing
- Artillery Command Academy in Xuanhua
- Artillery Command Academy in Langfang
- Chemical Defense Command and Engineering Academy, Yangfang, Beijing
- Communications Command Academy in Wuhan
- Engineer Command Academy in Xuzhou
- Logistics Command Academy in Beijing

In June 2004, the former Air Defense Force Academy at Zhengzhou was transformed into a command academy whose objective is to train both "primary and intermediate commanders, staff, and technicians in the air defense force."[41] A month later in July, the former Army Guided Missile Academy at Langfang was reformed to become the second Artillery Command Academy.[42] This new command academy will probably focus on training commanders and staff officers from company to brigade level for ground force missile units, including anti-tank guided missile, surface-to-air missile, and surface-to-surface missile units.

Senior level universities

The top of the PLA professional military education pyramid is formed by the National Defense University and National Defense Science and Technology University, both of which are under CMC direction. These two schools offer "courses on strategic studies and joint operations."[43] The NDU student body consists of senior PLA commanders, staff officers, and researchers, and senior civilian officials from government organizations above provincial level. Courses include the three-month "National Defense Course" (*guofang yanjiu xi*) for officers from Military Region headquarters, service headquarters, and other government ministries (this course is sometimes referred to as the "PLA Capstone Course"); senior officer's refresher course; higher command course (one year in length); overseas (foreign) student course (conducted at a separate campus from the main campus in northwest Beijing); and postgraduate study. In recent years, NDU has emphasized master's research in military science for leaders from PLA combat units. According to the *PLA Daily*, the NDU has awarded a total of more than 1,200 master's and doctorate degrees.[44] In 2004, the foreign student course was upgraded into a special department, the "Defense Affairs Institute," for training senior foreign officers.[45] Most of the NDU faculty are professional educators and researchers with little recent tactical experience. In 2003, the NDU received its first batch of 13 recent division, brigade, and regiment commanders from all services to provide their expertise to the teaching staff.[46]

National Defense Science and Technology University students are senior scientists, engineers, and commanders of technical units who attend senior level classes, as well as undergraduates just out of high school.[47] In 2003, the NUDT had 12,390 students, including 4,243 graduate students.[48] Subjects taught include optical engineering, information technology and communications, control science, computer science and technology, management science, aerodynamic optics, space information technology, information security, and space control engineering.[49] While the NDU focuses more on senior officers from the military, political, and logistics systems, NUDT students are mostly from (or about to enter) the armaments system or are technicians.

In the year 2000, the NUDT was the leading institution to implement a "4 + 1" pattern for training new officers. In that year, 400 "joint training" students were recruited into the NUDT. The new system includes four years at the university, where students receive a bachelor's degree, followed by a fifth year in "post" training where they receive instruction on specific military tasks. Disciplines offered in the first four years of education include science, technology, military, management, and philosophy courses. In the fifth year, students are transferred to one of the command academies to acquire "comprehensive" abilities. In 2004, the first group of students completed the bachelor's portion of the program. With a total of 1,800 students in the program, the NUDT has the largest enrollment of "4 + 1" students in the PLA education system.[50] Presumably, the last year at the command academy will expose the new technical officers to the rigors and intricacies of operational planning, tactics, and the requirements of field operations. With this introduction to operational matters, NUDT graduates can better support the needs of the troops in their future assignments, which most likely will focus on the research, development, testing, and maintenance of equipment.

Uniformed PLA civilians

Many instructors and research staff within the professional military education system are PLA civilians – uniformed members of the active duty PLA, but who do not have military rank. (In June 2005, regulations were issued to allow the PLA

Figure 3.3 PLA civilian collar insignia and epaulet

to hire civilian contract workers, who will also wear uniforms but *will not* be counted on active duty rosters.[51]) PLA civilians are categorized as specialist technical cadre, non-specialist technical cadre, and office or administrative personnel. Like PLA officers and NCOs they also have a system of numbered grades indicating their seniority. *Wenzhi ganbu* (uniformed PLA civilians) are identified by special collar insignia differing from the red star *bayi* or technical personnel insignia worn by the ground forces, as well as by their shoulder epaulets which have a single, large, red star *bayi* mounted in the center.

PLA civilians are found in a wide variety of jobs in research, engineering, medical, education, publishing, archives, cultural, and sports units. According to work requirements, PLA civilians may be transformed into officers.[52] Likewise, some PLA officers who have reached retirement age may become PLA civilians and stay on to perform similar functions as when they were commissioned officers. The number of PLA civilians on active duty has not been made public, but may have amounted to some 20 percent of the active duty force before the reductions that began in 1997.[53] This percentage is likely to have decreased as headquarters and administrative staffs were the targets of both the 500,000 and 200,000 man cutbacks.

The ratio of conscripts to NCOs to officers and PLA civilians on active duty has not been released publicly. The numbers and percentages are probably changing as the PLA continues to reduce its size and reform its organizational structure. A best guess at these percentages for the entire PLA may be: 30 percent conscripts, 20 percent NCOs, 33 percent officers, and 17 percent PLA civilians, give or take a few percentage points either way in each category. The ratios of enlisted to officers will vary among the services, with the army having more conscripts than the more technically-oriented air force, navy, and Second Artillery. Ratios will also differ among headquarters units, with more officers and senior NCOs assigned at higher levels. Nevertheless, all units and headquarters that deploy to the field will require a certain number of conscripts to perform physical tasks, like setting up tents, pulling electrical cables, performing guard duties, manning communications, feeding the troops, and refueling vehicles. Some functions formerly performed by soldiers are now being contracted out to civilian enterprises ("out-sourcing") as part of the reform of the PLA's logistics system, thus allowing for personnel billets to be reassigned to other functions or eliminated from the overall force structure.

PLA reserve unit personnel

One final element in answering the question "Who is the PLA?" concerns who makes up PLA reserve units. All reserve units have a small contingent of active duty personnel to serve as the backbone (*gugan*). The majority of reserve unit personnel, however, are civilians, only some of whom have been demobilized from the army. Other civilians with no military experience are recruited because they possess skills needed by the reserve units to perform their missions (this is especially true for more technical units). The rank structure for reserve personnel is similar to active forces, but the highest rank a reserve officer may attain is major general. Reservists wear uniforms similar to active PLA personnel and can be recognized by an elongated arm patch with a red star bayi and a large yellow "Y" for *yubeiyi*. The reservist "Y" insignia may also appear on the epaulets of some uniforms.

As the number of active duty personnel has been cut since 1997, the number of reserve units has increased moderately. However, the growth in the size of the reserve force has not been as great as might have been expected. It is a fact that not all demobilized military personnel enter into reserve service, nor are all deactivated units transformed into reserve units. Instead, like the active force, reserve units are seeking to improve the quality of their personnel, enhance training, and shorten the time it takes for them to assemble and deploy.

PLA personnel are assigned to headquarters and operational units stationed in all parts of China. The organizational structure and deployment of PLA ground force units provide insight into the expected missions for the military and potential enemies facing China in the twenty-first century.

4

WHERE IS THE PLA?

Before examining "where" the PLA ground forces are located throughout China, it is first necessary to ask "why" they are stationed where they are. Or, what are the missions of the units scattered all over the country? Generally speaking, PLA ground forces are garrisoned throughout the country to protect China's sovereignty from foreign and internal enemies, support national economic development, and assist in the maintenance of domestic stability. In this regard official Chinese statements provide the overall context for PLA dispositions, while details may be inferred from examination of geography and potential enemies.

In the post September 11 world, Beijing often categorizes China's most likely potential enemies as "terrorist, separatist, and extremist forces." This formulation includes a number of potential enemies:

- Both international and domestic terrorists, including radical Islamists, especially in China's western regions, but also in its metropolitan areas.
- Organizations seeking to split, separate, or prevent reunification of parts of China from Beijing's control, including movements advocating independence for Taiwan, Tibet, Inner Mongolia, and parts of western Xinjiang, as well as people or governments who support these movements.
- Organized groups of religious and political "extremists" who are perceived to challenge the central government's authority.

In order *not* to be characterized as "extremist" or illegal, religious or political groups must be authorized and approved by the central government. Official approval is intended to prevent individuals and groups from subverting the state's power or overthrowing the Chinese government and Chinese Communist Party. Many organizations, religious groups, or nascent political parties with visions that differ from those of the CCP do not accept the requirement for government approval, and are thus targeted by the Ministry of Public Security and Ministry of State Security. Examples of "extremist" or illegal organizations include the Falungong (which has been determined to be a dangerous "cult" by the Chinese government), the China Democratic Party, and the many "underground churches" found throughout the country. The PLA may be called on to help control *armed* "extremist" organizations, but for the most part civilian components of the Chinese security apparatus take the lead in monitoring and policing internal activities.

China's first two Defense White Papers of 1998 and 2000 repeated the PRC state constitution which outlines the tasks of the Chinese armed forces as "to consolidate national defense, resist aggression, defend the motherland, safeguard the people's peaceful labor, participate in national construction, and strive to serve the people."[1] In 2002, the first two of five "goals and tasks" of China's national defense were listed as "to consolidate national defense, prevent and resist aggression," followed by "to stop separation and realize complete reunification of the motherland."[2] In particular, the PLA was given the main task "to conduct operations of defense, and, if necessary, help to maintain social order in accordance with the law."[3]

In 2004, the Defense White Paper listed five "goals and tasks in maintaining national security":

- To stop separation and promote reunification, guard against and resist aggression, and defend national sovereignty, territorial integrity and maritime rights and interests.
- To safeguard the interests of national development, promote economic and social development in an all-round, coordinated and sustainable way and steadily increase the overall national strength.
- To modernize China's national defense in line with both the national conditions of China and the trend of military development in the world by adhering to the policy of coordinating military and economic development, and improve the operational capabilities of self-defense under the conditions of informationalization.
- To safeguard the political, economic, and cultural rights and interests of the Chinese people, crack down on criminal activities of all sorts, and maintain public order and social stability.
- To pursue an independent foreign policy of peace and adhere to the new security concept featuring mutual trust, mutual benefit, equality and co-ordination with a view to securing a long-term and favorable international and surrounding environment.[4]

A significant change between the specific "goals and tasks" enumerated in the 2002 and 2004 White Papers is the elevation of the task "to stop separation and promote reunification" to the number one position in 2004, up from second place in 2002. In effect, the 2004 White Paper merges two first two goals of the previous White Papers, now placing greatest emphasis on the Taiwan issue. "To stop separation" primarily refers to deterring or preventing a formal declaration of Taiwan independence or other moves Beijing perceives as interfering with its goal to reunify Taiwan with the mainland. The importance to the PLA of preventing Taiwan independence is underscored by the declarative statements:

It is the sacred responsibility of the Chinese armed forces to stop the "Taiwan independence" forces from splitting the country. . . . Should the Taiwan authorities go so far as to make a reckless attempt that constitutes a major incident of "Taiwan independence," the Chinese people and armed forces will resolutely and thoroughly crush it at any cost.[5]

While deterrence and prevention of Taiwan independence explains the composition, disposition, and training activities of many PLA ground forces, China maintains large forces in all corners of the country preparing to perform a variety of missions.

Identifying particular PLA units and their locations can be a frustrating endeavor. For operational security purposes, the Chinese government does not produce detailed lists of the names or numbers of PLA units and where they are stationed. Moreover, PLA units are known by a variety of designators which change periodically.

Unit identifiers

PLA units are identified by multiple names and numbers. First, units are given unique numerical designators, such as the 39th Group Army, 115th Mechanized Infantry Division, or 4th Subdepartment. Usually the type and size of the unit is specified after the numerical designator. If the type of unit, such as armor, artillery, air defense, etc., is not included in the unit designation, such as the 193rd Division, the unit is assumed to be infantry (except for logistics "subdepartments," which is a unique term applicable only to the logistics system).

Operational units down to regimental level are also assigned five-digit numbers, often called Military Unit Code Designators (MUCD, *budui daihao* or *junshi danwei daihao*).[6] The size and type of unit cannot be determined solely from the number itself, such as the 65521 unit, but subordinate units within larger units often have sequential numbers. The sequencing of MUCDs within an organization is sometimes lost as units are transferred from one headquarters to another as a result of reductions in force or restructuring. Chinese media reports commonly refer to military units using their five-digit designators, and the numbers (using either Chinese characters or Arabic numerals) are seen on unit signs outside their barracks areas and on unit flags, clothing, or stationery. The system of five-digit numbers was changed in October 2000 after the completion of the 500,000-man reduction and reorganizations begun in 1997.

Some units have been given honorary titles for past accomplishments, such as "Red Army Division" or "Linfen Brigade." Honorifics are conferred by order of the Central Military Commission. In a recent example, in June 2004 CMC chairman Jiang Zemin gave the name "Model Company Defending the Country and the Frontiers" to the Khunjerab Frontier Company of a frontier defense regiment in the Xinjiang Military District.[7]

Over the past decade, many divisions, brigades, independent regiments, and academies have created their own distinctive unit patches, which are worn on the sleeves of the field uniform. These unit patches have a combination of designs (often reflecting the type of unit) plus Chinese characters and/or initials from the *pinyin* names of the unit. The appearance of distinctive unit patches indicates an effort to create unit cohesiveness and increase morale among members of the unit. In previous decades, the PLA appeared to shy away from unit insignia worn on the uniform for operational security reasons.

PLA units are assigned military license plates for use on vehicles by the General Logistics Department. A new system of license plates was put into effect in late 2004, replacing the system that had been in effect for about a decade.[8] According to Chinese sources, the license plate system is changed on occasion to prevent the proliferation of fake license plates used by criminals to avoid inspection by civilian police forces.

Ground force organization and the Air Force's Airborne Army

To "conduct defensive operations" against a foreign enemy, PLA ground forces are organized into main force units that can be deployed throughout the country and local units responsible for defense of the regions in which they are stationed. Both active duty and reserve PLA units will be supported by local People's Armed Police units and militia units assigned to every province, autonomous region, and centrally administered city. In previous decades, a portion of the force was designated as rapid reaction (or response) units (RRU, *kuaisu fanying budui*) within Military Regions to be the first to deploy either in the local area or out-of-region in time of emergency. Now, as the PLA has grown smaller and more mobile, "rapid reaction" or rapid mobilization is a basic task practiced by all units in the active and reserve PLA as well as in the PAP and militia. The exact composition and designation of ground force RRUs is unclear, but is likely to take into account the formation of new SOF units and the improved rapid response capabilities found throughout the divisions and brigades remaining on active duty after recent reductions and reorganizations in the force structure.

The PLA Air Force's 15th Airborne Army is generally considered to be the primary national level rapid reaction unit in the PLA. The 15th Airborne's headquarters is in Xiaogan, north of Wuhan in Hubei. The 15th Airborne Army is composed of three airborne divisions: the 43rd Division stationed in Kaifeng, Henan, and the 44th and 45th Divisions also in the Wuhan area at Guangshui and Huangpi. Each division consists of about 10,000 personnel assigned to subordinate regiments, battalions, and companies. The majority of airborne troops are light infantry, supported by artillery, air defense, reconnaissance, engineer, chemical defense, communications, and logistics units. The 43rd also has a subordinate Special Operations Group. To lift the airborne army, the PLAAF has dedicated an air transport regiment of the 13th Transport Division to each division, each with some 25–30 transport aircraft.[9] The 15th Airborne is expected to be one of the first units to respond to almost any major military emergency that requires the insertion of ground forces quickly.

As outlined in Chapter 2, command flows from the Central Military Commission through the four General Headquarters Departments to the seven Military Region headquarters. The Military Regions exercise command over:

- group armies, naval and air forces, as well as a variety of independent ground force units in the region;
- logistics subdepartments consisting of a variety of hospitals, transportation units, supply and repair depots, bases, or centers, and the units that operate them; and
- Military Districts and garrison commands found in Beijing, Tianjin, Shanghai, and Chongqing that command Military Subdistricts and People's Armed Forces Departments, reserve, and militia units, as well as coastal, border, or frontier forces in the area.

In the middle of the first decade of the twenty-first century, PLA ground forces amount to roughly 1.6 million personnel. They are organized into 18 group armies, along with a number of independent units that do not belong to any group army. Maneuver forces (infantry and armored units) consist of approximately 40 divisions and about 43 maneuver brigades, supported by roughly 40 artillery, AAA, and air defense divisions and brigades, and by various other Special Operations Forces, reconnaissance, helicopter, engineer (combat and pontoon bridge), communications, chemical defense, electronic warfare, and "high technology" units. Most of the maneuver divisions are subordinated to group armies, with others subordinate to Military Region, Military District, or Garrison headquarters. (See Tables 4.1–4.7.) Over 30 logistics subdepartments (division level units) can be found in the seven Military Regions.[10] Local forces include many dozens of coastal defense divisions, brigades, and regiments and border (frontier) defense regiments along China's land boundaries.[11]

In addition to active ground force units, army reserve units include about 42 infantry, artillery, and AAA divisions; 16 infantry, artillery, and logistics support brigades; and seven chemical defense, engineer, and communications regiments.

Border security

The PLA shares responsibility with other government forces for securing China's borders. Both the CMC and State Council exercise joint leadership over this mission. Since 1996, the State Frontier Defense Commission has organized the construction of frontier defense infrastructure in nine inland provinces and autonomous regions.[12] Over the last ten years, more than 15,000 kilometers of roads, over 4,600 kilometers of wire netting, over 50,000 meters of iron fencing, and more than 300 frontier monitoring and alarm systems have been constructed along China's national boundaries to improve frontier defenses.[13] Monitoring and alarm systems include cameras, night vision devices, motion detectors, etc., linked to computers and improved communications systems at border outposts. These improvements have enabled the border to be patrolled more efficiently while allowing local civilians to conduct business and increase their living standards.

International agreements between the Chinese government and many of its land neighbors, most importantly with Russia, limit the size and types of forces that may be stationed within 100 kilometers of their borders. In general, Ministry of Public Security forces are primarily responsible for law enforcement activities along the border, with the PLA in support. According to a Chinese media report, the division of labor between PLA border guards and local authorities is defined as follows:

> Public security border defense units are responsible for exercising border administrative control according to law and for administrative law enforcement; detecting and investigating according to law suspected illegal immigration, smuggling, narcotics peddling and so on; checking and verifying persons and transportation means entering or leaving the border control zones.
>
> The duties of PLA border defense units are to defend the national borders; guard against and crack down on criminals and lawbreakers sneaking in and out and people trying to flee abroad; inspect and safeguard border markers; "get a handle" on the state of persons, vehicles, and vessels entering the border area and areas in dispute; meet the border defense organs of neighboring countries.[14]

PLA frontier defense units are organized into regiments and scattered, often in company-size outposts, along much of the length of the border. Life in these units can be austere and great effort has been made in recent years to upgrade the living conditions for troops performing these duties. As a result of advances in the country's electronics industry, computer and communications capabilities for both operational and quality of life purposes have been widely upgraded in border regions in the past decade.

Border troops routinely occupy permanent observation points and mount patrols between outposts. Some of these units use horses and snow mobiles in winter to patrol the border region. Border forces are lightly armed and would act as early warning of foreign movements into China, reporting back up the chain of command. They would not be expected to mount a formidable defense at the border. Because of the hardships associated with this mission, border defense units are featured prominently on the pages of Chinese military newspapers.

Missions for the Military Regions

Each of the seven Military Regions has a different mix of forces to achieve its primary mission in the defense of the Chinese mainland. In the northeast, the Shenyang Military Region originally was oriented to defend the traditional industrial center of Manchuria from Soviet attack (recalling particularly the multi-pronged Soviet armored advances at the end of World War II). Currently, in addition to training to defend China's northeast land borders, Shenyang Military Region units also practice amphibious operations. The region was the jumping off point for Chinese "volunteers" in support of North Korea in 1950, and today the local leadership is still mindful of conditions in that troubled neighboring communist state – especially the problem of refugees fleeing into China across the Yalu and Tumen rivers that separate the two countries. Over the past 15 years or more, however, the industrial might of northeast China has deteriorated considerably to the point where it is often called China's "rust belt." Central government policy has added the northeast to its list of areas that need special economic attention. PLA presence in the region helps deter disgruntled workers from taking steps beyond the thousands of peaceful protests and demonstrations that have occurred in recent years. For many years the Shenyang Military Region was assigned the second largest number of troops, exceeded only by the Beijing Military Region to its southwest. Now the force levels in these two regions are roughly equal.

The Beijing Military Region is primarily tasked to prevent foreign forces from entering the capital city from the north along avenues of approach from Manchuria and Inner Mongolia, and to a lesser extent from the south and east. While it is listed second in protocol order among the Military Regions (behind Shenyang), for decades the Beijing Military Region was assigned the largest number of main force units of all the Military Regions. In the reductions that began in 1997, of all the Military Regions, Beijing has lost the greatest percentage of its forces. These reductions indicate a shift in threat perception (toward "terrorist, separatist, and extremist forces") away from the danger of ground invasion from the Soviet Union of the 1960s and 1970s. Moreover, the reductions in the Beijing Military Region highlight the shift since the mid-1990s in defense priorities toward the task of reunification of Taiwan with the mainland. At the very minimum, the elevation in priority of deterrence of Taiwan independence calls for greater emphasis on readiness and training of forces in the Nanjing, Guangzhou, and Jinan Military Regions while the Beijing Military Region's relative importance decreases.

The Lanzhou Military Region is third in protocol order and originally was assigned to defend western China from the Soviet threat to the north and west. In order to do this, it was authorized only two group armies stationed well away from the border in Shaanxi and Gansu at the east end of the Gansu Corridor (a traditional route into China from central Asia), and a number of independent units further west. These deployments differ significantly from other regions (where troops are in closer proximity to China's borders), reflecting the impact of geography on China's strategic defenses. Obviously from the location of these troops, the mission of the Military Region was to "trade space for time" and weaken an invading force over the long, harsh distances between the border and central China. In the twenty-first century, the likelihood of invasion from Russia or the former states of the Soviet Union to China's west has diminished to minuscule proportion, but the threat of "terrorist, separatist, and extremist forces" is real in the vast territory of the Xinjiang Autonomous Region. There, and in neighboring countries, radical Islamic and ethnic nationalist groups are known to exist in greater numbers than anywhere else in China. Accordingly, PLA combat forces in the area have been reorganized within former headquarters, and their mobility has been increased with the addition of new equipment. Due to the threat and its remote location, the Xinjiang Military District has been organized to operate more independently than most other provincial Military Districts, especially in the logistics and armament support it can provide units in the region. Since the late 1990s, China's western regions have been granted high priority in economic development so that they may catch up with the progress found along the eastern seaboard, but in practice economic development has been haphazard. A unique civil–military organization, the Xinjiang Production and Construction Corps, is found in Lanzhou Military Region that has integrated agriculture and industrial production with security functions since the 1950s.

The Jinan Military Region is China's strategic reserve with forces that could be deployed to the north, west, or south as required. The region's forces will take advantage of being on or near many of the country's most important railroad hubs. As a reserve, the number of forces stationed in the Jinan Military Region is significant, but neither the largest nor smallest of the Military Regions.

The Nanjing Military Region follows in protocol order and remains oriented toward the east, especially toward Taiwan. The three group armies assigned to the region have not been reduced greatly in size and have been showered with new equipment and increased training opportunities in the last decade. Unlike all other Military Regions, the Nanjing Military Region has also been assigned a short-range surface-to-surface ballistic missile brigade that was transformed from a traditional artillery brigade in the late 1990s. This army-controlled missile unit is expected to augment the Second Artillery short-range missile brigades deployed in the area. Like other Military Regions along the coast, a number of local coastal defense units are active along the shore and on nearby offshore islands.

The Guangzhou Military Region is focused to the east toward Taiwan, as well as to the south toward Vietnam and the South China Sea. The region's two group armies have not undergone significant cuts, and, like the Nanjing Military Region, have received new equipment to transform a portion of their units to more mechanized, amphibious formations. The mountainous and jungle terrain of southern and southeastern China, along with the sandy soils near the coast, are not conducive to the movement of heavy equipment. Thus, many of the new lighter, armored vehicles, both wheeled and tracked, that have entered the force in recent years have been assigned to units in southern and southeastern provinces. Guangzhou Military Region forces, too, have been extremely active in military training since the turn of the century. While the Hong Kong and Macao garrisons are physically located in the region, they respond directly to command from the Central Military Commission and not Military Region headquarters in Guangzhou.[15]

Finally, in the southwestern border region the Chengdu Military Region is oriented toward mountain and high-altitude operations, particularly the local forces in Tibet. Though relations have improved with India since the turn of the century, Beijing still keeps an eye on a potential adversary to the south. The Military Region's two group armies located in Sichuan and Yunnan have not undergone significant cuts in recent years. Like the Xinjiang Military District, the Tibet Military District is organized to function relatively independently because of the difficulty in getting in and out of the region.

In the 1990s each Military Region created a Special Operations Force unit of regiment (*dadui*) level composed of about nine companies (organized into battalions) of roughly 100 personnel each. Each Military Region also has at least one helicopter regiment consisting of some 24–30 helicopters of all types – transport, armed, command and control, reconnaissance, medevac, and perhaps electronic warfare. A few helicopter regiments are assigned to group armies, while others remain under the command of the Military Region headquarters or are subordinate to the GSD (including a few training regiments). The number of helicopters in the force is still relatively small for such a large ground force. This implies that only a few army units routinely train in airmobile (heliborne) operations, and then likely at relatively low organizational level – perhaps up to battalion-size operations, but usually at company or platoon level. SOF units apparently receive priority over regular infantry units to train with the helicopters in each Military Region. Due to their small size, experienced personnel, and strategic importance, SOF units also receive the most modern equipment as it enters the PLA, such as advanced night vision devices, communications gear, and light weapons. Nevertheless, for an army as large as the PLA, its SOF capabilities are limited and focused mostly on commando-type missions.

Reductions, past and present

During the reductions that took place from 1997 to 2000, three group army headquarters were removed from the 24 in the pre-cutback PLA order of battle: the 28th Group Army in Datong, Shanxi in the Beijing Military Region; the 64th Group Army in Dalian, Liaoning in the Shenyang Military Region; and the 67th Group Army in Zibo, Shandong in the Jinan Military Region. In each of these three cases, in addition to the elimination of the group army headquarters, several divisions and other units, which were likely in lower-readiness categories, were disbanded. However, one or two divisions or brigades from each group army remained operational (and were possibly reorganized) and reassigned to other group army headquarters in the region.[16]

The three demobilized group armies came from Military Regions that previously had the largest concentrations of army units. The elimination of these units in north, east, and northeast China reflects the decrease in threat from Russian land forces. Although they had fewer ground forces to begin with, the number of group armies in Military Regions opposite from Taiwan and on China's western borders was not reduced. Existing unit structures within these group armies were, and continue to be, modified. The retention of previous numbers of army level organizations in these areas indicates Beijing's perception of the requirement to deter "terrorists, separatists, and extremists" by maintaining large standing ground forces near its borders.

In September 2003, a second reduction of an additional 200,000 personnel was announced to take place over a two-year period. These cuts were especially focused on streamlining headquarters and staff units. In particular, there were unsubstantiated reports that at least one Military Region headquarters may be eliminated. Similar rumors had been circulated in previous years; however, to date, there is no evidence of change to the basic Military Region structure.

Like the 1997 reduction, three group army headquarters were eliminated in the latest round of cuts: the 24th Group Army in Chengde, Hebei, and the 63rd Group Army in Taiyuan, Shanxi, both in Beijing Military Region, along with the 23rd Group Army in Harbin, Heilongjiang, in the Shenyang Military Region.[17] Other reductions include the deactivation of several divisions and brigades, the downsizing of additional divisions to brigades, and the transfer of a few divisions or brigades to the reserve force. Unlike the 1997 round of cuts, no army units were transferred into the PAP. (See "People's Armed Police in local force role" on pp. 87–88.)

After the two recent periods of force reductions, the Shenyang, Beijing, Jinan, and Nanjing Military Regions each have three group armies, while the Chengdu, Guangzhou, and Lanzhou Military Regions each control two. Despite the decrease in threat from the north, the PLA's two most powerful group armies, the 38th and 39th, are found in Beijing and Shenyang Military Regions.

An approximate ground order of battle

The Chinese government has not released a detailed listing of PLA ground forces and where they are stationed. Careful examination of the Chinese media over a period of years and decades can produce an unofficial approximation of the PLA order of battle. However, there may be a delay before many changes are reported in the Chinese press, if ever, and some details, such as the organization of sub-elements or specific equipment assigned to units, may never be acknowledged officially. The task is further complicated during periods of reduction and reorganization when units may be in the process of demobilization, structural change, or re-subordination for several months. Accordingly, unofficial orders of battle are not completely accurate or timely.

The following listing of PLA ground force units is based on the work of several organizations and individuals who have studied the PLA for decades.[18] It is as accurate as possible, but should not be construed as authoritative. A few operational divisions, brigades, or regiments are likely to have been overlooked or misidentified. Some units are known to have been reorganized or have been reassigned to other headquarters, but the specifics have yet to be confirmed.

Shenyang Military Region

The Shenyang Military Region has three group armies under its command in 2005: the 16th, 39th, and 40th (Table 4.1). The region's 23rd Group Army headquarters

Table 4.1 Shenyang Military Region forces

16th GA, Changchun, Jilin
- 46th Motorized Infantry Division, Changchun, Jilin
- 48th Motorized Infantry Brigade, Tonghua, Jilin
- 4th Armored Division, Meihekou, Jilin
- Artillery Brigade, Yanbian, Jilin
- AAA Brigade, Changchun, Jilin

39th Mechanized GA, Liaoyang, Liaoning
- 115th Mechanized Infantry Division, Yingkou, Liaoning
- 116th Mechanized Infantry Division, Haicheng, Liaoning
- 190th Mechanized Infantry Division, Shenyang, Liaoning
- Unidentified (UI) Mechanized Division (possibly double count of above)
- 3rd Armored Division, Siping, Jilin
- Artillery Brigade, Liaoyang, Liaoning
- Air Defense Brigade, Liaoning
- Chemical Defense Regiment
- Helicopter Regiment

40th GA, Jinzhou, Liaoning
- UI Motorized Infantry Brigade, Yixian, Liaoning
- UI Motorized Infantry Brigade, Chifeng, Inner Mongolia
- UI Armored Brigade, Fuxin, Liaoning
- Artillery Brigade, Jinzhou, Liaoning
- AAA Brigade, Jinzhou, Liaoning

Units Subordinate to MR or MD
- UI Motorized Infantry Brigade, Dandong, Liaoning MD
- 68th Motorized Infantry Brigade, Qiqihar, Heilongjiang (from 23rd Group Army)
- 69th Motorized Infantry Division, Harbin, Heilongjiang (from 23rd Group Army)
- ECM Regiment
- Special Operations Dadui, Huludao, Liaoning
- Psychological Warfare Unit
- High-Technology Unit

Logistics Subdepartments and units
- 1st Subdepartment, Jilin, Jilin (merged with former 3rd Subdepartment)
- 2nd Subdepartment, Shenyang, Liaoning
- 4th Subdepartment, Jinzhou, Liaoning
- 40th Subdepartment, Qiqihar, Heilongjiang
- Army Ship Transport Group

Reserve units
- Liaoning Army Reserve 192nd Infantry Division, Shenyang
- Liaoning Army Reserve 1st AAA Division, Shenyang
- Liaoning Army Reserve 2nd AAA Division, Dalian
- Liaoning Jinzhou Reserve Logistics Support Brigade
- Liaoning Army Reserve Communications Regiment, Anshan
- Jilin Army Reserve 47th Infantry Division, Jilin city
- Jilin Reserve Division, Yanbian
- Jilin Reserve Artillery Division, Changchun

Table 4.1 continued

- Jilin Reserve Anti-Tank Artillery Brigade, Baicheng
- Probable Reserve Artillery Brigade, Dunhua
- Jilin Army Reserve Communications Regiment, Tonghua
- Reserve Water Supply Engineer Regiment
- Heilongjiang Army Reserve Infantry Division
- Heilongjiang Army Reserve AAA Division, Daqing
- Reserve AAA Brigade, Jiamusi, Heilongjiang
- Heilongjiang Army Reserve Chemical Defense Regiment, Harbin

---

was deactivated during the 2003 reduction in force. The 68th Motorized Infantry Brigade and the 69th Motorized Infantry Division of the former 23rd Group Army appear still to be active, while the 67th Motorized Infantry Brigade, an armored brigade, and artillery brigade were demobilized. The 23rd Group Army's former AAA Brigade has been transferred to the reserves. The former Anti-Tank Missile Brigade at Baicheng, Jilin in the 16th Group Army was a unique formation within the PLA, recalling the armor threat from the Soviet Union. This unit was transferred to the reserve force during the 2003 reduction cycle and is now known as the Jilin Reserve Anti-Tank Artillery Brigade. This move reflects the lesser need for a large, standing anti-tank force in the northeast after the demise of the USSR.

The region's 39th Group Army is one of the two most powerful formations in the Chinese ground force, consisting of all mechanized or armored divisions and an organic helicopter regiment. The 39th was not downsized during the recent reduction and had its former AAA brigade upgraded to an air defense brigade by the addition of short-range surface-to-air missiles. On the other hand, the 40th Group Army is one of the few group armies with an all-brigade maneuver force (infantry and armored units), and has no subordinate divisions.[19]

As will be seen in other Military Regions, most group armies have the bulk of their forces stationed in a single province, but a few subordinate elements of a group army may be located in adjacent provinces.

Beijing Military Region

The Beijing Military Region commands three group armies, the 27th, 38th, and 65th, and the Beijing and Tianjin Garrison Commands (Table 4.2). During the 2003 reduction cycle, the region's 24th Group Army headquarters and the 63rd Group Army headquarters were eliminated. (Prior to the details of these demobilizations becoming known, some reports speculated that the 27th Group Army, not the 24th, would be deactivated.) Over the course of this period, the 114th Mechanized Division of the 38th Group Army, the 70th Division of the 24th Group Army, two artillery brigades, and an AAA brigade appear to have been dropped from the force. In 2005, two new reserve AAA brigades were formed from what appear to be previously active units.[20]

Table 4.2 Beijing Military Region forces

27th GA, Shijiazhuang, Hebei
- 235th Mechanized Infantry Brigade, Xingtai, Hebei
- 80th Mechanized Infantry Brigade, Luquan, Hebei
- UI Armored Brigade, Handan, Hebei
- Artillery Brigade, Handan, Hebei
- AAA Brigade, Shijiazhuang, Hebei

38th Mechanized GA, Baoding, Hebei
- 112th Mechanized Infantry Division, Baoding, Hebei
- 113th Mechanized Infantry Division, Baoding, Hebei
- 6th Armored Division, Nankou, Beijing
- 6th Artillery Brigade, Pinggu, Beijing
- Mechanized Air Defense Brigade, Shijiazhuang, Hebei
- Chemical Defense Regiment
- Helicopter Regiment, Baoding, Hebei

65th GA, Zhangjiakou, Hebei
- 193rd Division ("Red 1st Division"), Xuanhua, Hebei
- 194th Motorized Infantry Brigade, Huai'an County, Hebei
- 207th Motorized Infantry Brigade, Wanquan, Hebei
- UI Armored Brigade, Zhangjiakou, Hebei
- 14th Artillery Brigade, Huailai, Hebei

Beijing Garrison
- 1st Garrison Division
- 3rd Garrison Division, Shunyi

Tianjin Garrison
- 196th Infantry Brigade, Yangcun, Tianjin municipality
- 1st Armored Division, northern Tianjin municipality (the subordination of this unit to Tianjin Garrison is speculative)

Other units subordinate to MR or MD
- Armored Brigade, Datong, Shanxi, for the Combined Arms Training Base in Inner Mongolia
- UI Motorized Infantry Brigade, Hohhot, Inner Mongolia
- UI Mechanized Infantry Brigade, Taiyuan, Shanxi
- UI Motorized Infantry Brigade, Datong, Shanxi (from 65th Group Army)
- Artillery Brigade
- AAA Brigade
- Special Operations Dadui, Daxing, Beijing
- Engineer Brigade, Nankou, Beijing
- Engineer Water Supply Regiment

Logistics Subdepartments and units
- 5th Subdepartment, Taiyuan, Shanxi
- 6th Subdepartment, Fengtai, Beijing
- 7th Subdepartment, Shijiazhuang, Hebei
- 8th Subdepartment, Tianjin

Table 4.2 continued

Reserve units
- Hebei Army Reserve Infantry Division, Shijiazhuang
- Hebei Army Reserve Artillery 72nd Division, Tangshan
- Army Reserve Artillery Brigade, Qinhuangdao
- Army Reserve Antiaircraft Artillery Brigade, Zhangjiakou
- Langfang Army Reserve Logistics Support Brigade
- Shanxi Army Reserve Infantry 83rd Division, Xinzhou (from 63rd Group Army)
- Shanxi Army Reserve Infantry Division (possibly newly formed)
- Neimenggu Army Reserve Division, Hohhot
- Beijing Garrison Reserve AAA Division
- Beijing Garrison Reserve Chemical Defense Regiment
- Tianjin Army Reserve AAA Division

The 38th Group Army, like the 39th in Shenyang Military Region, consists of all mechanized or armored divisions and an organic helicopter regiment. Its 112th Mechanized Division has relocated south to Baoding from its former location at Xincheng, Hebei. The 27th Group Army remains active and is composed of two infantry brigades, both of which were recently transformed from motorized into mechanized units, and an armor brigade.

The Central Guard Regiment, responsible for the personal security of senior PLA and government leaders, is stationed in various locations in and around Beijing and responds to direction from the General Staff Department. It would coordinate closely with the Beijing Garrison headquarters and PAP forces in the capital city in performing its routine duties.

Lanzhou Military Region

The Lanzhou Military Region has two group armies under its command: the 21st and 47th (Table 4.3). The 47th Group Army is the third of the group armies composed entirely of maneuver brigades. The Military Region headquarters also has several independent combat divisions farther west in Xinjiang that do not belong to a group army. In May 2004, *Jiefangjun Bao* reported one of these divisions as having transformed into a mechanized infantry division (along with converting one of its infantry regiments into an armored regiment), but the specific unit identification or location is unknown.[21] Seven identified logistics subdepartments support the Military Region, an unusually high number of logistics units, but necessary to support the combat forces scattered throughout such a large chunk of the country.

Jinan Military Region

The Jinan Military Region has three group armies assigned, the 20th, 26th, and 54th (Table 4.4). It also has a fairly large number of logistics subdepartments, which

Table 4.3 Lanzhou Military Region forces

_____

21st GA, Baoji, Shaanxi
- 61st Division ("Red Army Division"), Tianshui, Gansu
- 55th Motorized Infantry Brigade, Zhangye, Gansu
- 12th Armored Division, Jiuquan, Gansu
- Artillery Brigade
- AAA Brigade, Gansu

47th GA, Lintong, Shaanxi
- 139th Mechanized Infantry Brigade, Weinan, Shaanxi
- 56th Motorized Infantry Brigade
- UI Motorized Infantry Brigade
- UI Armored Brigade, Chengcheng, Shaanxi
- Artillery Brigade
- AAA Brigade, Pucheng, Shaanxi
- Engineer Regiment
- Communications Regiment

Units subordinate to MR or MD
- 4th Division ("Red Army Division"), Xinjiang MD
- 6th Motorized Division, Shache County, Xinjiang MD
- 8th Motorized Infantry Division, Tacheng, Xinjiang MD
- 11th Motorized Division, Urumqi, Xinjiang MD
- UI Armored Division, Nanjiang, Xinjiang MD
- Artillery Brigade, Xinjiang MD
- Artillery Brigade, Qinghai
- AAA Brigade, Xinjiang MD
- Helicopter Regiment, Xinjiang MD
- Special Operations Dadui, Qingtongxia, Ningxia
- ECM Regiment, Lanzhou, Gansu
- High-Technology Bureau

Logistics Subdepartments and units
- 25th Subdepartment, Xining, Qinghai
- 27th Subdepartment, Lanzhou, Gansu
- 28th Subdepartment, Xi'an, Shaanxi
- 29th Subdepartment, Xinjiang
- 30th Subdepartment, Xinjiang
- 31st Subdepartment, Xinjiang
- 32nd Subdepartment, Yecheng Xian, Xinjiang
- Motor Transport Regiment, Xinjiang MD

Reserve units
- Shaanxi Army Reserve Infantry Division
- Shaanxi Army Reserve AAA Division, Xi'an
- Shaanxi Baoji Army Reserve Logistics Support Brigade
- Gansu Army Reserve Infantry Tianshui Brigade
- Gansu Army Reserve AAA Division, Lanzhou
- Xinjiang Army Reserve Infantry Division
- Qinghai Army Reserve Infantry Division
- Qinghai Army Reserve Brigade

_____

Table 4.4 Jinan Military Region forces

20th GA, Kaifeng, Henan
- 58th Mechanized Infantry Brigade, Xuchang, Henan
- 60th Motorized Infantry Brigade, Minggang, Xinyang, Henan
- UI Armored Brigade, Nanyang, Henan
- Artillery Brigade, Queshan, Henan
- AAA Brigade, Shangqiu, Henan
- Engineer Regiment, Xinyang, Henan

26th GA, Weifang, Shandong
- 138th Motorized Infantry Brigade
- 199th Motorized Infantry Brigade, Zibo, Shandong
- 77th Motorized Infantry Brigade, Haiyang, Shandong
- 200th Motorized Infantry Brigade, Tai'an, Shandong
- 8th Armored Division, Weifang, Shandong
- 8th Artillery Brigade, Weifang, Shandong
- Air Defense Brigade, Jinan, Shandong

54th GA, Xinxiang, Henan
- 127th Light Mechanized Infantry Division, Luoyang, Henan
- 162nd Motorized Infantry Division, Anyang, Henan
- 160th Motorized Infantry Brigade, probably in Zhumadian, Henan
- 11th Armored Division, Xinyang, Henan
- Artillery Brigade, Jiaozuo, Henan
- Air Defense Brigade, Xingyang, Zhengzhou, Henan

Units subordinate to MR or MD
- Army Aviation Regiment, Xinxiang, Henan
- Special Operations Dadui, Laiwu, Shandong
- Electronic Warfare Regiment, Zhoucun, Shandong
- Technical Rapid Reaction Unit, Jinan, Shandong
- UI Technical Dadui
- Pontoon Bridge Regiment, Pingyin, Shandong
- Pontoon Bridge Regiment, Mangshan, Luoyang, Henan
- Chemical Defense Regiment

Logistics Subdepartments and units
- 9th Subdepartment, Zaozhuang, Shandong
- 10th Subdepartment, Laiyang, Shandong
- 11th Subdepartment, Jinan, Shandong
- 33rd Subdepartment, Zhengzhou, Henan
- 34th Subdepartment, Xinyang, Henan

Reserve units
- Shandong Army Reserve 76th Infantry Division, Yantai
- Shandong Reserve Artillery Division, Jining
- Shandong Reserve AAA Division, Qingdao
- Shandong Reserve Army Logistics Support Brigade
- Henan Army Reserve 136th Infantry Division, Kaifeng
- Henan Army Reserve Artillery Division, one regiment at Sanmenxia
- Henan Army Reserve AAA Division, Zhengzhou

due to their central locations could be used to support operations to the north or south of the region. During the force reduction started in 2003, the 26th Group Army's 138th Motorized Infantry Brigade, 199th Motorized Infantry Brigade, and 8th Artillery Brigade were created from divisions and the AAA brigade transformed into an air defense brigade.

In the 54th Group Army, the 127th Light Mechanized Infantry Division was one of the first complete motorized infantry divisions to be converted into a mechanized division in which armored personnel carriers are used to transport infantry squads and platoons. The 127th's conversion started in 1997 and took about three years before the division was evaluated to be combat effective with its new equipment. Likewise, the 58th Mechanized Infantry Brigade of the 20th Group Army was one of the first brigades in the PLA to be transformed from a truck-mobile unit to one using armored personnel carriers. The 20th Group Army also has an all-brigade structure (the fourth group army consisting only of brigades in this listing).

Nanjing Military Region

The Nanjing Military Region is composed of three group armies, the 1st, 12th, and 31st, the Shanghai Garrison, and several coastal defense units (Table 4.5). The 1st Group Army's 1st Amphibious Mechanized Infantry Division was the army's first division to be transformed into an amphibious unit. (A second such division is found in the Guangzhou Military Region.) The division's conversion began in 2000 and took approximately two years to complete. An amphibious armored brigade is also assigned to the region. These units have exercised extensively on amphibious operations annually since the spring and summer of 2001, as have elements from all the group armies in the region. As mentioned earlier, the Nanjing Military Region has the ground force's only surface-to-surface short-range ballistic missile brigade. All three group armies in the region have converted their former AAA brigades into mixed gun and surface-to-air missile air defense brigades. This modernization reflects the perceived air and cruise missile threat to the region.

Table 4.5 Nanjing Military Region forces

1st GA, Huzhou, Zhejiang
- 1st Amphibious Mechanized Infantry Division, Hangzhou, Zhejiang
- 3rd Motorized Infantry Brigade, Jinhua, Zhejiang
- UI Armored Division, Suzhou, Jiangsu
- 9th Artillery Division, Wuxi, Jiangsu
- Air Defense Brigade, Zhenjiang, Jiangsu

12th GA, Xuzhou, Jiangsu
- 34th Motorized Infantry Brigade, Chuzhou, Anhui
- 36th Motorized Infantry Division, Suqian, Jiangsu
- 179th Motorized Infantry Brigade ("Linfen Brigade"), Nanjing, Jiangsu
- UI Armored Division, Xuzhou, Jiangsu
- UI Artillery Brigade, Xuzhou, Jiangsu
- Air Defense Brigade, Huai'an, Jiangsu

Table 4.5 continued

31st GA, Xiamen, Fujian
- 86th Division, Fuzhou, Fujian
- 91st Motorized Infantry Division, Zhangzhou, Fujian
- 92nd Motorized Infantry Brigade, Nanping, Fujian
- UI Amphibious Armored Brigade, Changtai, Fujian
- Artillery Brigade, Quanzhou, Fujian
- Air Defense Brigade

Shanghai Garrison
- UI Coastal Defense Brigade
- UI Coastal Defense Brigade
- UI Coastal Defense Brigade

Other units subordinate to MR or MD
- UI Coastal Defense Division, Jinjiang, Fujian MD
- 12th Coastal Defense Division, Changle, Fujian MD
- UI Coastal Defense Division, Shishi, Fujian MD
- UI Coastal Defense Brigade, Fujian MD
- Helicopter Regiment
- Pontoon Bridge Brigade, Jiangsu MD
- Pontoon Bridge Brigade
- Special Operations Dadui
- Surface-to-Surface Missile Brigade, Shangrao, Jiangxi

Logistics Subdepartments and units
- 13th Subdepartment, Wuxi, Jiangsu
- 15th Subdepartment, Huai'an, Jiangsu
- 16th Subdepartment, Nanjing, Jiangsu
- 17th Subdepartment, Yingtan, Jiangxi
- 18th Subdepartment, Fuzhou, Fujian
- Army Ship Transport Group

Reserve units
- Shanghai Army Reserve AAA Division
- Jiangsu Army Reserve Infantry Division
- Jiangsu Reserve AAA Division, Nanjing
- Anhui Army Reserve Infantry Division, Hefei
- Fujian Army Reserve AAA Division, Fuzhou
- Fujian Zhangzhou Reserve Logistics Support Brigade
- Jiangxi Army Reserve Infantry Division, Nanchang
- Zhejiang Reserve Infantry Division
- Zhejiang Reserve Chemical Defense Regiment

Guangzhou Military Region

The Guangzhou Military Region commands two group armies, the 41st and 42nd, and has the Hong Kong and Macao Garrisons located within its boundaries (Table 4.6), but does not command them. The army's second amphibious mechanized division, the 124th, is found in the 42nd Group Army and was formed in 2001.

Table 4.6 Guangzhou Military Region forces

41st GA, Liuzhou, Guangxi
- 121st Infantry Division, Guilin, Guangxi
- 123rd Motorized Infantry Division, Guangxi
- UI Armored Brigade, Guilin, Guangxi
- UI Artillery Brigade, Liuzhou, Guangxi
- UI AAA Brigade, Henyang, Hunan

42nd GA, Huizhou, Guangdong
- 124th Amphibious Mechanized Infantry Division, Boluo, Guangdong
- 163rd Division, Chaozhou, Guangdong
- UI Armored Brigade, Guangzhou, Guangdong
- UI Artillery Division, Oujiang, Guangdong
- Air Defense Brigade, Chaozhou, Guangdong

Hong Kong Garrison
- Infantry Brigade
- Logistics Base, Shenzhen

Macao Garrison

Other units subordinate to MR or MD
- 132nd Infantry Brigade, Wuzhishan, Hainan
- UI Brigade, Shantou, Guangdong
- Army Aviation Regiment
- Special Operations Dadui, Guangzhou, Guangdong
- 32nd Pontoon Bridge Brigade, Hubei MD
- Electronic Warfare Regiment
- Technical Rapid Reaction Unit/MR Informationalized Unit

Logistics Subdepartments and units
- 19th Subdepartment, Hengyang, Hunan
- 20th Subdepartment, Guilin, Guangxi
- 21st Subdepartment, Guangzhou, Guangdong
- Army Ship Transport Group

Reserve units
- Hunan Army Reserve Infantry Division, Changsha
- Hunan Hengyang Army Reserve Logistics Support Brigade
- Guangdong Reserve AAA Division
- Guangxi Army Reserve Infantry Division, Nanning
- Hainan Army Reserve Division
- Hubei Army Reserve Infantry Division, Yichang
- Yichang Army Reserve AAA Brigade
- Shenzhen Reserve Chemical Defense Regiment

The two marine brigades of the PLA Navy (one of which was transformed from an infantry division during the 1997 reductions) are also located in the region in Zhanjiang. The army's two recently converted amphibious mechanized divisions (the 1st and 124th) now outnumber in personnel and equipment strength the two

PLAN marine brigades. This development points to the ground force leadership's efforts to maintain their relevance in times of changing threat and strategic environment. A significant component to the logistics forces stationed in the region is an "Army Ship Transport Group," which is composed of a variety of small transport ships and craft used to transport ground force troops and equipment. "Army Ship Transport Groups" are also found in the Shenyang and Nanjing Military Regions to augment the amphibious lift capability of the PLA Navy. The Yichang Army Reserve Anti-Aircraft Artillery Brigade was formed in 2005 by reorganizing and expanding the AAA regiment in the Hubei Army Reserve Infantry Division.[22]

Chengdu Military Region

The Chengdu Military Region has two group armies assigned: the 13th and 14th (Table 4.7). It also commands the Chongqing Garrison and a significant number of independent and border forces in Tibet. Both the General Headquarters Departments and the Chengdu Military Region expend great efforts to make sure the forces in Tibet are supplied adequately, primarily by road, but sometimes also by aircraft. (Construction on the first railroad linking the rugged Tibetan plateau with Qinghai began in 2001 and is scheduled for completion around 2006 or 2007.) No logistics subdepartment has been identified in Tibet, which suggests that the Tibet Military District headquarters has dedicated logistics and armament units responsible for providing services for troop units in the autonomous region. The difficulty in getting large equipment in and out of the Tibetan plateau encourages the Military District to have its own repair capacity to reduce the requirement for damaged equipment to be transported over difficult roads in extreme weather conditions.

Reserve unit order of battle

As the active force underwent force reductions from 1997 to 2000, the PLA reserve unit force also was involved in a major reorganization, encompassing the consolidation and restructuring of many old units and creation of new units with the province or centrally administered city as a basis. Before this reorganization, the PLA reserve force was estimated to consist of approximately 43 divisions and two regiments, smaller than the current structure of 42 divisions, 16 brigades, and seven regiments identified above.[23]

As can be seen from the orders of battle for each Military Region, a reserve infantry division has been identified in every province (except for Jilin, which has two divisions; Gansu, which has a brigade; and Sichuan, which has a division and a brigade) and autonomous region (except for Tibet, where no reserve units have been identified). The four centrally administered cities have established reserve anti-aircraft artillery divisions, but *not* reserve infantry divisions. Reserve artillery and AAA divisions, along with a few engineering, chemical defense, and communications regiments, are also found in several provinces in addition to infantry forces. Reserve divisions are now organized along provincial lines with subordinate regiments found in major provincial cities and surrounding areas. Organization on

Table 4.7 Chengdu Military Region forces

13th GA, Chongqing
- 37th Division, Chongqing
- 149th Motorized Infantry Division, Leshan, Sichuan
- UI Armored Brigade, Pengzhou, Sichuan
- UI Artillery Brigade, Chongzhou, Sichuan
- UI AAA Brigade, Mianyang, Sichuan

14th GA, Kunming, Yunnan
- UI Division, Dali, Yunnan
- UI Division, Kaiyuan, Yunnan
- UI Armored Brigade, Kunming, Yunnan
- UI Artillery Brigade, Yunnan
- UI AAA Brigade, Kunming, Yunnan
- Chemical Defense Regiment

Chongqing Garrison

Other units subordinate to MR or MD
- 52nd Mountain Infantry Brigade, Nyingchi, Xizang
- 53rd Mountain Infantry Brigade, Nyingchi, Xizang
- Army Aviation Regiment
- "Cheetah" Special Operations Group, Chengdu, Sichuan
- Special Reconnaissance Group
- Electronic Warfare Regiment
- High-Technology Unit
- Chemical Defense Technical Group

Logistics Subdepartments and units
- 22nd Subdepartment, Kunming, Yunnan
- 37th Subdepartment, Chongqing
- 38th Subdepartment, Chengdu, Sichuan

Reserve units
- Sichuan Army Reserve Infantry Division, Chengdu
- Sichuan Leshan Reserve Infantry Brigade
- Chongqing Reserve AAA Division
- Chongqing Army Reserve Logistics Support Brigade
- Guizhou Army Reserve Infantry Division
- Yunnan Army Reserve Division

---

a provincial basis is consistent with the peacetime chain of command for reserve units running through provincial Military District headquarters.

Prior to 1998, no brigades were found in the reserve force. As part of the PLA logistics modernization program, a reserve logistics support brigade was created in each Military Region starting in 1999. Logistics support brigades include transportation, supply, POL, medical, and maintenance and repair units along with command, control, and communications elements. These seven brigades have been active in their relatively short lifespan supporting both active and reserve forces in training. Other newly formed reserve brigades include the anti-tank artillery, artillery, and AAA brigades in Shenyang Military Region.

In time of war, reserve units may operate independently or be assigned to supplement active duty units. Some individual reservists may also be assigned to active units to fill manpower vacancies.

People's Armed Police in local force role

In addition to PLA forces and reserve units, another local force that may be called upon to provide support to the PLA in wartime is the internal security arm of the People's Armed Police. (The PAP is a component of the Chinese *armed forces*, but is not an element of the PLA.) Other elements of the PAP will likely also perform local defense missions in time of war, but internal security units are the largest and most appropriate force for the mission. PAP forces are organized, trained, and equipped as light infantry and routinely practice infantry missions in addition to their internal security functions. Each mainland province, autonomous region, and centrally administered city has a PAP internal security *zongdui*, equating to a division-size light infantry force – adding roughly 30 divisions to support PLA operations. (No PAP units are stationed in Hong Kong or Macao.) Each *zongdui* is composed of several *zhidui*, or regimental-size units, based in large cities, the number of which varies according to local circumstances. While these are mostly light infantry-type forces using trucks for transportation, many PAP units throughout the country have been issued a few armored personnel carriers primarily for anti-terrorist and domestic security missions. Some units also have access to anti-tank and heavier weapons, which are not necessary or appropriate for domestic security roles. PAP *zongdui* are named after the province where they are assigned (such as the Sichuan *zongdui*) and *zhidui* by the cities. Some *zhidui*, such as those found in *zongdui* in the centrally administered cities, will be numbered (such as the Beijing *zongdui* 10th *zhidui*).

During the PLA's 1997 reduction in force, 14 army divisions were transferred to the PAP. Most of the officers and men of these divisions changed uniforms and missions and were incorporated into the PAP chain of command. These 14 divisions are identified by four-digit numerical designators assigned to them by PAP headquarters (replacing the five-digit numbers belonging to their predecessor PLA units) and can be found in many parts of the country. Subordinate *zhidui* to these new four-digit *zongdui* are identified by sequential numbers to the *zongdui*'s base number. For example, the 8680 *zongdui* will have the 8681, 8682, 8683, and 8684 *zhidui* subordinate to it. The 14 PAP *zongdui* converted from former PLA divisions are found in Table 4.8.

In time of war, the 44 total internal defense PAP *zongdui* (30 provincial level and 14 former PLA units) will be able to perform missions in the rear areas of PLA formations, such as security and population control, allowing the active duty units to concentrate on other operational requirements. Other civilian and paramilitary forces will also be available to support PLA operations in wartime.

Table 4.8 Four-digit PAP *zongdui*[24]

PAP Unit	Location
8610 *zongdui*	Probably in Jinzhou, Liaoning
8620 *zongdui*	Xingcheng, Huludao, Liaoning
8630 *zongdui*	Tianjin
8640 *zongdui*	Dingzhou, Baoding, Hebei
8650 *zongdui*	Taiyuan, Shanxi
8660 *zongdui*	Yining, Xinjiang
8670 *zongdui*	Pingliang, Gansu
8680 *zongdui*	Gongyi, Henan
8690 *zongdui*	South Jiangsu
8710 *zongdui*	Putian, Fujian
8720 *zongdui*	Wuxi, Jiangsu
8730 *zongdui*	Leiyang, Hunan
8740 *zongdui*	Nanchong, Sichuan
8750 *zongdui*	Mengzi, Yunnan

Militia forces

The paramilitary people's militia is the third arm of the Chinese armed forces (distinct from the PLA and PAP) and has the mission to support the PLA in time of war and provide protection to the locales in which militia units are located. Like the PLA, the militia has undergone serious reform since the early 1990s, particularly in readjusting its size and missions to meet contemporary requirements. In years past many militia units were "paper" units composed of names on lists, without proper equipment, who conducted little or no training. In the past decade, emphasis has been on reducing the size of the ordinary militia while building up and modernizing the primary militia to perform new roles. The militia of a previous era, known best for the strong backs and legs of its peasant troops to haul supplies to the front and damaged equipment and wounded personnel to the rear, is no more.

The 2004 Defense White Paper states that the total number of personnel currently on the rolls of the primary militia is 10 million, but does not specify a number for the ordinary militia.[25] No order of battle listing is available for either militia force. Within a single militia battalion or higher level organization, both primary and ordinary subordinate units may be found. The number of subordinate units in militia battalions and regiments may be less than the number of elements in a similar size unit in the active PLA.[26]

The number and type of militia units in any region varies according to size of the areas they support and local needs. Traditional militia units for local defense, such as infantry, air defense, and chemical defense, continue to be prevalent throughout the country. For instance, more than 1,400 counties in China have established "People's Air Defense" organizations.[27] Militia units will help in population and traffic control in PLA rear areas, as well as perform rear area security functions. For example, a sample infantry division logistics defense plan shows a militia battalion integrated into the rear area defense scheme of a typical PLA division deployed in the field with each of the battalion's three companies given a separate mission to accomplish.[28]

Emergency high-technology and logistics militia units of battalion size and smaller are becoming numerous, numbering in the thousands throughout the entire country. Representative examples of new militia units include anti-terrorist, information technology, electric power control, equipment repair, road and bridge repair, railroad repair, vehicle and ship transport, POL support, camouflage, medical, and mobile and satellite communications units. People's Armed Forces Departments deliberately seek to recruit personnel for their militia forces with the special skills needed for their locales. Prior military service is not required. Recently, building the "Urban Militia" to defend Chinese cities from long-range attack and repair infrastructure damaged in air raids has been the focus of much national and local effort.

Both the active and reserve PLA force rely heavily on militia and other civilian resources to provide logistics support, particularly transportation assistance, when they are outside of their home garrisons. Command of militia units is exercised through joint civil–military headquarters that have been created and equipped with modern communications since the late 1990s.

The Xinjiang Production and Construction Corps

In China's western region, a unique paramilitary organization exists in a form similar to its predecessor of another era. The Xinjiang Production and Construction Corps (*xinjiang shengchan jianshe bingtuan*, abbreviated in Chinese as the *bingtuan*), which is also known as the China Xinjiang Group, was first created in 1954 when most PLA units in the region were ordered to transfer to civilian work. Then in 1975 the Corps was dissolved but reestablished in 1981. According to the 2003 Chinese White Paper on Xinjiang, the mission of the Corps is "cultivating and guarding the frontier areas entrusted to it by the state."[29] It is a "special social organization" under the dual leadership of the central government and the Xinjiang Uygur Autonomous Region. The total number of personnel assigned to the Corps amounts to 2,453,600, including 933,000 workers organized into 14 divisions and 174 regimental farms, which have established an unknown number of militia units.

The total number of personnel in the Xinjiang Production and Construction Corps *cannot* be considered as part of China's armed forces, though it is organized along military lines. Individual elements of the Corps are known by their military designations (for example, the "No. 102 Regiment" of the Corps) and its leaders are addressed as "commanders." An unknown number of the nearly one million workers in the Corps, however, are part of its militia forces, in the same way a large factory or village may form militia units. Some estimates put the number at about 100,000 workers who have undergone military training.[30] All 100,000 workers who have received this training, however, would not necessarily still be on the Corps' militia rolls; or others may have been newly trained since these reports. The exact situation is uncertain.

Along with local PLA and PAP units, as well as with local citizens, the Corps has established a "four-in-one" joint defense system aimed at "resisting internal and external separatists' attempts at sabotage and infiltration, and in maintaining the stability and safety of the borders of the motherland."[31] Militia units from the Corps routinely work with PLA and PAP forces in a variety of missions, including border defense, internal security (including anti-riot training), and disaster relief. While elements of the Xinjiang Production and Construction Corps definitely are involved in domestic and external security, as a whole the Corps primarily is engaged in economic and production work and is not a formal part of the PLA or the Chinese armed forces.

Where the PLA is located and how it is organized provides some insight into how it will fight. Traditional Chinese sources, such as Sun Zi's (or Sun Tzu's) *The Art of War*, and Mao Zedong's military thought (which introduced the concept of "People's War") are the foundation for PLA's current military doctrine, along with influences from the study of modern military campaigns – primarily those waged by the United States and its allies in the late twentieth century. Many influences from the Soviet army have receded in importance from a high point in prior decades. Because of China's geography, economic and technological conditions, and large population, Chinese military doctrine emphasizes the integration of civilian personnel and material assets into military operations in the defense of China or its sovereignty. While the PLA has not developed unique "principles of war" unto itself, it does approach fighting differently than other more technologically advanced militaries. Once again, there is both change and continuity in Chinese military doctrine as the PLA prepares for potential contingencies in the twenty-first century.

5
HOW WILL THE PLA FIGHT?

In the quarter century since the PLA's last major ground campaign against a foreign enemy, the technology and complexity of war have increased dramatically. Although slow to accept many of the potentials of modern technology, in the 1990s the PLA acknowledged the new efficiencies, extended ranges, and lethality of advanced weapons systems and modified elements of its modernization process to better integrate new equipment into its force structure and planning. The PLA also took advantage of advances in China's civilian and dual-use technology base to provide capabilities undreamed of a generation ago, particularly in the realms of command, control, communications, and computers. By the end of the twentieth century, the PLA had developed a new doctrine to fight Local Wars Under Modern High Technology Conditions on China's periphery. Joint operations (*lianhe zuozhan*, operations involving the employment of forces from two or more services) and combined arms operations (*hetong zuozhan*, operations involving more than one branch of a service, such as the combination of infantry, tanks, artillery, and helicopters) became the focus of the PLA's new approach to war. The PLA recognized that it must be prepared to fight in a multidimensional environment integrating operations on land and sea, in the air and space, as well as in the electromagnetic spectrum.

At the same time, Chinese military planners continued to study traditional Chinese sources, such as *The Art of War* by Sun Zi, and Mao Zedong's concept of "People's War" (*renmin zhanzheng*). While many technological factors have changed, Chinese military leaders understand that China's geography, population, economic development, and natural resources still have a major impact on the way the PLA intellectually and physically approaches warfare. Therefore, the PLA is in the process of integrating old ideas and unavoidable realities with new concepts and technologies to prepare to fight in a manner it has never attempted in its recent history. (PLA writings acknowledge that its only true *joint* combat operation against an enemy force was the January 1955 amphibious operation in the Dachen island group to "liberate" Yijiangshan island from Nationalist forces. Although the campaign did indeed employ ground, naval, and air forces, it was of relatively small scale involving only about 10,000 men of all services, of which about 3,000 army troops were landed.[1])

While the PLA has a general vision of how it wants to employ its forces in future conflicts (often called an "aspirational" doctrine by foreigners[2]), it is likely there will be a gap between what the PLA strives to do and what it actually can accomplish for some time to come. Because of the size of the force, selected units will acquire equipment and capabilities faster than others. Due to the 1999 promulgation of new regulations for fighting and training, officers, NCOs, and conscripts now have an official outline of the capabilities the PLA ground forces are seeking to achieve. Closing the gap between actual unit proficiencies and theoretical standards is a major goal of the current phase in the Chinese military modernization process.

The PLA has drawn from classic Chinese studies of war, its own experiences, and the study of modern campaigns to create its current operational doctrine. Many details, such as specific planning factors, frontages, and depths for various size units, may not be available to the public, but the guiding principles which provide the framework for "how the PLA will fight" can be found in a variety of Chinese sources.[3]

The Art of War

Many general tenets of how the PLA intends to fight in the future can be discovered in *The Art of War*, written some 2,000 years ago. These ideas are very broad in nature and are not unique to China, but can be applied in the contemporary era using technologies and tactics currently available. Sun Zi is not the only classical Chinese source studied by the PLA, but *The Art of War*, in its many translations, is more accessible to foreigners than most other Chinese texts. Another source frequently mentioned by Chinese military thinkers is the 36 military strategies or stratagems – the last of which is "Running Away as the Best Choice. Evade the enemy to preserve the troops. The army retreats: No blame. It does not violate the normal practice of war."[4] Other stratagems emphasize deception, ingenuity, and stealth – many of the same characteristics found in *The Art of War* and later in the works of Mao Zedong. These ancient and modern texts provide the PLA with a military heritage that is imprinted on soldiers before they enter the service through their social roots and then throughout their professional military education experience.

Sun Zi begins *The Art of War* by proclaiming: "War is a matter of vital importance to the State . . . It is mandatory that it be studied thoroughly."[5] For communists trained in the study of dialectical materialism, a methodical, objective approach to thinking about war is accepted readily. The study of war includes the PLA's detailed examination of its own operations, as well as the wars of other nations. The PLA demonstrates this idea in practice by the degree of planning it undertakes prior to any military operation, whether an exercise or actual deployment.

The first of five factors Sun Zi recommends to be studied is "moral influence . . . that which causes the people to be in harmony with their leaders" (I.4). The relationships of war to the state and the army to the Chinese people are fundamental precepts adopted by Mao which live on today in the PLA's ever-adaptable understanding of "People's War." Sun Zi continues by emphasizing the importance of man to war (i.e., the way man thinks about and organizes for battle) and the training of both officers and men (I.7, 8, 12). Before speaking of the destruction of the enemy, however, Sun Zi stresses the use of deception:

- All warfare is based on deception.
- Therefore, when capable, feign incapacity; when active, inactivity.
- When near, make it appear that you are far away; when far away, that you are near.
- Offer the enemy a bait to lure him; feign disorder and strike him.
- When he concentrates, prepare against him; where he is strong, avoid him.
- Anger his general and confuse him.
- Pretend inferiority and encourage his arrogance (I.17–23).

These concepts can be applied either on the battlefield at the tactical and operational levels or at the national-strategic level of war. Then as now, they can be accomplished by the actual or notional deployment of troops, the use of camouflage, concealment, and speed in movement, or they can be accomplished by manipulating the use of information.

While "victory is the main object in war" (II.3), Sun Zi discourages protracted warfare (II.4, 5, 7) and attacks against enemy cities (III.7) (what would now be considered enemy "strong points"). Sun Zi instead argues the "best policy is to take a state intact" (III.1), and, in one of *The Art of War*'s most memorable lines, declares, "to subdue the enemy without fighting is the acme of skill" (III.3). Thus, while overt military strength is important, other aspects of national power are also essential to waging war. In modern China, calculations of "comprehensive national power," including factors such as political, economic, geographic, scientific and technological conditions, as well as military might, are commonly used to judge the relative power of nations and inform national decision-makers. In fact, for Sun Zi, political, diplomatic, and economic means are preferred methods to achieve victory:

- Thus, what is of supreme importance in war is to attack the enemy's strategy.
- Next best is to disrupt his alliances.
- The next best is to attack his army.
- The worst policy is to attack cities. Attack cities only when there is no alternative.
- Thus, those skilled in war subdue the enemy's army without battle. (III.4, 5, 6, 7, 10)

Attacking an enemy's strategy and alliances primarily can be accomplished through means other than the use of force; use of military force against the enemy's strength is a third-level preference.

Sun Zi provides guidelines for actions to take after comparing military strength, including surrounding, attacking, or dividing the enemy. However, "If weaker numerically, be capable of withdrawing; And if in all respects unequal, be capable of eluding him" (III.16, 17). A leader should not throw away his troops for political gain; the preservation of one's forces is fundamental. Accurate knowledge and understanding of the situation through detailed planning and analysis are essential. Wise commanders strive for situational awareness: "Know the enemy and know yourself; in a hundred battles you will never be in peril" (III.31).

Sun Zi categorizes forces as "normal" (*zheng*), that use the "direct approach," and "extraordinary" (*qi*) that use the "indirect approach" and should be employed to win on the battlefield (V.5). He urges to deploy troops "without ascertainable shape" (VI.24) and repeatedly emphasizes attacking the enemy's weaknesses: "Now an army may be likened to water, for just as flowing water avoids the heights and hastens to the lowlands, so an army avoids strength and strikes weakness" (VI.27). Flexibility is key, for "there are in war no constant conditions" (VI.29).

Sun Zi spends considerable time on how to analyze terrain, how to conduct maneuver and marches, employ firepower, and the use of spies and importance of intelligence. Much can be summarized in a single passage: "Speed is the essence of war. Take advantage of the enemy's unpreparedness; travel by unexpected routes and strike him where he has taken no precautions" (XI.29). None of these tasks can be accomplished without proper intelligence and planning.

Many of the details found in *The Art of War* are not directly applicable to modern conditions, but Sun Zi consistently returns to the importance of man and moral strength on the battlefield: "Pay heed to nourishing the troops; do not unnecessarily fatigue them. Unite them in spirit; conserve their strength. Make unfathomable plans for the movements of the army" (XI.32).

The relationship between civilian and military leaders Sun Zi described would be recognized today:

> "And therefore it is said that enlightened rulers deliberate upon the plans, and good generals execute them. If not in the interests of the state, do not act. If you cannot succeed, do not use troops. If you are not in danger, do not fight" (XII.16, 17).

Mao Zedong adopted many of Sun Zi's principles and applied them to the conditions China faced in the mid-twentieth century. Because of the situation confronting the Red Army in the 1930s, however, he developed a theory of protracted war, contrary to Sun Zi's advice, which would conserve communist strength while biding time until he could resume the offensive. Guerrilla warfare was a major component of Mao's strategy and one by which the Red Army gained international fame, but it was not the only method used by Chinese communist forces. Mao agreed with Sun Zi about the need to protect his own forces, but gave equal attention to annihilation of the enemy. "The object of war is specifically 'to preserve oneself and destroy the enemy' . . . Attack is the chief means of destroying the enemy, but defense cannot be dispensed with . . . If war is taken as a whole, attack remains primary."[6] Like Sun Zi, however, Mao recommended avoiding attacks on the enemy's strength, especially in cities. Nevertheless, offensive operations, at the tactical, operational, and strategic levels of war, continue to be the basis for Chinese warfighting – once the political decision to go to war has been made.

The military thought of Mao Zedong and
People's War

Mao produced a significant body of military works, which has been studied by professional and paramilitary forces throughout the world for over half a century. His military writings include "Problems of Strategy in China's Revolutionary War" (December 1936), "On Protracted War" (May 1938), "Problems of Strategy in Guerrilla War Against Japan" (May 1938), "Problems of War and Strategy" (6 November 1938), and "The Present Situation and Our Tasks" (25 December 1947), all of which are readily available in many languages.

Mao's military writings have been accorded the highest level of respect in Chinese communist literature by being labeled "Thought" (*sixiang*). Central to his thinking is the concept of People's War. Initially People's War was envisioned as defense of the Chinese mainland (continental defense) from a more advanced invader. People's War takes advantage of China's inherent strengths (a large population and vast land mass), while employing traditional Chinese fighting skills of speed, surprise, deception, and stratagem. In particular, Mao emphasized the role of man over weapons, mobilization of the population, and use of guerrilla tactics until enough combat power could be accumulated for a transition to conventional operations.

After the development of nuclear weapons, Mao and the Chinese leadership expected China to be a target of nuclear attack, and new technological developments were incorporated into Mao's theories. As China developed industrially in the 1950s and 1960s, modern weapons, including air, naval, missile, and nuclear forces, were incorporated into the concept of People's War in defense of the mainland and the name eventually was changed to "People's War under Modern Conditions" after a prolonged internal debate within the PLA. Following Deng Xiaoping's declaration in 1985 that the likelihood of a major war was remote and Local War would be the most likely form of future combat, the principles of People's War lived on and have been adapted into the twenty-first century. Every senior PLA leader continues to uphold the importance of People's War. For Chinese military planners, the most likely form of contemporary combat, Local Wars Under Modern High Technology (or Informationalized) Conditions on China's periphery, will be fought with the tenets of People's War in mind. The Chinese see no contradiction in using the most advanced weapons and technology available to them in conjunction with existing, often antiquated, weaponry to fight a Local War on China's borders using the principles of People's War. People's War still is often referred to as China's "secret weapon."

A major component of Mao's Military Thought is the "Active Defense" (*jiji fangyu*), which is sometimes now called China's "military strategy" or "strategic guideline." A fundamental rule of "Active Defense" asserts that China will strike only after the enemy has struck. However, the line between accepting the enemy's first strike and the use of preemption to defend China from an immediate attack is blurred. In 1936, Mao defined "Active Defense" as:

Active defense is also known as offensive defense, or defense through decisive engagements. Passive defense is also known as purely defensive defense or pure defense. Passive defense is actually a spurious kind of defense, and the only real defense is active defense, defense for the purpose of counter-attacking and taking the offensive. . . . Militarily speaking, our warfare consists of the alternate use of the defensive and the offensive. In our case *it makes no difference whether the offensive is said to follow or to precede the defensive*, because the crux of the matter is to break the "encirclement and suppression."[7]

(emphasis added)

Mao's emphasis on the offensive is consistent with much western military thinking from the nineteenth and twentieth centuries from Clausewitz to B.H. Liddell Hart. The decisive nature of the offensive was demonstrated by German, Japanese, Soviet, Israeli, British, and American campaigns in the last century, all of which have been studied in depth by the PLA.

In 1947 Mao compiled ten "principles of operation" that had been learned through two decades of his (and the PLA's) own combat experience. These principles stressed the Red Army's "style" of fighting and emphasized annihilation of the enemy through concentration of forces, situational awareness, and detailed preparation. Some details were at variance with Sun Zi, but most of Mao's guidance was consistent with the thinking of the ancient writer:

(1) Attack dispersed isolated enemy forces first; attack concentrated strong enemy forces later.

(2) Take small and medium cities and extensive rural areas first; take big cities later.

(3) Make wiping out the enemy's effective strength our main objective; do not make holding or seizing a city or place our main objective. Holding or seizing a city or place is the outcome of wiping out the enemy's effective strength, and often a city or place can be held or seized for good only after it has changed hands a number of times.

(4) In every battle, concentrate an absolutely superior force (two, three, four and sometimes even five or six times the enemy's strength), encircle the enemy forces completely, strive to wipe them out thoroughly and do not let any escape from the net. [Note: Sun Zi recommends "To a surrounded enemy you must leave a way of escape" (VII.31).] In special circumstances, use the method of dealing the enemy crushing blows, that is, concentrate all our strength to make a frontal attack and an attack on one or both of his flanks, with the aim of wiping out one part and routing another so that our army can swiftly move its troops to smash other enemy forces. Strive to avoid battles of attrition in which we lose more

than we gain or only break even. In this way, although inferior as a whole (in terms of numbers), we shall be superior in every part and every specific campaign, and this ensures victory in the campaign. As time goes on, we shall become superior as a whole and eventually wipe out the entire enemy.

(5)   Fight no battle unprepared, fight no battle you are not sure of winning; make every effort to be well prepared for each battle, make every effort to ensure victory in the given set of conditions as between the enemy and ourselves.

(6)   Give full play to our style of fighting – courage in battle, no fear of sacrifice, no fear of fatigue, and continuous fighting (that is, fighting successive battles in a short time without rest).

(7)   Strive to wipe out the enemy when he is on the move. At the same time, pay attention to the tactics of positional attack and capture enemy fortified points and cities.

(8)   Concerning attacking cities, resolutely seize all enemy fortified points and cities that are weakly defended. At opportune moments, seize all enemy fortified points and cities defended with moderate strength, provided circumstances permit. As for all strongly defended enemy fortified points and cities, wait until conditions are ripe and then take them.

(9)   Replenish our strength with all the arms and most of the personnel captured from the enemy. Our army's main sources of manpower and materiel are at the front.

(10)   Make good use of the intervals between campaigns to rest, train and consolidate our troops. Periods of rest, training and consolidation should not in general be very long, and the enemy should as far as possible be permitted no breathing space. These are the main methods the People's Liberation Army has employed in defeating Chiang Kai-shek. They are the result of the tempering of the People's Liberation Army in long years of fighting against domestic and foreign enemies and are completely suited to our present situation . . . our strategy and tactics are based on a People's War; no army opposed to the people can use our strategy and tactics.[8]

With the promulgation of new regulations to fight Local War Under Modern High Technology Conditions in 1999, Mao's basic military principles were updated to conform to the military developments and technology of the late twentieth century.[9] Many traditions from Sun Zi through Mao are apparent in the PLA's "new" approach to warfare.

On military campaigns

After the PLA's new fighting regulations were issued, the National Defense University published a book entitled *Zhanyi Xue*, or *On Military Campaigns*, to be used as a text to instruct PLA officers on their new doctrine.[10] This book provides detailed insights as to how the PLA intends to conduct operations at group army and higher levels in future military campaigns (i.e., the operational level of war). Campaigns are defined as "combat operations consisting of a series of battles conducted by army corps-level units under a unified command to achieve a local or an overall objective in a war."[11] Though *Zhanyi Xue* does not focus on tactics, some tactical techniques can be inferred from the larger principles addressed in the book and other PLA literature.

As discussed in Chapter 2, in time of war or national emergency War Zone headquarters will be established based on the structure of existing Military Regions to command forces from all services in their respective regions. Accordingly, War Zone headquarters are "joint" organizations, as are Military Region headquarters. However, War Zone boundaries will be drawn according to the strategic task(s) to be accomplished and may not conform exactly to existing Military Region boundaries – being larger or smaller than Military Regions depending on the mission. Likewise, the commander and staff of the Military Region may be replaced or augmented by senior personnel from the four General Headquarters Departments.

Within a War Zone a main effort or direction (*fangxiang*) will be designated as well as supporting directions (to accomplish secondary missions) and sub-campaigns with specific functions (for example, air offensive campaign, ground defense, anti-airborne campaign, etc.). Subordinate to the overall War Zone commander will be a commander for the main direction or lead service, along with "campaign corps" commanders from the services participating in the operation. The smallest "campaign corps" level organization in the ground force is the group army (i.e., an "army corps level unit").

Operations will be divided into phases organized according to tasks to be accomplished, terrain to be taken, or time. While campaign operations are likely to be joint operations involving more than one service, current PLA doctrine retains the option for single service campaigns. Campaigns may employ mobile warfare in which there are no fixed lines, positional warfare in which the PLA and/or the enemy fights from fixed positions, or guerrilla war conducted by guerrilla forces (or main force units) behind enemy lines or along the flanks to complement main force operations. War Zone commanders will utilize a combination of main force units, local forces (including People's Armed Police units), and militia augmented by civilian support.

Study of *Zhanyi Xue*'s content reveals how many of the principles discussed by Sun Zi and Mao are still incorporated into the way the PLA plans to fight in the twenty-first century. The PLA's current general warfighting tenets are found in the ten "Basic Principles of Military Campaigns"[12] (brief excerpts from the explanatory text follow):

- Know the enemy and know yourself (*zhi bi zhi ji*)

In modern military campaigns, the battlefield is vast, problems are numerous, and information is overwhelming; situations change fast, and there is a higher demand for timely and accurate intelligence; the reconnaissance and counter-reconnaissance struggle is intense with trials of strength both in technology and in wits. As a campaign commander, therefore, one must be fully in command of the enemy's conditions in various aspects as well as those of one's own. . . . Based on such understandings and analyses, one should make comprehensive analyses of and comparison between the enemy forces and one's own forces, discover their respective strength and weaknesses, make realistic judgments and correctly plan and organize the campaign accordingly. During the execution of the campaign, a campaign commander must constantly follow the changes in various aspects of the enemy and one's own forces, acquire new information in a timely manner, and make appropriate modifications or even changes to the campaign intent, and adjustments to campaign plans.

- Be fully prepared (*chongfen zhunbei*)

Campaign preparations are made up of two parts – peacetime preparation and advance combat preparation. Peacetime preparation is the foundation while advance combat preparation is critical. . . . The main components of advance combat preparation include massing campaign forces, carrying out reconnaissance and intelligence collection, revising campaign operational plans and campaign plans, and organizing campaign coordination, conducting various forms of pre-combat training and mock maneuvers according to pre-determined plans, completing and perfecting various battlefield and position fortifications, replenishing and reserving sufficient war materiel, carrying out thoroughly spiritual mobilization, organizing in a comprehensive manner various support functions, carrying out necessary military actions and adopting necessary measures to disrupt the enemy's preparations to create conditions for a smooth execution of the campaign, etc. Campaign preparations must be made based on the worst-case or most complex case scenario. They must be done in a meticulous and complete fashion . . . One must be prepared for domestic pacification while defending against foreign aggression, and for defending against foreign aggression while pacifying domestic disturbances. And one must be prepared to fight both domestically and externally.[13] One must be prepared to fight with a powerful enemy and at the same time prepared to combat a weak enemy with a looming threat of foreign intervention. . . . One must strive to achieve decisive victory quickly, but at the same time, be prepared for a protracted struggle.

- Be pro-active (*jiji zhudong*, demonstrate initiative, activism and creativeness)

The essence of being pro-active is to establish the consciousness for active offense. In an offensive campaign, actively and flexibly selecting directions, places and timing of attacks, striking at the enemy by surprise and catching it unprepared, thus disrupting the enemy's campaign deployment are effective ways to seize the initiative in the campaign. In a defensive campaign, stressing the consciousness of active offensive operation is of particular significance. One must adopt offensive operations of various scales and types to actively attack the enemy in various sectors of the battlefield and at various stages of the campaign in order to disrupt the pace and deployment of the enemy's offensive operations and to damage the overall structure of the enemy's offensive system. The ultimate objective is to achieve the defensive objectives through active offensive operations. . . . One must take full advantage of one's superiority and strength to focus on the struggle for the control of some key areas. The strategy of active defense determines that the PLA has the favorable conditions to take full advantage of the collective superiority in waging a People's War. The PLA can fully realize and utilize favorable factors in the theater in such areas as politics, economy, diplomacy, culture, and geography, and it can flexibly adopt various operational forms and tactics in the execution of the campaign. These are the areas where the PLA's basic superiority lies. . . . One should stress subduing the enemy through pre-emptive operations.

- Concentrate forces (*jizhong liliang*)

Concentrating force and striking at a weak enemy with a strong force is a universal military law. A superior campaign force is an important material condition for achieving campaign victory. Campaign execution under modern conditions relies even more on high quality crack forces and highly capable high tech weapon systems and equipment. Hence, in modern campaigns, when one's overall technology level of weapon systems and equipment is inferior, it is even more imperative to stress the importance of concentrated employment of crack troops and high tech weapons so as to develop a local superiority and to destroy the enemy forces one by one. . . . It is particularly important to concentrate crack troops and high tech weapons to develop a superior force for concentrated strikes at the decisive direction, areas and main targets and at critical junctures. Concentrated employment of forces must be able to deliver a powerful first strike capability, while at the same time it must also be able to support sustained follow-up operations and provide powerful deterrence. . . . The objective of concentrating force is to develop local superiority vis-à-vis the enemy force. . . . One must pay special close attention to the functions, characteristics and weaknesses of the enemy's high tech weapon systems and equipment and concentrate troops, weapons and technologies that would effectively overcome the enemy. In addition, concentrating force should also require physically dispersing disposition of troops and weapons while keeping a high degree of concentration in terms of combat effectiveness. . . . Concentration and dispersion are a unity of the opposites. The objective of developing superiority over the enemy force can be achieved either by concentrating one's own forces or by effectively dispersing the enemy's forces. . . . One should strive to achieve rapid mobility. Rapid mobility is essential to a highly effective concentration of forces.

- In-depth strikes (*zongshen daji*)

To mount in-depth strikes is to employ all available forces and means to launch simultaneous strikes against the full depth of the enemy campaign. . . . In executing in-depth strike, one should attack the enemy's first echelon, at the same time also hit its follow-up echelons, important in-depth targets, the enemy's rear and its command system. One should also at the same time try to secure one's own campaign depth and rear from enemy attacks. In terms of space, one should be able not only to attack the enemy's depth, but also to protect one's own depth, not only on the ground, but also in the air, the sea and even in outer space. . . . On the basis of a People's War, one should pay attention to the implementation of the principle of in-depth strike. First, in terms of targeting, one should mainly pick those vital but fragile targets. Attacking such targets should have great significance in crippling and paralyzing the overall structure of the enemy's operational system, and they should be easy to destroy and destroying them should be highly cost effective. Such targets should include the enemy's command system, rear support system, airports, ports, transport and communication hubs, high tech weapon platforms, heavy troop concentration, important battlefield facilities etc. Secondly, in the employment of forces, one should mainly rely on high tech "magic weapons" [*shashoujian* – sometimes also translated as "trump cards" or assassin's mace" weapons] while at the same time maximizing one's superiority in conducting a People's War and mounting wide-spread special operations in the enemy's depth. Thirdly, in terms of methods, one should mainly rely on close quarters engagement, night fighting, and surprise attack while at the same time using various tactics of special operations to strike at the enemy flexibly and by surprise. Fourthly, in term of space, one should focus mainly on shallow depth, with long-range depth strikes as a complementary operation. And one should pay close attention to crippling and degrading the enemy's effort aimed at realizing its superiority in high tech weapon systems and equipment. Fifthly, in terms of timing, one should select the most critical juncture to mount in-depth strikes and strive to maintain sustained strikes throughout the campaign.

- Take the enemy by surprise (*chu di bu yi*)

Taking the enemy by surprise is to mount a surprise attack against the enemy at places and times, and by means and methods that are not anticipated by the enemy. Taking the enemy by surprise would catch it unprepared and cause confusion and huge psychological pressure on the enemy, and would help one win relatively large victories at relatively small costs. . . . To be able to command and assess the battlefield conditions in a timely, comprehensive and accurate manner is an important pre-requisite for achieving the goal of taking the enemy by surprise. . . . To well disguise one's own intent is an important element in taking the enemy by surprise. The objective of disguising one's intent can be achieved through camouflage, deception, feint and under bad weather. Although it has become more difficult to disguise one's intent under modern con-ditions, modern campaign practice has proved that it is still possible to take the enemy by surprise through excellent stratagem, smart camou-flage, deception, feint and under bad weather conditions. . . . Resolute, fast pace and unconventional combat operations are the basic requirement for realizing surprise. Faced with fast changing battlefield conditions, one must make quick decisions, quick organization, quick preparations, quick re-deployment, fast mobility and quick transition between offense and defense. Whenever necessary, one must also dare to break the convention and adopt unconventional combat methods. . . . Under modern conditions, it is difficult to sustain surprise, which can only exist at the initial period of time. Therefore, once surprise is achieved, one must move quickly to exploit and expand the initial battle success . . .

- Unified coordination (*xietiao yizhi*, unified command, objective, and planning)

Unified coordination refers to the coordination of various combat forces, combat methods and combat operations in various battlefields under a unified command, based on a unified objective and through unified planning, macro-control and cooperation. . . . The missions, timing and space of various combat operations must be clarified and set in accordance with the campaign objective. There must be a focus in coordination and a clear definition of what are the principal operations and what are sub-ordinate operations. . . . Firepower in a modern campaign has a significant impact on campaign operations. Therefore, special attention should be directed toward the coordination between powerful firepower assault and troop attack so as to ensure that troop attack can take full advantage of the effect of firepower assault. . . . There is a high degree of intensity and complexity in modern campaigns. Mistakes can occur easily in the coordination of various units, which in turn could lead to deviations from coordinating objectives. Thus, based on actual battlefield conditions, one should be able to foresee as early as possible likely changes and make timely adjustments, restoration or changes to the coordination plan . . . In order to have smooth well coordinated campaign operations, the campaign commander must be thoroughly familiar with actual conditions, such as the operational characteristics of various units, the technical and operational capabilities of major weapon systems etc.

- Continuous fighting (*lianxu zuozhan*)

Continuous fighting refers to the capability to carry out sustained combat operations and execute non-stop, consecutive operations. A military campaign is the sum of a series of combat operations. A campaign [covers] vast battlefields and can last an extended period of time. . . . Continuous fighting requires a demonstration of the spirit of bravery, tenacity, no fear of sacrifice and no fear of fatigue in carrying out non-stop and unremitting attacks against the enemy. . . . To implement the principle of continuous fighting, one must pay close attention to the following: first, there should be careful planning and unified employment of forces . . . Secondly, one must set up a strong reserve force . . . Thirdly, . . . one should stress the demonstration of the spirit of courage and bravery in fighting . . . Fourthly, one should strive to maintain the troops' high combat spirit through political education and battlefield mobilization.

- Comprehensive support (*quanmian baozhang*[14])

Comprehensive support refers to a series of support measures that one takes to ensure the smooth execution of a campaign and its final victory. It includes operational support, logistic support, and equipment support. . . . In exercising comprehensive support, one should take advantage of the favorable conditions of fighting a People's War and the superiority of fighting on one's home territory by fully mobilizing the potential of civilian support capabilities. By combining civilian support with military support capabilities, one can create a military-led united civil–military support system to provide comprehensive support. . . . One should adopt methods that integrate regional support with institutional support, and general supply with special supply, and should build a multi-layered support system with multiple channels, multiple means and multiple support measures on each level. . . . One should concentrate the main support force, materiel, instruments and equipment in the main campaign direction, the main battlefield and at the critical campaign stages in order to ensure the completion of the main combat mission. . . . In modern campaign operations, support for areas such as intelligence, communication, air defense, logistics, and mobility are particularly important. The campaign commander should give necessary attention to the provision of personnel and technical equipment and help solve related problems. . . . There should be ample materiel and troop and equipment reserves so as to ensure the accomplishment of key support missions and maintain sustainable support capabilities. . . . During peacetime one should strengthen battlefield construction and materiel preparations. Particularly in areas of road transportation and communication facility construction, one should seek an integration of peacetime and wartime construction, and military and civilian use construction. In the area of logistic and equipment support, there should be a well-targeted effort to strengthen the construction of production lines for logistics, weapons and equipment, and the building of storage and depot facilities. . . . In particular, one should integrate degrading and crippling the enemy's support capabilities with enhancing and strengthening one's own capabilities so as to be able to carry out comprehensive support in intense conflicts and to ensure the smooth execution of the military campaign.

- Political superiority (*fahui zhengzhi youshi*)

A modern military campaign is not only a trial of strength in terms of military and economic power, but also a trial of strength in terms of political and spiritual power. To win victory in a campaign mainly depends on two major factors – man and weaponry. Spiritual power can turn into tremendous fighting capabilities. . . . One should strive to strengthen coordination between military struggle and national political, economic and diplomatic struggles, to correctly apply relevant international rules, and to take full advantage of favorable international and domestic situations to ensure campaign operations are conducted with justification, to one's advantage and with limit. . . . A modern military campaign is a joint campaign waged by multiple services and arms. Victory depends on the realization of the joint operational power of various participating services and arms. Thus, it is necessary to educate participating forces that they must abandon the idea of winning victory by relying on a single service, and that they should establish, instead, the concept of joint operations and the consciousness for integrated combined arms operations in terms of active cooperation, mutual support and close coordination, in order to maximize the combined power of participating forces. In addition, one should strengthen broad links with local governments, promote military–government and military–civilian unity, maximize the superiority of a People's War, and attack the enemy with unified purpose and in concert with one another. . . . To maximize political superiority, one should attach importance to the struggle of waging "psychological warfare" against the enemy and of countering the enemy's "psychological warfare."

Integrated operations, key point strikes

The "Basic Principles of Military Campaigns" were formulated in order "to carry out the basic military campaign guidance concept of 'integrated operations, key point strikes.'" *Zhanyi Xue* defines "integrated operations, key point strikes" (*zhengti zuozhan, zhongdian daji*) as follows:

- Bring into full play the overall superiority of a People's War by uniting the military with the government, the military with police and civilians.
- Integrate the military struggle with struggles on the political, economic and diplomatic fronts.
- Synergize all the essential campaign factors such as strength, space, time, means, etc. to form an integrated operational force.
- Take destroying and paralyzing the overall structure of the enemy's operational system as the starting point.
- Move forward and to seek resolution of the overall campaign situation by concentrating crack forces in the main direction of the campaign, at the critical junctures and in important operations.
- Adopt flexible and adaptable methods to execute active and focused integrated strikes aimed at those targets that are critical in sustaining and supporting the overall enemy operational system.
- Strive to paralyze the enemy force first and annihilate it later.
- Pursue battles of annihilation.
- Strive to fight quick battles with fast resolution so as to accomplish campaign objectives as soon as possible.[15]

Thus, the Chinese national leadership will seek to employ political, diplomatic, and economic means along with military force, and to integrate the Chinese armed forces with civilian police and civilian support forces to achieve its strategic objectives in the twenty-first century. Beijing would prefer to accomplish its political objectives without the use of force, though it retains military means as an option and a tool of coercion. Consequently, Beijing may be expected to threaten the use of military force to deter or dissuade a political opponent from taking undesired actions or coerce him into doing something favorable to Chinese objectives.

The ten "Basic Principles of Military Campaigns" are the general rules based on the precepts of People's War by which the PLA will seek to annihilate an enemy by using its best ("crack" or elite) forces and most advanced weapons in a series of rapid battles against critical points focused on a primary campaign direction (main effort). Chinese military planners will aim to bring any campaign to a quick conclusion and attempt to "win the first battle" no matter who strikes first; however, they will be prepared for prolonged conflict. Not only is the political support of the Chinese population important, the mobilization of civilian resources is essential to future military campaigns, especially to their logistics support and sustainment. (Prior to conflict, the Chinese leadership may seek to make civilian mobilization less observable when strategic or operational surprise is sought, or it may highlight these efforts to demonstrate its resolve.) *Zhanyi Xue* identifies four important military operations that are crucial to future PLA campaigns: information warfare, integrated firepower, campaign mobility, and Special Operations.

Information warfare

Zhanyi Xue calls information warfare a "new kind" of combat operation that has come into being mostly since the 1970s when new information technologies became available on the battlefield.[16] These technologies include advanced forms of communications (satellites, optical fiber, microwave, etc.), portable and inexpensive computers, reconnaissance and surveillance platforms (various radars, airborne and space-based optical and signals intelligence systems), modern navigation tools (positioning satellites, detailed maps, etc.), night vision devices, and precision-guided munitions, to name a few. Information operations are defined as:

> Integrated combat operation targeting the enemy's information detection resources, information channels, and information processing and decision-making systems, with the aim of seizing and maintaining information superiority and damaging the enemy's information controlling capability, while maintaining our information controlling capability. . . . Therefore, it has become the primary task of modern campaigns to seize informa-tion superiority and to take away the enemy's capability of getting information.[17]

Information operations have both offensive and defensive components and are conducted continuously and throughout the battlefield. The enemy's information system is the primary target of integrated attack by various methods including electronic warfare, psychological warfare, and physical destruction (by raids, missiles, or other forms of firepower). Offensive information operations are aimed at enemy "vital points" and are especially important at the beginning of a campaign. The initial goal is the destruction or paralysis of the enemy's command and control and early warning systems. Coordinated attacks against "vital points" are divided among those targeted for "soft kill," using electronic warfare, computer attack, and psychological warfare, and "hard kill" through physical destruction. Defense against information attack is recognized as extremely difficult and hard to organize. Deception, camouflage, and decoys, as well as air defenses and local security forces, help protect friendly information systems.

Perhaps most importantly, *Zhanyi Xue* recognizes "information warfare is a *means*, not a goal" (emphasis added). By itself, information warfare is unlikely to be decisive. Instead, the PLA intends to use information operations in conjunction with other combat methods to create the conditions for victory. While information warfare has a number of outspoken advocates within the PLA (as it does in other countries), official PLA doctrine considers information operations similar to what is known as a "force multiplier" in the US military: "A capability that, when added

106

to and employed by a combat force, significantly increases the combat potential of that force and thus enhances the probability of successful mission accomplishment."[18] This definition is also appropriate for the larger class of weapons and techniques under which information warfare may be categorized – *shashoujian* or secret weapons, "trump cards," or "assassin's mace" weapons.

As is apparent from the earlier discussion of this concept in *Zhanyi Xue*, *shashoujian* are intended to be employed as an element of People's War in conjunction with other operations such as firepower, mobility, and special operations. When successfully employed, *shashoujian* are envisioned as giving the PLA an early advantage which Chinese commanders would then exploit with other, additional military means. "Trump card" weapons, in official PLA doctrine, are *not* an end in themselves that will single-handedly, magically defeat the enemy and eliminate the need for other forms of combat. Thus, the need to emphasize firepower, mobility, and Special Operations.

Firepower operations

Integrated firepower operations include attack by artillery, air forces (of the various services), and missile strikes supported by information operations:

> The main goal of firepower combat is to control battlefield space, to damage the war potential and important infrastructure of the other side, to destroy and paralyze the combat system of the other side, to reduce its combat capability, to create conditions for decisive combat, or to accomplish certain campaign and strategic goals.[19]

At the operational level of war, firepower may be delivered by ground, naval, air, or missile forces and must be under the unified command of the campaign commander. Modern firepower has four major characteristics: (1) it is capable of attacking the enemy at great depths and may target any part of the enemy's force at anytime in the battle; (2) it can be used at any phase of the campaign because of the variety of ways firepower can be delivered on target; (3) it can be highly efficient (i.e., accurate) allowing for fewer platforms (aircraft, ships, artillery tubes, etc.) to deliver fewer munitions to achieve results faster and with fewer civilian casualties than in previous wars; and (4) it can be delivered by a diverse set of weapons systems from all the services which permit commanders to choose from a variety of weapons appropriate to the situation (weather, terrain, civilian population, etc.) and type of target.

Firepower operations have three main forms: air raid, missile attack, and artillery attack. *Zhanyi Xue* lists four major types of air attacks. First is the "combined air raid" conducted by multiple aircraft of multiple types, such as ground attack, fighter, airborne command and control, refueling, electronic warfare, and air rescue. Next are "remote" and "sudden stealth" attacks launched from bases far from the battlefield. Finally, "continuous" attacks take place in all weather conditions during both day and night. All of these missions are described as pre-planned, centrally controlled efforts.

Conspicuous in its absence is any discussion of air power in direct support of front line troops, which is controlled by ground observers and flexible in its ability to react to changing conditions on the battlefield. In western terms, such missions are called "close air support" (CAS) and have been conducted and refined over a 60-year period. CAS is different from "air interdiction," which focuses on attacking pre-planned targets not in the immediate vicinity of friendly troops. CAS operations require specialized aircraft and munitions, direct ground-to-air communications, decentralized control, effective doctrine and procedures, and extensive training on the part of both the ground and air components. There is little evidence that the PLA Air Force has adopted close air support as a mission to support PLA ground forces.[20] The few army attack helicopters available most likely also fly missions against pre-planned targets with only minimal real time coordination with forces on the ground in contact with the enemy. As the PLA continues its training program, it seems reasonable that ground and air forces eventually will attempt to perfect methods of close air support, but any CAS capability will take a number of years to develop and be common throughout the entire force.

The second form of firepower operations is missile attack, which uses guided munitions and takes advantage of remote sensing and other electronic techniques to "fundamentally change the nature of the conventional firepower combat." *Zhanyi Xue* discusses the various forms of missiles available for combat, including conventional surface-to-surface missiles and land attack cruise missiles. These weapons may be fired from long distances and achieve great accuracies, effectively producing similar effects of several aircraft with "high cost-effectiveness." Missile attack is praised for its all-weather surprise and shock value, as well as the covert aspects of mobile missile launchers firing from scattered locations.

Use of ground artillery is the third form of firepower operations. It is the army's main means of firepower and has not been supplanted by air or missile attack. For ground troops, artillery is the most timely, reliable, and sustainable form of firepower and, because of its modern mobility, it can accompany ground forces as they move on the battlefield. At the operational level (group army and above), centralized organization and control of firepower assets is essential to concentrate fires and maximize destructive effect. Unified control allows the commander to select the proper weapon from the various assets assigned to attack targets and to integrate intelligence information on enemy targets derived from the reconnaissance assets available. The campaign commander will concentrate firepower to support the main operational direction. Because of the longer ranges of modern artillery, it is no longer necessary to physically locate artillery units in close proximity to each other. Rather, fires can be concentrated from dispersed locations. Modern systems can also be employed in all-weather, day and night conditions. At the same time, it is necessary to protect friendly artillery forces from enemy counterbattery fire or air attack through movement and by using local security, dispersal, camouflage, and protection provided by the terrain or defensive positions.

Operational artillery missions include long-range firepower attacks against large area targets in the enemy's rear area; interdiction fires, including the use of artillery-delivered mines, to block enemy deployments (especially the deployment of reserve forces), isolate a battle area, or cut off logistic supply; destruction of key points in the enemy rear area; artillery counterattack (counterbattery fire) to neutralize enemy firepower to protect friendly operations; firepower blockade directed at key transportation targets (such as roads, bridges, harbors, airports, etc.) to block enemy movements and destroy infrastructure; and firepower feints or decoy operations to mislead the enemy and create a favorable situation for friendly forces.

Mobility

Campaign mobility is the movement of troops, weapons, and firepower in order to gain the initiative or create a favorable situation. *Zhanyi Xue* calls mobility "the most important combat operation of a campaign."[21] Mobility allows the concentration of superior force and can be used to achieve surprise. Friendly forces may be employed in deception operations by showing false movements while hiding real intentions. Both sides will attempt to increase the range and ease of their own movements while conducting anti-mobility operations against the other.

Campaign mobility should attempt to identify and avoid hitting the enemy's strong points. Rather, forces should be concentrated on the enemy's weak points using both air and ground movements. Careful reconnaissance and analysis of the battlefield situation are necessary to determine the enemy's areas of strength and weakness. Campaign mobility also requires rapid and sudden attack to disrupt the enemy's rhythm and freedom of action. Mobility operations should be continuous using multiple routes and having multiple dimensions, such as air and ground movements. It will often be necessary to fight while on the move to counter enemy actions. Seizing and maintaining local control of the air is a priority, as is protection of the flanks, especially from enemy armored attacks. Reserve forces may be positioned to protect threatened flanks.

Basic forms of mobility operations include forward movement; deep envelopment focused on forces in the enemy rear area (including single flank or double encirclement – i.e., a pincer movement); deep and distant outflanking maneuver focused on a geographical location; penetration using elite forces against weak points in the enemy forces; vertical envelopment bypassing enemy strong points using troops inserted by parachute or landed by aircraft or helicopter; and retreat or withdrawal, either while in contact with the enemy or while not in contact with the enemy.

Special Operations

Special Operations are characterized by their covert nature, the preciseness of their objective and actions, and their high efficiency, which includes a relatively low cost in terms of manpower and equipment. *Zhanyi Xue* defines Special Operations as:

> Irregular combat operations conducted by specially organized, trained, and equipped elite troops with special tactics in order to achieve certain campaign and strategic goals on the battlefield. Its goals are mainly to attack the enemy's critical targets, to paralyze the enemy's combat systems, to reduce enemy combat capability, to interfere, delay, and destroy the enemy's combat operations, and to create favorable conditions for the main force.[22]

Special Operations missions include:

- Raids to kill or capture enemy command personnel (including military and government leaders), or destroy small units in the enemy's rear area or key command and control, intelligence, or logistics systems.
- Sabotage operations to destroy command and control, intelligence, early warning, transportation and communications, and logistics facilities.
- Ambushes to destroy enemy high technology weapons or forces during movement to disrupt the enemy's combat operations.
- Harassing attacks to dispirit the enemy and cause him to divert forces to the rear away from the main PLA effort.
- Special technology attacks, such as attacks against enemy computer and communications systems and navigation and guidance systems.
- Psychological attack to destroy the enemy's will to fight and cause commanders to make bad decisions by spreading false information and propaganda. Psychological attack may also be directed at enemy civilian leaders and population.
- Long-range reconnaissance operations to "complement the insufficiency of [China's] high tech reconnaissance" capabilities. These operations include both identifying targets for strike and assessing the extent of damage after strikes have been conducted [known as battle damage assessment].[23]

Based on these missions, Special Operations are conducted not only by Special Operations Force units (found in every Military Region) but also by newly formed "High Technology" units and Psychological Warfare units. All such units are relatively small and composed of highly trained soldiers who use special equipment and techniques to accomplish sensitive operations against key enemy targets. Because Special Operations missions are operational or strategic in nature, they are under the direct command of the campaign (or higher level) commander; however, once deployed the SOF units themselves are expected to act with individual initiative, surprise, and flexibility to accomplish their missions.

Special Operations Forces depend heavily on stealthy means of insertion (such as by parachute, helicopter, or small boat at night or during inclement weather) and reliable forms of communications to report the results of their activity on the ground. Members of SOF units are trained in many specialties and units have multiple capabilities. Usually Special Operations will be conducted by small groups of soldiers numbering from "several to a few dozen" (i.e., from smaller than a squad to platoon size), but, if necessary, small groups may be concentrated to seize key targets or locations in support of the main force. *Zhanyi Xue* explicitly notes that Special Operations are very different from guerrilla warfare because, among other reasons, Special Operations are designed to strike at critical enemy *strong* points.

Ground force campaigns

Ground force or army campaigns may be conducted independently by ground forces only, though *Zhanyi Xue* recognizes only a small possibility for such independent campaigns under modern conditions. More likely ground force campaigns will be joint operations, supported by and in cooperation with forces from other services.[24] The smallest unit to conduct a campaign is a group army; multiple group armies may also be combined to form a campaign-level ground force. (Operations by units smaller than a group army, i.e., division and below, are considered to be at the tactical level of war.)

Campaigns may be offensive or defensive in nature with offensive campaigns having several different forms: mobile warfare, positional warfare, landing (or amphibious) campaign, urban offensive, and frontier counterattack campaign. (Airborne campaigns are considered joint offensive campaigns that may be under-taken on their own or as a part of a larger joint campaign.[25] Airborne operations include parachute delivery of personnel and equipment and air transport, and land-ing of personnel and equipment using either fixed wing or helicopters. SOF units and some army reconnaissance units may use parachutes to enter the battle area, but the primary PLA airborne formation is the 15th Airborne Army that belongs to the PLA Air Force. Airborne, SOF, reconnaissance, and some PLA ground force units train in airmobile or heliborne operations in which troops are transported into the battle zone using helicopters. But, because of the limited numbers of helicopters in the PLA, Chinese airmobile operations – from squad up to perhaps battalion size – are limited to the tactical, not the campaign or operational, level of war.)

Defensive campaigns include mobile, positional, coastal, and urban defense campaigns. As could be expected, the descriptions in *Zhanyi Xue* of these various campaign types emphasize and repeat the general principles described earlier and provide examples of how the principles may be applied under varying circum-stances. The need to shift from defensive operations to offensive operations in order to regain the initiative is emphasized frequently.

Detailed planning is key, so for each kind of operation forces are organized into an assortment of groups, such as "assault groups" or "fire support groups," to accom-plish specific tasks. For example, many operations may form "anti-airborne groups" to protect against enemy attacks using paratroopers or heliborne forces. Such a group may have air forces tasked to intercept incoming aircraft and ground forces designated to counterattack if an enemy landing is made.

The PLA recognizes that Chinese ground forces are particularly vulnerable to long-range air and missile strikes. Therefore, they are highly dependent on other services to provide extended defense from such weaponry. Though not mentioned specifically in *Zhanyi Xue*, in the first decade of the twenty-first century PLA forces have used the slogan "three attacks and three defenses" (i.e., strike at stealth aircraft, cruise missiles, and helicopter gunships; defend against precision strikes, electronic jamming, and reconnaissance and surveillance) as a guide for nearly all training exercises. Soldiers and units are urged to find innovative ways to attack these modern threats and defend themselves from their effects using both active and passive means, such as camouflage, concealment, and deception. While ground force units have responsibility for local, short-range defenses against these threats, due to the limited range of their own air defense weapons they must depend primarily on the PLA Air Force, and to a lesser extent the PLA Navy, to defend at longer distances.

Missile attack

PLA conventional ballistic missile attack (i.e., short- or medium-range ballistic missiles armed with *non-nuclear* warheads) is recognized as an important part of any joint campaign. Under special conditions, a conventional missile attack may be conducted independently. *Zhanyi Xue* specifies that conventional missile attack is initiated *first* in a campaign sequence to maximize its shock effect on the enemy.[26] (Doctrine for a Second Artillery conventional missile attack was only issued in April 1998, ten years after the Central Military Commission assigned it the mission in addition to its nuclear retaliatory strike role. Promulgation of non-nuclear missile attack doctrine came less than ten years after the creation of the first conventional missile units in the PLA.[27])

A Second Artillery campaign corps is composed of three or more conventional missile brigades and supporting units, such as air defense and ground security, under command of the overall campaign commander.[28] Close coordination among Second Artillery forces, and other means of delivering long-range firepower, is essential. Missile attacks must be concentrated against the most critical, threatening, and vulnerable enemy targets in order to paralyze its combat systems and set the conditions for the remainder of the campaign. Conventional missiles may also be used to conduct "firepower blockades" as a "low intensity" operation to disrupt the enemy's flow of troops and supplies. They may also be used in random and small-scale attacks to disturb the enemy's daily life and apply psychological pressure. In all cases of missile combat it will be necessary to fire from dispersed locations and move after launch. Missile forces will hide from the enemy using camouflage, concealment, decoys, and electronic warfare.

Conventional missiles are one of the most commonly identified Chinese *shashoujian*, secret weapon or trump card. However, it is apparent from the discussion in *Zhanyi Xue* that the PLA does *not* plan for a missile attack alone to be decisive in battle. Rather, while conventional missile attacks may start a campaign, and be used in subsequent phases, Chinese military planners fully intend to employ air, naval, and ground forces to achieve victory. Again, like information warfare, the efficacy of conventional missile attacks is highly praised by some writers and thinkers within the PLA (as well as by some foreign observers), but *doctrinally*, under most circumstances, Chinese military planners intend for missile strikes to be one part of a much larger, integrated campaign utilizing many types of forces and methods of combat.

Amphibious operations

The following sections discuss major elements of several joint campaigns incorporating the use of ground forces as described by *Zhanyi Xue*. Among the many types of campaigns the PLA may conduct are amphibious (also called sea-crossing or landing operations), border counterattack, airborne, and anti-landing campaigns.

Amphibious operations are considered highly difficult operations and are composed of a series of component land, air, and sea campaigns divided into three phases: initial combat operations; concentration, loading, and sea-crossing; and assault of the beach.[29] Initial combat operations are conducted primarily by PLA air, naval, and missile forces to gain control of the information environment, as well as the air and sea in the area of operations. Initial combat operations aim to destroy the enemy's defense systems, consume the enemy's fighting strength, clear obstacles from the landing area, and isolate, blockade, or interdict the landing area in order to create favorable conditions for the landing force. These operations provide cover for the beginning of the second phase of the amphibious operations – concentration, loading, and sea-crossing.

This second phase of the amphibious operation is extremely logistics-intensive and calls for detailed advanced planning and on-the-ground preparation on the friendly shore. First, landing forces must be assembled at a number of "embarkation points," which are selected to be "relatively close to the landing area." These activities are organized and executed by an "embarkation zone command post" in coordination with the local government and landing force commander. "Embarkation points" are chosen with their defense in mind and forces are organized to protect against air raids and harassment attacks by enemy special forces. In order to move troops from their home bases to assembly areas at the "embarkation points" all forms of transportation will be used, but the primary means of transport will be rail and road. At the same time, the military and civilian vessels to conduct the sea movement must be assembled, organized, and prepared for loading. At each "embarkation point" a comprehensive support team will be deployed to assist the landing troops to inspect, repair, prepare, and load equipment; replenish supplies; attend to sick and wounded; and provide support until the troops depart. Actual loading should be carried out as quickly and safely as possible, according to schedule, from concealed positions. Once loaded, vessels move away from the "embarkation points" and assemble in designated locations until the time comes to begin the movement toward the opposite shore.

The sea-crossing calls for a high degree of organization and discipline in the fleet. This phase is commanded by the commanding officer of the joint landing group. After all boats and ships have assembled, they will set out on a wide front, in pre-arranged order, maintaining close contact with each other, in a multi-column movement. During this stage of the assault, the transport groups must be alert for enemy interdiction.

Landing operations are considered the most critical and complicated phase of the operation. Approaches must be cleared of obstacles, then landings across the beach must be coordinated with helicopter and airborne assaults to the enemy's rear. Fire assaults and electronic warfare will be concentrated at the beachhead to support the first landing echelon. Landings will be conducted on a wide front from multiple directions supported by SOF units on the flanks or in the enemy rear area. Landing forces will breach enemy lines of defense and prepare to defend the beachhead from counterattack. Second echelon units will land shortly after the first wave and seek to expand the beachhead.

A forward logistics support element accompanies the landing forces and sets up positions to deliver ammunition and supplies, evacuate the wounded, and rescue and repair damaged equipment. The forward logistics support element will also support the unloading of additional personnel, equipment, and materiel, and assist in expanding the beachhead and pushing operations farther inshore. Because of the lack of depth on the beachhead, several layers of logistics and armament support are likely to be compressed into fewer organizational structures than on the mainland.

As the beachhead is being consolidated and expanded, air and missile attacks will be directed against enemy mobile forces. SOF units will also be used to harass the enemy and create conditions for follow-up attacks.

Border counterattack

Border counterattack operations are designed to drive out and destroy an attacking enemy and regain lost territory.[30] Usually the scale, area, and goals of an attacking enemy are limited, so the PLA will conduct operations in the same area in support of political goals determined by the senior Chinese leadership. Border areas are particularly sensitive because of minority populations who live in the region and the possibility that ethnic separatists may collude with foreign enemies. Moreover, most border regions are mountainous, desert, or forest areas with limited transportation networks; this greatly complicates operations. Most Chinese forces also are stationed in peacetime at some distance from border areas making logistics support to counterattack operations difficult. Meticulous planning and intelligence is required to account for these factors as commanders prepare options to respond quickly to enemy actions.

Border counterattacks *usually* start after the enemy attacks and the PLA is forced to be on the defensive. However, a main goal of the campaign commander is to regain the initiative and resume the offensive. During the campaign, many shifts between offense and defense are expected. Elite forces and high-technology weapons will be concentrated to achieve local or overall superiority. Mobile forces will be used for counterattacks; civilian support forces for logistics and security operations are to be included, especially in rear areas. Civilian police, government, and party organizations cooperate with military forces to suppress riots and sabotage conducted by separatists in the area of operations.

Long-distance transportation will primarily be conducted by rail supplemented by road and air movements. Short distances will be covered mainly using wheeled or tracked vehicles, and also on foot. Helicopters are used to enhance transportation capabilities. A campaign mobility corridor should be set up to ensure that troops may safely move, fight, and be supported. Such a mobility corridor requires good air and ground defenses, reliable communications, and logistics and repair facilities. Activities conducted in this phase of the operation include anti-reconnaissance, air defense, and electronic countermeasures.

When a war is clearly unavoidable, the PLA may take preemptive measures to seize the initiative before the enemy strikes. Elite forces and long-range firepower are essential to operations designed to paralyze enemy command and control and disrupt his attack plans. It is also important to expose the enemy's intentions to the international community, but not let him gain the initiative by striking first.

If the enemy does attack first, it is difficult to stop him at the border. Key strategic points must be identified, occupied, and defended, while mobile forces delay the main enemy offensive and protect the flanks. Enemy second echelon forces can be disrupted by deep attacks employing firepower from all services and the use of airborne and SOF forces behind enemy lines. Enemy units should be searched out, destroyed, and pursued for decisive defeat. Sometimes, however, it is possible that the campaign objective is not fully achieved, though the military situation is favorable. Then, because of political requirements, the campaign may be ended.

Airborne operations

Zhanyi Xue states that airborne operations are highly complex joint operations, which make use of speed, surprise, and shock, but are vulnerable to interdiction and the effects of weather, and are highly dependent on intelligence.[31] Airborne operations can be conducted as a joint campaign themselves or as a component of a joint campaign; however, because of the light nature of the force, air cover, fire support, and timely resupply is required.

Airborne missions include capturing "political, military and economic centers"; supporting offensive operations; sabotage; preventing enemy reserves from entering the battle and eliminating defenses; seizing airfields and ports; and degrading enemy capabilities by destroying missiles sites, command and communication centers, and logistics hubs. Concentration of force on enemy vital points is essential. Units involved in airborne operations are divided into "groups," all of which must be under a unified command. These groups include airborne (landing) assault, air transport, air cover, air–ground attack, support (including reconnaissance, electronic warfare, airborne control, and weather), missile attack, logistics support, and air defense (including surface-to-air missiles, anti-aircraft artillery, and radars).[32]

Loading of troops and equipment should take place under cover of darkness or during inclement weather; troops may be delivered by parachute drop or air-landed by fixed-wing aircraft or helicopters. The air transport phase is recognized to be the most "tense and complex" time of the operation. Under normal conditions, one air corridor is necessary to transport an airborne infantry regiment, while an airborne division requires two corridors, separated by about 30–40 kilometers. Fire preparation of drop zones or landing zones should be conducted shortly before the insertion of troops. An airborne force supporting an amphibious assault normally would be landed 10–30 kilometers beyond the shore, while an airborne operation supporting a ground attack could occur 30–50 kilometers beyond the front lines.

The operational area for an airborne division is approximately 800 square kilometers, and about 80 square kilometers for an airborne regiment. Using a single lift, an airborne division requires from 9–12 drop zones (DZs), an airborne regiment three to four, and an airborne battalion one. If multiple lifts are used, the number of DZs may be decreased. A battalion DZ is normally about 4 square kilometers in size. For night drops, the size should be increased. In addition to primary drop zones, alternatives should be selected. When helicopters are used to transport troops, a battalion landing zone (LZ) is about 3 square kilometers, composed of three to four company landing zones, each about 300 by 200 meters. If transport aircraft are used to land troops in a single lift, a division requires two to four airfields, though that number may decrease if multiple lifts are used.[33] Forces should be landed as close to the objective as possible in order to achieve surprise and shock the enemy. *Zhanyi Xue* stresses the need for the airborne landing force to establish communications with all elements of the campaign as soon as possible after insertion.

When the airborne landing force commander decides on transition to defensive operations, it is the responsibility of the campaign commander to organize support and cover operations to protect the airborne force. *Zhanyi Xue* specifically cites the World War II Allied airborne operation "Market Garden" in September 1944 as an example of the need for a rapid link-up between airborne and ground forces.

Anti-landing campaigns

Anti-landing campaigns are joint defensive operations conducted against an enemy amphibious operation. The main tasks of an anti-landing campaign are to defend key islands; block straits (water channels); defend key regions in coastal areas, coastal cities, naval bases, and key harbors; cover key access to national strategic locations; consume and destroy enemy landing forces; and foil an enemy landing offensive.[34] In addition to main force army, navy, air, and missile units, local forces, including paramilitary and civilian elements, are important to anti-landing campaigns. Though *Zhanyi Xue* specifies the need for unified command of the various service campaign corps, it does not recommend which service element should have the lead role and assume overall command.

Preparation of multi-layered, fixed positions, such as tunnels and bunkers, and anti-landing obstacles is stressed, along with the formation of a strong reserve force to counter enemy actions. At the "favorable time," counterattacks against enemy weak points will be conducted in order to crush the landing force. Long-range firepower, including tactical surface-to-surface missiles and cruise missiles, is employed at all stages, particularly while the enemy is "still on the other side of the water." The enemy is most vulnerable as he approaches the Chinese coast and his forces shift among vessels to begin the assault. Once the enemy lands, PLA forces will counterattack the enemy's flanks and at the point of his foothold when he "backs to the water." A primary concern for PLA forces in this phase of the operation is defending against enemy air attacks as he attempts to control the air. It is important to prevent the enemy from seizing ports, airports, transportation hubs, and coastal cities in the region. *Zhanyi Xue* summarizes the main anti-landing operations as the "three-anti's" (anti-air raid, anti-landing, and anti-airborne) and "four attacks" (attack when the enemy is still on the other side of water, attack when the enemy is in water, attack when the enemy backs to water, and attack the enemy's deep area).

Logistics support

Zhanyi Xue recognizes the importance of adequate logistics and armament (equipment) support to all the PLA's modern combat operations and devotes two full chapters (out of a total of 21 chapters) to those tasks.[35] Main logistics and armament support operational principles include:

- The PLA "should take advantage of the favorable conditions of fighting a People's War and the superiority of fighting on one's home territory by fully mobilizing the potential of civilian support capabilities." Combining civilian support with military support capabilities, the PLA "can create a military-led united civil-military support system to provide comprehensive support." Stress should also be placed on enhancing support capabilities, which requires strengthening battlefield construction and materiel preparations during peacetime.
- Support forces must be under a unified command and should be employed to ensure the completion of the main combat mission. The main support force, materiel, and equipment should be concentrated in the main campaign direction at critical stages. Support systems should be structured with "multiple channels, multiple means, and multiple support measures" at each level. Mobile support must be combined with fixed support.
- Support forces are made up of organic (i.e., units directly subordinate to a specific headquarters), reinforcing (i.e., units from higher headquarters to

augment lower-level organizations), and local civilian support forces. Support may be provided using the traditional hierarchical method of higher-level unit to subordinate unit, or skip-echelon support may also be provided as appropriate. Higher-level headquarters should organize mobile support forces to provide forward support for subordinate units. Reinforcing units from higher headquarters should be integrated into organic units according to their specialties. Local support teams can either be integrated into units or perform independent missions.

- Railway and highway transport are the main transport means in campaign logistics transportation. Such transport lines should be extended as far as possible to the front, so as to carry out more transport missions. Oil pipelines are the main means for campaign logistic fuel transport. Civilian assets, especially ships and aircraft, must be integrated with military transportation.
- Defense of the support system, and attack of the enemy's logistics, must be an integral part of any campaign plan.

Within a War Zone, several logistics support zones will be created from logistics subdepartments assigned to the region, and may be reinforced by additional assets from other Military Regions. Logistics support zones will be organized according to road, rail, and water lines of communications to be mutually supporting to adjacent zones. Support will flow both vertically (i.e., from rear to front) and horizontally among logistics support zones. Each logistics support zone will be composed of systems for:

- command and control of logistics and armament elements performed by a system of "rear" (logistics/armament-related) command posts;
- general support, primarily provided by the Military Region Joint Logistics system;
- special support, primarily provided by the Military Region armament system and the armament systems of the individual services; and
- defense of the support area incorporating the organic defenses of logistics and armament units; support or augmentation from higher headquarters, such as air defense; and support from local forces, including militia units.

Military Region logistics subdepartments will form *ad hoc* "logistics support brigades" (sometimes called "emergency logistics support brigades" or "armament support units") from their various subordinate units, supply depots, and bases. These units will be assembled according to the mission, terrain, and type of forces to be supported. They will displace from their garrison locations and establish forward, fixed field supply points, medical facilities, and repair depots, as well as dispatch sub-elements to provide mobile support to operational units, such as group armies and lower level forces. Civilian and militia assets, incorporating both personnel and material resources, will be integrated into PLA logistics and armament support operations. Supply will be pushed as far forward as possible and repairs made "on-the-spot" when feasible. Group armies, divisions, brigades, and regiments will establish "field service centers" and "field armament centers" to act as medical, supply, repair, and transportation hubs for their respective units.

Within this structure, support units will move among the different locations to pick up and drop off supplies, personnel, and equipment, as well as evacuate wounded and return damaged equipment to the rear, according to pre-arranged time schedules. To assist in these actions, the PLA has taken advantage of communications advances and is experimenting with the use of long distance video and teleconferencing links to guide repairs on the battlefield and emergency medical procedures by specialists in remote areas.

Engineer units and militia units are critical in repairing roads, runways, and other infrastructure damaged by hostile forces or suffering from age and the effects of weather. Engineer units also have primary responsibility to build decoys, dig shelters, or employ an assortment of other methods to conceal and protect operational units and their logistics tail. PLA studies of foreign conflicts often take note of the number (usually in the thousands or tens of thousands) of precision-guided munitions (such as land attack cruise missiles, laser- or GPS-guided bombs, etc.) employed, and frequently comment on how effective relatively inexpensive camouflage and deception measures can be to protect forces on the ground from highly accurate, long-range weapons. Other methods discussed to protect against precision-guided munitions include the use of localized jammers (to block GPS signals) or the use of smoke to obscure targets and disrupt laser guidance.

The Military Training and Evaluation Program

In order to guide training for the PLA's new doctrine a "Military Training and Evaluation Program" (MTEP, *junshi xunlian yu kaohe dagang*, also called the "Outline for Military Training and Testing") was promulgated by the General Staff Department and became effective on 1 January 2002. (Similar outlines had been issued before, but this was the first based entirely on recently updated doctrine.) The MTEP sets uniform standards and establishes procedures for evaluation of training for all types of units. The many various types of units and headquarters throughout the PLA all have their own MTEP standards to guide training. Units disseminate MTEP requirements and procedures through a series of meetings and classes. According to news reports, unit training stresses:

- the "Five Capabilities" of rapid reaction, information countermeasures, field survival, combined arms operations, and comprehensive logistics support;
- joint operations;
- information warfare;
- "three attacks and three defenses";
- new equipment training.[36]

Also prominent among training topics in the new MTEP are amphibious operations and emergency rescue and relief operations.[37] Twenty-five percent of specialized technical and tactical training is to take place at night.[38] The new MTEP is a giant step in getting the PLA ready to fight future wars.

Senior Chinese military leaders can see the progress the PLA has made in the past two decades of its modernization program, especially since 1999. Nevertheless, they are also realistic in their evaluations of the hard work remaining ahead. Frequently, senior PLA officers give speeches or write essays in praise of the advances achieved to date. Often, after the praise, they add critiques of shortfalls and obstacles to overcome. These latter passages usually provide outsiders with the most revealing insights into the actual state of the PLA. *Zhanyi Xue* has such an example early on:

> The PLA will be able to defeat the enemy only by proceeding from its actual conditions, taking advantage of the concept of the People's War, of the fact that it is fighting on home territories, and of its superior political work, and by carefully integrating various factors of a campaign into an organic whole and mounting joint combat operations. . . . Although the weapon systems and equipment of the PLA have seen great improvement from the past, there is and will continue to be in the future a considerably large gap when one compares them with those of forces of developed countries. Therefore, we must accelerate the development of advanced weapon systems and equipment so as to narrow this gap, while at the same time we must get prepared to overcome the enemy based on existing weapon systems and equipment.[39]

Foreign observers are well advised to temper enthusiastic press reports with actual conditions within the PLA. Closing the gap between aspiration and capability is a long, continuing process that must be repeated constantly as new personnel and equipment enter the system. The capability of individual units to apply the principles discussed above to realistic battlefield conditions will vary throughout the force depending on the training the units have received, equipment and technology available, and the leadership abilities of officers and soldiers subjected to the extreme pressure of the modern battlefield.

6
WHAT EQUIPMENT DOES THE PLA USE?

According to the series of Chinese Defense White Papers, since 1997 the amount of money available for equipment purchases in the announced Chinese defense budget has almost tripled from about $3 billion to nearly $9 billion in 2004. The sum total of procurement funds over these eight years amounted to approximately $44 billion.[1] The Chinese government does not, however, explain how these funds are divided among the services or exactly what is included in this budgetary category. Nor do these figures account for "purchase power parity" advantages obtained through what remains of the planned economic policies in the Chinese civilian defense industrial sector or for some research and development funds available to the defense industries.[2] Such calculations *may* increase the value of Chinese goods and equipment purchased by the PLA by two or threefold.

It is also generally accepted outside of China that most foreign equipment purchases are not included in the officially announced defense budget; rather they come from special allotments from the central government, including the use of barter trade. According to the Stockholm International Peace Research Institute, 90.77 percent of arms deliveries to China over the past decade have come from Russia. Over the eight years from 1997 to 2004, China imported a total of $13.146 billion in arms from Russia. In 1997, deliveries amounted to $545 million; in 2004, that figure had grown to $2.161 billion (with even higher figures of $2.917 billion in 2001 and $2.379 billion in 2002).[3] Thus, while PLA purchases of domestic equipment have increased significantly since the late 1990s, deliveries from Russia have grown at an even higher rate. The Chinese navy and air force received the lion's share of weapons and equipment from Russia, with the ground force primarily benefiting from the import of Mi-17-series helicopters.

The vast majority of equipment in the PLA ground forces is produced by the Chinese defense industries. Much of the ground force's weaponry is based on Soviet designs of the 1950s and 1960s, which have been modified and upgraded for contemporary use. In the late 1990s, many newer models and modifications of weapons and equipment began entering the force. Most of the new equipment is based on designs of the 1980s and 1990s, some of which were the result of indigenous research and development while others were derived from reverse-engineering small numbers of weapons acquired from foreign sources. Newer, commercially available civilian or dual-use technologies, especially electronics, have been incorporated in many recent modifications and designs. The PLA has also benefited from military electronics produced by the Chinese defense industries; for example, frequency-hopping radios have been introduced into the force along with global positioning (GPS) receivers. Additionally, a large assortment of new command vehicles and mobile shelters, field communications vehicles, support equipment (high-mobility vehicles, trucks, POL transports, field kitchens, electricity generators, etc.), repair vans, and material handling equipment (such as forklifts, material containers, oil pipelines, and POL bladders) has been issued to units to improve command and control and provide logistics support to future operations. As new equipment enters active duty PLA forces, some of the older, retired weapons will be assigned to the reserves and militia.

While there are many sources of technical data for the assortment of weapons, equipment, and vehicles produced by Chinese factories, authoritative information on exactly what equipment is assigned to what units in what number is scarce.[4] The problem of determining the distribution of equipment in the PLA is compounded by the different names (nomenclatures) that may be used by various data sources to identify the same piece of equipment. Further complicating the problem is the defense industry's propensity to build a few prototype items, publicize them, and offer them for export. Many Chinese-made weapons are intended for foreign use only and are never deployed to the PLA – others eventually may reach the force, but long after the industry brochures advertise them for sale. Once new equipment is introduced into the force, it is often difficult to determine how widespread its distribution is. Because of the size of the PLA, it may take years for any single item of equipment to be distributed to all units, if it is intended for universal use. For example, new Kevlar-style helmets were introduced into ground force units in the late 1990s, yet over five years later older-style "steel pots" are still worn by some units.

Chinese language sources often refer to Chinese-made equipment as *guo chan*, or "made in China," followed by a type or designation. The type of equipment is identified often by a year, for example, 69 or 85, followed by the character "*shi*" for "type." Other designators include *pinyin* initials, such as WZ (*wuzhuang*, "armed") or HQ (*Hongqi*, "Red Flag"), which identify the general category of equipment or its name, followed by a series number. For many weapons, both the "year-type" and "category/name-series number" may be followed by a size (caliber) of gun, type of weapon (howitzer, mortar, etc.) and "self-propelled" if mounted on a vehicle. Often some or all of these name combinations may be strung together.

Modifications to equipment types may be identified by the addition of an A, B, C, etc. or I, II, III, etc. to the basic designator. Modifications come in many forms, some of which are more visible than others, like changes to the size of main guns or the addition of laser range finders. Other modifications are less visible, like improved engines or the installation of computers and other electronic gear. After a number of modifications, an equipment type may evolve into a "new" type, which may receive a new year-type or other designation.

Some weapons or modifications to basic equipment types are intended primarily for export and usually have the designator "M" in their name. (Perhaps the best known "M" series weapons are the short-range ballistic missiles M-9 and M-11, which are known in China by the *Dong Feng* (DF, East Wind)-15 and DF-11 designators.) Models and prototype weapons are often displayed at Chinese and foreign arms shows. Brochures prepared by the Chinese defense industries, aimed at potential buyers, are a main source of technical data for these weapons. However, the existence of a weapon system, its photograph or model, does *not* mean the weapon has entered the PLA inventory. In some cases, the Chinese defense industries display prototypes with the hope that foreign buyers will help cover further design and production costs. This strategy has not proved very successful, as China has remained in the mid-ranks of arms suppliers to the world.[5]

Some weapons or vehicles are the basis for a "family" of different categories of equipment. In the case of vehicles, these "variants" use a basic chassis and are modified for different purposes. For example, the WZ-551 six-wheeled armored personnel carrier has mortar, ambulance, and armored recovery vehicle variants, as well as a four-wheeled anti-tank guided missile vehicle and an eight-wheeled variant, which mounts a 122-mm howitzer or 120-mm anti-tank gun. In the case of small arms, several families of weapons are based on a single caliber standard, for example 5.8 mm or 7.62 mm, with numerous modifications to perform specific functions, such as sniper or assault weapons.

The mix of equipment in the PLA changes almost daily as new items are distributed and older models retired. New weapons entering a ground force division are likely to go to each of the subordinate regiments on a staggered schedule over a period of months, extending to a year or more. In the end, not all subordinate units in some large formations may receive the newest equipment available. New equipment may also be introduced into units in small numbers for training purposes before the full inventory arrives.

The London-based International Institute for Strategic Studies annual publication *The Military Balance* is the best concise single source for an *estimate* of the overall numbers and types of weapons and equipment in the PLA (as it is for most other militaries). It does not, however, provide insight into which specific units have what type of equipment. Chinese sources (those with photographs in particular) sometimes link certain equipment with certain Military Regions, but rarely does the mainland identify specific units with specific equipment. Such associations can sometimes be made if other factors are known, such as unit histories, names of officers, or garrison locations.

This chapter identifies and describes briefly the primary weapons and vehicles in the PLA ground forces at the beginning of the twenty-first century. Most of the following sections begin by citing *The Military Balance* for approximate numbers of various sorts of equipment in the PLA inventory. Subsequently, the various names associated with many weapons systems and short descriptions are provided, but detailed technical data for each piece of equipment is not included. Categories of weapons systems addressed are tanks; infantry fighting vehicles/armored personnel carriers; field artillery; multiple rocket launchers; anti-tank weapons; air defense weapons; helicopters; unmanned aerial vehicles and battlefield electronics; small arms, machine-guns, and mortars; and light vehicles and other equipment.

Each section concludes by highlighting equipment included in the 1 October 1999 military parade in Beijing. This parade was well documented by the Chinese media and is a good source for information about much of the new equipment entering the PLA at the time.[6] Several other Chinese-made weapons systems included below, that had been advertised in defense industry brochures and magazines (for example, several new models of multiple rocket launchers), *were not* included in the parade, suggesting they had not been introduced into the force in significant numbers in late 1999. Nevertheless, the parade was a good indicator of many of the weapons then entering the PLA to form the basis of the ground force in the twenty-first century. (The last big military parade was held on 1 October 1984 and, likewise, was a good source of information about PLA weaponry in the late 1980s and 1990s.) New equipment and modifications not included below undoubtedly will enter the PLA's inventory in coming years.

Tanks

The Military Balance lists "some 7,580" medium and main battle tanks in the PLA ground force inventory. These are broken down as 5,000 Type 59 I/II, 300 Type 79, 1,000 Type 88A/B, 1,200 Type 96, and 80 Type 98A. Additionally, another approximately 1,000 light tanks, including some 400 Type 62/62I, 200 Type 63, and 400 Type 63A, are found in the force.[7] The list that follows correlates the various names and designators for the Chinese tanks mentioned by *The Military Balance*:[8]

- *Type 59.* The Type 59 (WZ-120) is the Chinese copy of the Soviet T-54/55, with a 100-mm rifled main gun and a four-man crew. The Type 59I has a laser range finder and improved 100-mm main gun. The Type 59II (WZ-120B) has a 105-mm main gun, and its Type 59IIA variant (also known as the M-1984) has a thermal sleeve over the main gun. The Type 59 series continues to be upgraded (including new engines, fire control systems, reactive armor, etc.) and is still in use in the PLA. One experimental version was fitted with a 120-mm main gun.
- *Type 69/Type 79.* The Type 69 series (WZ-121) is an upgraded Type 59 with a 100-mm smoothbore main gun, aimed at the export market. The smoothbore gun was replaced by the Type 59's 100-mm rifled gun on the Type 69II, along with a new fire control system. The Type 69III (WZ-121D) is also known as the Type 79 and is equipped with a 105-mm main gun with thermal sleeve and a British fire control system. Like the Type 59 series, the Type 69/79 series tanks have five road wheels and Soviet-style "Christie" suspension (i.e., no support rollers), with a large gap between the first and second road wheels.
- *Type 80/Type 88.* The Type 80 series (export version) is also known as the Type 88 series (for domestic use). The early models of the Type 80/Type 88

series retain the round, cast steel turrets of previous Chinese tanks and are armed with 105-mm rifled main guns. Unlike previous Chinese tanks, the Type 80/Type 88 series has six road wheels and three support rollers (which usually are not visible because of side skirts). As offered for export, the series was known as the Type 80I and Type 80II; within China, the series has the designators Type 88A and Type 88B, depending on the type of 105-mm gun mounted. This series, like others, may also be fitted with reactive armor for additional protection.

- *Type 85II/Type 88C/Type 96.* The Type 80/Type 88 series developed into the Type 85II/Type 88C series when the old-style rounded turret was replaced by an angular welded turret. Early versions of the Type 85 (Type 85/85I/ 85II/85IIA) were still fitted with a 105-mm main gun. The Type 85IIM (also known as the Type 85III) replaced the 105-mm main gun with a 125-mm smoothbore gun and autoloader. Several hundred Type 85IIM (also known as the Type 85IIAP) were exported to Pakistan, while domestic versions were designated Type 88C, later changed to Type 96. The US Department of Defense estimates a total of about 1,500 Type 96 tanks to be deployed to PLA forces by 2005.[9] The Type 88C/Type 96 is similar in appearance and performance to the Type 98 main battle tank, but can be distinguished by the driver location on the left side of the vehicle.

- *Type 98/Type 99.* The Type 98 (WZ-123 or ZTZ-98) resembles the Soviet T-72, especially in the location of the driver (centered in the middle of the tank under the main gun tube) behind a distinctive "V" on the front of the glacis plate. The Type 98 is equipped with a 125-mm smoothbore gun, which is capable of firing laser-guided anti-tank rounds, and autoloader. The Type 98 also mounts a laser warning and laser self-defense system on top of its welded turret. Recently, a newer version of the Type 98, called the Type 98I or Type 99 (ZTZ-99), has a modified turret and improved protection over its frontal arc.[10] Fewer Type 98/Type 99 are currently in the force than the Type 96 main battle tank, and fewer are expected to enter the force, primarily because of the higher cost of the newer tank.

- *Type 90-II.* The Type 90-II series, with a welded turret, 125-mm main gun, and driver centered under the main gun tube, was developed in the early 1990s based on older Chinese models and the Soviet T-72. However, the Type 90-II series did not enter into service with the PLA. The Type 90-II was advertised heavily for export and the Type 90-IIM, also known as the MBT-2000, was the basis for the license production of the Al-Khalid main battle tank in Pakistan.

- *Type 62 Light Tank.* The Type 62 is basically a smaller, lighter Type 59 designed for the mountain regions and sandy soils of southern China. It is armed with an 85-mm main gun, but has relatively thin armor. The Type 62I upgrade is fitted with a laser range finder.

- *Type 63 Light Amphibious Tank.* The Type 63 (WZ-211) has a hull similar to the Soviet PT-76 amphibious light tank but with the turret and main gun of the Type 62 Light Tank. Often a laser range finder is mounted above the main gun.

The Type 63I has been upgraded to a 105-mm main gun and computer fire-control system.

- *Type 63A Light Amphibious Tank.* The Type 63A (also known outside of China as the Type 99 Light Amphibious Tank) has an elongated, boat-like hull and welded turret. Its main armament is a 105-mm gun, which is reported to be capable of firing laser-guided anti-tank rounds. The Type 63A has been deployed to both army and marine units.

To summarize, several external features help to differentiate among the Chinese main battle tanks. As seen above, each major tank type also has many modifications, some of which are not readily apparent. Major features to help distinguish tank types include:

- round, cast turret (Type 59/69/79/80/88A/88B) or angular, welded turret (Type 85II/88C/96/98/99);
- size and type of main gun, 100-mm, 105-mm (with or without thermal sleeve), or 125-mm;
- type of suspension (often not visible because of side skirts) and number of road wheels: Christie with five road wheels (Type 59/69/79) or support roller with six road wheels (Type 80/85/88/96/98/99);
- location of driver (on left side of tank for all models, except for Type 98/99 where driver is located in center of the vehicle behind a "V" on the glacis plate).

The October 1999 military parade in Beijing in commemoration of the 50th anniversary of the founding of the PRC was a showcase for many new types of equipment coming into the PLA inventory, as well as for a number of older weapons. Units from all over the country traveled to Beijing prior to the event and spent months preparing to move at a precise speed in formations of 18 vehicles each. (Each ground force unit was marked with a letter from A to P, with vehicles numbered 001 to 018.)

The first three units to pass in review were tank formations. Type 80/Type 88B tanks (with the letter "A" on their turrets) led the parade, identified as being from an armored regiment in the Beijing Military Region, which was most likely the 1st Armored Division. The second formation was composed of Type 88C/Type 96 tanks (marked with the letter "B") from a battalion of an armored regiment of a "Red Army Division," in the Jinan Military Region, likely the 127th Light Mechanized Infantry Division. The third unit to pass in review was identified as a "mixed formation" composed of two new types of tanks (with the letter "C"). Ten Type 98 tanks led the way, followed by eight Type 88C/Type 96 tanks. The unit was from the Beijing Military Region (and received foreign visitors), making it the 6th Armored Division of the 38th Group Army. The fact that the formation had only ten Type 98 tanks indicated the limited degree to which the tank had been issued to the PLA. The number of ten tanks is also highly suggestive of a three-tank

Plate 1 Ministry of Public Security police (foreground) are responsible for law enforcement. They are supported by the People's Armed Police (background in helmet) in domestic stability operations. The PLA is the third line of defense for domestic stability. Civilian MPS police uniforms, insignia, and organization are distinct from the Chinese armed forces. (Photo: Getty Images.)

Plate 2 People's Armed Police squad in Tiananmen Square. PAP uniforms are distinctive from those of the People's Liberation Army in many ways, including color, insignia on hats and collars, color of epaulets, and piping on sleeves and trouser legs. (Photo: Getty Images.)

Plate 3 People's Armed Police first lieutenant (center) and NCO Grade 1 in winter uniforms. New chest badge and shoulder patch are visible. (Photo: Getty Images.)

Plate 4 People's Armed Police squad exercising in the Forbidden City. PAP and PLA units throughout the country have similar apparatus for physical training. (Photo courtesy Susan M. Puska.)

Plate 5 PLA NCO Grade 3 in field camouflage uniform wearing tanker's helmet. (Photo courtesy Susan M. Puska.)

Plate 6 PLA lieutenant general visiting Pearl Harbor in spring/autumn uniform. Note cap and collar insignia. Name tags may be worn while on foreign visits, but normally are not worn in China. (Photo courtesy Susan M. Puska.)

Plate 7 Former US defense attaché to China, Brigadier General G.O. Sealock, with PLA lieutenant general (far right) in summer uniform and beret. Also pictured are a PLA colonel (far left), and a major general and lieutenant colonel (second row). (Photo courtesy G.O. Sealock.)

Plate 8 Civilian MPS anti-riot police were dispatched to Haiti as part of the UN Peacekeeping force in 2004. These civilian police are distinguished by their uniform and patches and wear the UN blue beret and helmet. (Photo: Getty Images.)

Plate 9 PLA uniformed civilian (female) and senior colonel in spring/autumn uniform. Note civilian collar and epaulet insignia. (Photo Dennis J. Blasko.)

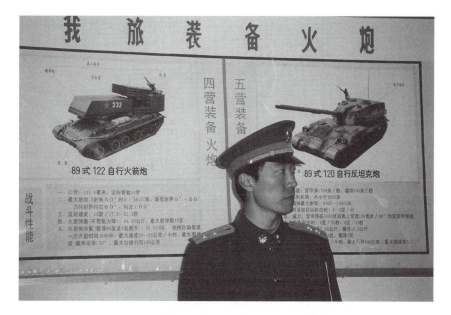

Plate 10 PLA first lieutenant of 6th Artillery Brigade in winter uniform. Charts behind him show Type 89 SP MRL in the brigade's 4th Battalion and Type 89 SP anti-tank gun in the 5th Battalion. (Photo Dennis J. Blasko.)

Plate 11 Type 89 SP anti-tank gun training simulator in 6th Artillery Brigade. (Photo Dennis J. Blasko.)

Plate 12 Type 96 main battle tank at the October 1999 military parade in Beijing. The Type 96 is the most widely distributed modern tank in the ground force inventory. Identification numbers on the turret were for this parade only. (Photo: Getty Images.)

Plate 13 Many units have constructed inland amphibious training areas near their barracks. This company-size training area consists of landing craft (left), beach with obstacles, and objectives on shore. (Photo Courtesy Susan M. Puska.)

Plate 14 Mortar platoon comes ashore in drill at amphibious training area. Note assault platoon has taken up positions beyond the wall. (Photo courtesy Susan M. Puska.)

Plate 15 PLA cadets at Nanchang Academy practice close combat (grenade throwing) in an urban training area. (Photo courtesy Susan M. Puska.)

Plate 16 PLA ground force Honor Guard in ceremonial uniform. The distinctive red epaulets and collar insignia for this uniform may cause confusion with PAP uniform. (Photo Courtesy Susan M. Puska.)

platoon, ten-tank company organization (three tanks in each of three platoons with a tenth tank for the company commander – see Chapter 2).

No light tanks appeared in the parade, signifying that the Type 63A Light Amphibious Tank had not yet begun entering the PLA inventory in operational numbers. By the early years of the twenty-first century, deployment of the Type 63A was widely observed in the Chinese press. Some Chinese media reports of recent military exercises suggest new light tank units may be composed of four tanks per platoon for a total of 12 or 13 tanks per light tank company.

Both tracked and wheeled armored personnel carriers followed the tank formations on 1 October.

Infantry fighting vehicles/armored personnel carriers

The Military Balance holds a total of over 4,500 armored infantry fighting vehicles (IFVs) and armored personnel carriers (APCs). They are divided among 2,300 Type 63A/I/II/C, 200 Type 77-II (BTR-50PK), 1,000 Type 86A (WZ-501), 300 Type 89I (modified Type 85), 100 WZ-523, and 600+ Type 92 (WZ-551).[11] This list includes both tracked and wheeled IFVs and APCs. In order to enhance their amphibious capabilities, some older APCs (such as the Type 77) have been modified with bow and stern extensions to make them more seaworthy.

- *Type 63 Armored Personnel Carrier.* The Type 63 (YW-531 or A531) tracked APC is a lightly armored, distinctive box-like vehicle of indigenous Chinese design with four road wheels. From the 1970s onward, it was and continues to be the most numerous APC in the PLA inventory, though it is gradually being retired as new vehicles enter the force. The vehicle can transport an infantry squad and has been modified to perform many other roles, including command vehicle, mortar transport, self-propelled howitzer, multiple rocket launcher, and ambulance (each variant has its own specific nomenclature). The most common version is the Type 63C (YW-531C). The vehicle was widely exported to Third World countries.
- *Type 77 Amphibious Armored Personnel Carrier.* The Type 77 is similar to the Soviet BTR-50 and has two main versions, the Type 77-I and Type 77-II. As an APC it can carry up to 20 troops; it can also mount or tow anti-tank guns or artillery. The Type 77 has been issued to both army and marine units.
- *Type 85/Type 89 Armored Personnel Carrier.* The Type 85 APC was developed from the Type 63 (YW-531C) and is sometimes called the YW-531H. The Type 85 is longer than the Type 63 and has five road wheels (compared to four on the Type 63). The Type 85 is deployed in the PLA as the Type 89 (YW-534, WZ-534, or ZSD89) with a variety of turrets and gun systems, along with a number of variants such as 122-mm howitzer self-propelled artillery, mortar carrier, ambulance, and armored recovery vehicles. The most common gun system on the APC variant is a 12.7-mm machine-gun in a lightly armored, shoulder-high, open cupola. The Type 85 also had variants

known as the NVH-1 and NVH-4 for export purposes fitted with different gun systems.

- *Type 86 Infantry Fighting Vehicle.* The Type 86 IFV (WZ-501) is the Chinese version of the Soviet BMP-1. Though the vehicle has undergone some experimental modifications primarily in its main armament, it is usually seen equipped with the BMP-1 turret mounting a 73-mm gun and HJ-73 (*hongjian*, "Red Arrow") anti-tank guided missile. The Type 86 has also been offered for export. The Chinese defense industries may also have acquired a few BMP-3 IFVs or BMP-3 technologies, which they may be attempting to integrate into new indigenously produced infantry fighting vehicles.

- *Type 90 Armored Personnel Carrier.* The Type 90 APC (YW-535) was offered for export in the 1990s and has some similarities to the BMP design (though it is commonly seen with a 12.7-mm machine-gun open cupola found on the Type 89 APC instead of a BMP turret and 73-mm gun). Like other APCs it is the basis for a family of vehicles, including a command vehicle, mortar carrier, self-propelled artillery, ambulance, and armored recovery vehicle. The Type 90 does not appear to have been deployed to the PLA.

- *Airborne Combat Vehicle.* In 2004, an airborne combat vehicle of Chinese design was observed on Chinese television. This vehicle appears to be based on other tracked Chinese armored personnel carriers and is equipped with a 30-mm cannon, 7.62-mm machine-gun, and HJ-73 anti-tank guided missile. The vehicle apparently has been deployed in limited number in the 15th Airborne Army.[12] It is possible a few Russian BMD-3 airborne combat vehicles have been sold to China and were used in the development of this Chinese vehicle; however, there is no verifiable evidence of the deployment to the Chinese airborne of a large number of BMD-3s (for example, the 100 vehicles needed to equip a regiment).

- *WZ-523 Wheeled Armored Personnel Carrier.* The WZ-523, a six-wheeled (6X6) APC, was first seen in the 1984 military parade and identified as a reconnaissance vehicle. Other names associated with this vehicle include "Cheetah," M-1984, WZ-553, and ZFB-91. It appears to be issued only in limited numbers in the PLA. Most visibly, the WZ-523 has been assigned to the Hong Kong and Macao Garrisons. The WZ-523 is recognizable by a large gap between the front wheels and the second and third wheels.

- *WZ-551 Wheeled Armored Personnel Carrier.* The WZ-551 (Type 90, ZSL 90) is a six-wheeled (6X6) APC, identified by equal spacing between all wheels. Variations deployed in the PLA are also known as the Type 92 and Type 92A (ZSL 92, ZSL 92A). Additional variants include a four-wheeled (4X4) anti-tank guided missile carrier and an eight-wheeled version. It can mount a number of turrets and main armament systems and has self-propelled AAA, surface-to-air missile, mortar-howitzer, ambulance, and armored recovery vehicle variants. People's Armed Police units have been issued WZ-551 APCs painted white. The first PLA unit reported to be equipped with this vehicle was the 127th Light Mechanized Infantry Division in the 54th Group

Army in the Jinan Military Region, with others deployed to units in Xinjiang, Tibet, and the Beijing Military Region.[13]

Three formations of infantry fighting vehicles and armored personnel carriers were on display in the 1999 military parade. Following the tanks, the fourth formation (marked with the letter "D") consisted of Type 86/WZ-501 infantry fighting vehicles from the Beijing Military Region. They were followed by Type 85/Type 89 (YW-534) APCs also from the Beijing Military Region (identified by the letter "E"). The last formation of armored personnel carriers was composed of WZ-551s from the Jinan Military Region (marked with the letter "F").

Field artillery

The Military Balance lists some 14,000 towed artillery pieces and another estimated 1,200 self-propelled pieces; however, it is less precise about the exact numbers of each type of weapon. Among the towed category are Type 59 100-mm field/anti-tank guns; Type 54-1, Type 60, and Type 83 122-mm howitzers; Type 59 and Type 59-1 130-mm guns; Type 54 and Type 66 152-mm howitzers; and 150 Type 88 (WAC-21) 155-mm gun-howitzers. Self-propelled artillery includes 200 Type 70I and 500 Type 89 122-mm howitzers, and 500 Type 83 152-mm howitzers.[14] Additionally, *The Military Balance* notes that an assortment of anti-ship surface-to-surface cruise missiles are found in the force – most likely in the coastal defense units along China's eastern and southern seaboard.

* *Towed 100-mm field/anti-tank guns.* The Type 59 100-mm field/anti-tank gun listed in *The Military Balance* is probably a misprint for the Type 86 100-mm smoothbore anti-tank gun. Its predecessor was the Type 73 100-mm smoothbore anti-tank gun. Both models are probably being phased out of the inventory and replaced by 120-mm anti-tanks guns and anti-tank guided missiles. (See "Anti-tank Weapons," pp. 133–35.)
* *Towed 122-mm howitzers.* The Type 54-1 122-mm howitzer is based on the Soviet M-38 and is distinguishable by its short gun tube with no muzzle brake. The Type 60 122-mm howitzer is based on the Soviet D-74 and has a longer barrel than the Type 54-1 and a muzzle brake. The Type 83 listed by *The Military Balance* is the Type 85 or D-30 Type 122-mm howitzer based on the Soviet D-30. This weapon is easily recognized by its three-trail carriage, which folds forward under the barrel so it can be towed by a lunette under the muzzle brake. In its firing position, the three trails are spread at 120 degree angles, with the gun and wheels jacked up off the ground to allow for a 360 degree traverse. A variant of the Type 85, with a conventional two-trail configuration, apparently has been developed and may be deployed to the force.
* *Towed 130-mm field gun.* The Type 59 130-mm field gun is a copy of the Soviet M-46 130-mm field gun. The Type 59-I (Type 59-1) has a modified carriage making it lighter than the Type 59. The gun is distinguished by its very long barrel, which gives it exceptional range capability. The maximum range of

27 kilometers can be extended to over 30 kilometers by firing enhanced-range projectiles.

- *Towed 152-mm gun and gun-howitzer.* The Type 66 152-mm gun-howitzer is a copy of the Soviet D-20. It is recognized by its thick, stocky barrel with large muzzle brake and is one of the most common artillery pieces in the PLA inventory. A few Type 54 152-mm guns, copies of the Soviet M-37/ML-20, may still be in the inventory. Likewise, a few Type 83 152-mm field guns may also be assigned to the PLA. The Type 83 is an indigenous design from the 1980s recognizable by a long barrel that rotates to the rear to fold over its two trails when being towed. The Type 83 was not issued to the PLA in great numbers, but was replaced by towed 155-mm gun-howitzers.[15]

- *Towed 155-mm gun-howitzers.* The Chinese defense industries developed their 155-mm gun-howitzers from the Austrian GNH 45 155-mm howitzer. The GM-45 Type 155 gun-howitzer mounted the GNH 45 weapon on the two-wheel carriage of the 130-mm field gun. Though publicized, the GM-45 does not appear to have entered the PLA inventory. Instead, the PLL-01 155-mm gun-howitzer, also known as the W-88 or the WA-021 or WAC-021 for export, has been deployed to some PLA artillery units, likely at echelons above division level. (Various sources also give it either a Type 88 or Type 89 nomenclature.) The barrel of the PLL-01 folds over its trails for towing on a four-wheel carriage. In its firing position, all four wheels are forward with the two trails spread to the rear of the gun. Its normal maximum range of 24 kilometers can be extended to 39 kilometers using advanced, extended range munitions.

The PLL-01 155-mm gun-howitzer was the only towed field artillery piece to be displayed in the 1999 military parade. The formation was marked by the letter "N" and was reported to be from the Beijing Military Region. At the time only about 36 of the pieces were believed to be in the PLA; now, as seen in *The Military Balance* numbers above, that number has grown fourfold. Two types of self-propelled artillery were included in the parade.

- *122-mm self-propelled artillery.* The Chinese defense industries have developed several types of 122-mm self-propelled (SP) howitzers. The Type 70 122-mm SP howitzer integrates a Type 54-1 122-mm howitzer on a Type 63 APC chassis and may still be in limited service in the PLA. The Type 85 122-mm SP howitzer, also known as the D-30 Type 122-mm SP howitzer, puts a D-30 122-mm howitzer on a Type 85 APC chassis, but is not known to have been deployed to the PLA. A more successful weapon, the Type 89 122-mm SP howitzer, began entering the force in the 1990s (and was also offered for export). The Type 89 mounts a 122-mm howitzer derived from the D-30 in a turret on the back of a tracked amphibious chassis. The Chinese defense industries have developed and publicized at least two more 122-mm self-propelled howitzers, one using an eight-wheeled WZ-551 chassis with large center-mounted turret and the other with a rear-mounted turret on a new eight-wheeled chassis. These new wheeled 122-mm SP howitzers were probably designed for the lighter mechanized forces being developed in the PLA, as well as for potential export.

- *152-mm self-propelled artillery*. The Type 83 152-mm SP gun-howitzer has been deployed in the PLA for approximately two decades. The system has a large rear-mounted turret on a tracked chassis with six road wheels.
- *PLZ-45 155-mm self-propelled howitzer*. The PLZ-45 155-mm SP howitzer mounts a WAC-021 155-mm howitzer in a large rear turret on a modified Type 80 tank chassis. The system has been exported to Kuwait, but is not confirmed to be deployed in the PLA. Photographs on the Internet in 2005 of the system with Chinese markings rekindled debate as to whether it has been deployed to the PLA.
- *203-mm self-propelled artillery*. The Chinese defense industries may also have attempted to develop or continue to develop a 203-mm howitzer in either self-propelled or towed versions. There is no indication that development has been completed or the system deployed to the PLA.

The Type 89 122-mm SP howitzer was the eighth formation (identified by the letter "H") in the 1999 military parade. The Type 89 was assigned to an artillery regiment in an armored division of the Beijing Military Region, likely the 6th Armored Division. The tenth formation in the parade (marked by the letter "J") was composed of Type 83 152-mm SP gun-howitzers from an armored division also in the Beijing Military Region. This division's predecessor unit was described as "the first tank unit in the Chinese PLA"[16] and thus is likely to be the 1st Armored Division.

In addition to the self-propelled artillery listed above, in recent years the Chinese defense industries have also publicized several other guns mounted on wheeled vehicles: a 105-mm assault gun mounted on a six-wheeled WZ-551 APC chassis, the "BK 1990 combat vehicle" on an eight-wheeled APC chassis, a 120-mm assault gun also mounted on an eight-wheeled WZ-551 APC chassis, and a WAC-021 155-mm howitzer mounted on the back of a flatbed six-wheeled truck. None of these weapons are known to be deployed to the PLA, but some could eventually enter the inventory.

The Chinese defense industries are reported to have purchased and produced Russian Krasnopol laser-guided artillery projectiles, which are capable of being fired from both 152-mm and 155-mm guns and howitzers. These precision-guided munitions (PGM) require a laser target designator (LTD) that enables extremely accurate fire at individual targets, such as armored vehicles or fortifications, or at the center-of-mass of larger targets. The Krasnopol round can be very expensive (some 30 to 50 times as expensive as a conventional round), but is estimated to be 20 to 50 times as effective as a conventional round.[17] It is not known how many LTD are available to PLA forward observers, and techniques to employ the round properly must be practiced and refined through training both forward observers and gun crews. Reliable communications between forward observers and artillery units is essential. Laser warning detectors (as found on the Type 98 tank) and smoke grenades (now found on most Chinese tanks and armored vehicles) are used to counter the Krasnopol and US Copperhead PGMs. Though expensive, if available in sufficient quantity, PGMs, such as the Krasnopol, exponentially increase the effectiveness of properly trained and equipped ground forces.

Multiple rocket launchers

The Military Balance counts 2,400 multiple rocket launchers (MRL) broken down among the Type 81 122-mm MRL and Type 89 122-mm self-propelled MRL; Type 70 130-mm self-propelled MRL and Type 82 130-mm MRL; Type 83 273-mm MRL; and Type 96 320-mm MRL. No specific numbers are listed for each type.[18] In addition to the MRLs identified by *The Military Balance*, it is likely that a number of smaller 12-tube 107-mm MRL systems, either towed or mounted on vehicles, remain in the force, primarily in light infantry units.

- *122-mm multiple rocket launchers*. The Chinese defense industries have taken the basic design of the Soviet BM-21 40-tube 122-mm multiple rocket launcher and mounted it on a variety of wheeled and tracked vehicles. The Type 81 122-mm MRL is the basic truck mounted version. The Type 89 122-mm self-propelled MRL uses the same tracked chassis as the Type 83 152-mm self-propelled gun-howitzer with the significant addition of a reload pack mounted in front of the launchers. This modification increases the speed of reloading and allows for two volleys to be fired in rapid succession. Both the Type 81 and Type 89 MRLs are in the PLA inventory in artillery regiments at division and higher levels. In the 1990s, the Chinese defense industries offered a truck-mounted version of the 40-tube launcher with a reload mounted in front, known as the Type 90. This version of the 122-mm MRL weapon system is not known to be issued to PLA units.
- *130-mm multiple rocket launchers*. Several types of 130-mm MRL are deployed to the PLA. The earliest version, the Type 63 19-tube 130-mm MRL is mounted on the back of a truck. A similar 19-tube system mounted on top of a Type 63 APC is known as the Type 70 130-mm MRL. A 30-tube version mounted on a truck is called the Type 82 130-mm MRL; when the same 30-tube system is mounted on a Type 85 APC it is called the Type 85 130-mm MRL. The 130-mm MRL has a range about half as long as the 122-mm MRL and is therefore likely found in the artillery battalions of infantry and armored regiments.
- *273-mm multiple rocket launchers*. The Type 83 273-mm MRL (WM-40) is a four-tube system mounted on the back of a tracked carrier developed in the 1980s. The rocket tubes themselves appear as long rectangular boxes placed together side by side in a single row. Reported range of the Type 83 is 40 kilometers. In the 1990s, a wheeled eight-tube 273-mm MRL was marketed as the WM-80 with an advertised range of over 80 kilometers. While the

Type 83 reportedly is deployed in limited numbers in the PLA, the WM-80 has been offered for foreign sale, but is not known to be in the PLA inventory.

- *300-mm multiple rocket launcher.* The A-100 300-mm MRL is a 10-tube system mounted on an eight-wheeled truck. The weapon system appears to be very similar to the Russian 12-round Smerch 300-mm MRL. Minimum range for the system is 50 kilometers with a maximum of 100 kilometers, with a longer range 70 to 180 kilometer version under development. The A-100 is reported to be deployed in the Guangzhou Military Region.[19]
- *320-mm multiple rocket launcher.* The WS-1 eight-tube 320-mm MRL and WS-1B (Type 96) four-tube 320-mm MRL have been developed by the Chinese defense industries. Both systems are mounted on six-wheeled flatbed trucks. The WS-1 has a range from 20 to 80 kilometers while the WS-1B has a range from 80 to 180 kilometers.[20]
- *B611* Zhenmu *short-range, tactical missile system.* The B611 short-range, tactical missile system was offered for export at the 2004 Zhuhai International Aviation and Aerospace Exhibition. The missile system, with advertised range of 150 kilometers, was mounted in two canisters on the back of a Chinese-made 6X6 truck. The missile reportedly uses Russian GLONASS satellite positioning system technology and has both fragmentation and cluster munitions warheads. It is not known if the system has entered into serial production or has been deployed to the PLA.[21]

Two MRL systems were on display in the 1999 parade: the truck-mounted Type 81 122-mm MRL and the tracked Type 89 122-mm self-propelled MRL. The Type 89 passed first, with the letter "K" on the reload pack on each vehicle. The unit was from the artillery regiment of a mechanized infantry division in the Beijing Military Region. Later, the wheeled Type 81s (marked with the letter "M") were identified as subordinate to an artillery regiment in the Beijing Military Region.[22] None of the newer, longer-range, multiple-launch rocket systems, such as the WM-80, A-100, or WS-1B, were featured in the parade. The absence of these systems implies that they had not yet entered into PLA operational units in 1999 in enough time for them to be ready for the parade. It is likely that these systems are assigned in relatively small numbers only to artillery brigades and divisions at group army and higher level.

Anti-tank weapons

Anti-tank weapons include anti-tank guns, recoilless rifles, anti-tank rockets, and anti-tank guided missiles (ATGM). *The Military Balance* includes the Type 73 and Type 86 100-mm guns and 300+ Type 89 self-propelled anti-tank guns. Recoilless rifles include the Type 56 75-mm recoilless rifle; Type 65 and Type 78 82-mm recoilless rifles; and Type 75 105-mm recoilless rifle. ATGM are listed with a total number of 7,200, broken down among HJ-73A/B/C (Soviet *Sagger*-type), HJ-8A/C/E (TOW/*Milan*-type), and 24 HJ-9.[23]

133

- *Anti-tank guns.* As discussed in the Field Artillery section, towed Type 73 and Type 86 100-mm smoothbore anti-tank guns have been deployed to the PLA but are probably being phased out of the inventory. Since about the mid-1990s, the Type 89 120-mm self-propelled anti-tank gun (or tank destroyer) has entered the force. The Type 89 mounts a 120-mm gun in a turret located at the rear of the same tracked chassis as the Type 83 152-mm self-propelled gun-howitzer. The 120-mm assault gun mounted on an eight-wheeled WZ-551 APC chassis mentioned earlier has the potential to be used in an anti-tank role, but is not known to be deployed in the PLA.

- *Recoilless rifles and anti-tank rockets.* The most commonly seen recoilless rifle in the PLA today is the jeep-mounted Type 75 100-mm recoilless rifle. Though still seen in some units, the Type 75 is being replaced by vehicle-mounted anti-tank guided missiles. (Though likely to be ineffective against most modern armor, the Type 75 is used in demonstrations by PLA units probably because it makes a lot of noise when fired and is much cheaper than launching an anti-tank guided missile. Given the proper circumstances and ammunition, the Type 75 could be effective against personnel, battlefield fortifications, and unarmored vehicles.) *The Military Balance* lists the Type 56 75-mm recoilless rifle and Type 65 and Type 78 82-mm recoilless rifles still in the PLA inventory. These weapons would be found at the infantry battalion and company level, but are probably being phased out for the PF-98 120-mm anti-tank rocket, which is man-portable using a two-man crew. The PF-89 and PF-89A 80-mm light anti-tank weapons are individual, one-round anti-tank rockets available to PLA units since the 1990s. The PF-89 series replaces the earlier Type 70 62-mm anti-tank rocket and Type 69-1 40-mm rocket launcher (similar to Soviet the RPG-7 series).

- *Anti-tank guided missiles.* Three families of ATGM are currently deployed in the PLA. All are known by their "HJ" designator. The HJ-73 is derived from the Soviet *Sagger* wire-guided anti-tank guided missile and modified with a Chinese guidance system. It can be man-packed and ground-launched by a three-man team or mounted on a vehicle. It is commonly seen mounted over the 73-mm gun on the Type 86/WZ-501 (BMP-1) IFV. The second-generation Chinese ATGM, the HJ-8 series, is similar to the US TOW and French *Milan* systems. The HJ-8 can be launched from a tripod on the ground, or mounted on a jeep, armored vehicle, or helicopter. The latest anti-tank guided missile in the PLA inventory is the HJ-9. The HJ-9 has several modifications, including both optically guided and "fire and forget" millimeter wave seekers and semi-active laser beamriding seekers.[24] The HJ-9 was first seen at the 1999 military parade mounted on a four-wheeled version of the WZ-551 APC.

The HJ-9 ATGM was the seventh formation in the 1999 military parade (marked with the letter "G"). It was identified as subordinate to an anti-tank missile regiment in the Nanjing Military Region (which could be an element of the artillery division in the 1st Group Army). The HJ-73 was seen mounted on the WZ-501s in the parade.

The Type 89 120-mm self-propelled anti-tank gun also took part and was identified as being from the artillery brigade of a group army in the Beijing Military Region.[25] This unit, identified by the letter "I," was the 38th Group Army's 6th Artillery Brigade.

Air defense weapons

Air defense weapons include anti-aircraft artillery and surface-to-air missiles. *The Military Balance* lists some 7,700 AAA guns, including Type 80 23-mm; Type 85 25-mm; 50+ Type 90 35-mm; Type 55/65/74 and Type 88 self-propelled 37-mm; Type 59 and Type 80 self-propelled 57-mm; Type 56 85-mm; and Type 59 100-mm. Surface-to-air missiles found in the force include the man-portable HN-5A/B (SA-7 type), QW-1, QW-2, FN-6, 24 HQ-61A, 200 HQ-7A, and 60 SA-15 (Tor-M1 from Russia).[26] Though *The Military Balance* lists the SA-15 in the ground force, the system is more likely found operating in conjunction with the SA-10 SAMs the PLA Air Force has purchased from Russia. The SA-15 provides close-in, low altitude coverage the SA-10 is not capable of and thus is necessary to complement the larger, longer-range system.

Smaller caliber AAA guns (23 mm to 57 mm) will be found in maneuver divisions, brigades, and regiments, with larger calibers (37 mm, 57 mm, and higher) in AAA divisions and brigades. (The PLA Air Force also has air defense units equipped with 85-mm and 100-mm AAA guns.) Many of the older, large caliber guns are gradually being phased out of the inventory as newer systems and SAMs enter the force.

- *23-mm and 25-mm anti-aircraft guns.* The single-axle, towed Type 80 23-mm dual anti-aircraft gun is similar to the Soviet ZSU-23-2. It is also the basis for the 25-mm dual anti-aircraft gun, known as the Type 85 or Type 87 (Type PG87). In the 1990s, the Type 95 quad 25-mm gun/SAM SP system (PGZ 95) began entering the PLA. This tracked vehicle has four 25-mm guns on a turret (two per side mounted over the top of each other), along with four QW-2 short-range surface-to-air missiles. Each gun/missile vehicle has a fire control radar on the turret and each firing battery (probably composed of four or six gun/missile vehicles) has a separate tracked vehicle with larger target acquisition radar.

- *35-mm anti-aircraft guns.* The Type 90 twin 35-mm anti-aircraft gun on a two-axle towed carriage is reportedly based on the German Gepard 35-mm self-propelled AAA gun, and uses Oerlikon 35-mm gun technology acquired by China in the 1980s.[27] A self-propelled version, mounted on a tracked chassis with a large turret that also mounts fire control radars, has been developed for display. The towed Type 90 apparently has entered the PLA in limited numbers as a replacement for some of the more numerous 37-mm AAA systems.

- *37-mm anti-aircraft guns.* The Chinese defense industries developed several types of twin 37-mm anti-aircraft guns mounted on towed, two-axle carriages:

Type 65, Type 74, and P793 (the systems are distinguished primarily by their rates of fire). These guns were deployed extensively to ground force maneuver units to provide close-in air defense for infantry and tank units. The Type 88, a track-mounted self-propelled twin 37-mm gun system, was also developed, but did not enter service with the PLA. The JP-113 twin 37-mm mounted in a round turret on a two-axle carriage was developed for export as part of an integrated gun-missile short-range air defense system.

- *57-mm anti-aircraft guns.* The Type 59 57-mm anti-aircraft gun is derived from the Soviet S-60 57-mm anti-aircraft gun. The Type 59 is a towed, single-barrel gun mounted on a two-axle carriage and was deployed extensively in the PLA. The Type 80 self-propelled 57-mm is similar to the Soviet ZSU-57-2, but does not appear to have entered service with the PLA.

- *85-mm and 100-mm anti-aircraft guns.* The Type 56 85-mm anti-aircraft gun and Type 59 100-mm anti-aircraft gun are derived from Soviet models of the same caliber. Both are single-barrel systems, mounted on two-axle carriages. It is unclear how many are still in PLA units.

- *Man-portable surface-to-air missiles.* Several types and modifications of man-portable, shoulder-fired SAMs are available to PLA units in significant numbers. Man-portable systems may be modified for use on vehicles. The HN-5, with modifications A, B, and C, is based on the Soviet SA-7. The HN-5C consists of eight HN-5A SAMs mounted on a truck. China's second-generation shoulder-fired SAM is the QW-1 (*Qianwei*, "Vanguard"), reported to be similar to the US Stinger. The QW-2 appears to be the SAM mounted on the Type 95 quad 25-mm gun/SAM self-propelled system. In 2004, a new self-propelled wheeled SAM system incorporating what also appears to be the QW-2 was publicized. The CQW-2 mounts a search radar, fire-control radar, electro-optical tracker, and eight short-range SAMs on a four-wheeled APC. The system would be able to accompany maneuver units in the field or provide point protection for fixed facilities.[28] The publication of photographs of this system does not indicate that it has been issued to the PLA, however. The FN-6, a second-generation, man-portable shoulder-fired SAM, has also been publicized.

- *HQ-61.* The HQ-61A is truck-mounted a medium-range SAM. *The Military Balance* lists them in the PLA inventory, but not in large numbers. The HQ-61 has been offered for export and is in service with the PLA Navy; in 2005 photographs on the Internet showed it deployed to an air defense brigade in the Beijing Military Region, along with the HQ-7.

- *HQ-7.* The HQ-7 (FM-80) is a short-range SAM based on the French *Crotale* missile system, recognized by its blunt-nosed, tubular canister mounted two on each side of a small fire-control radar. The HQ-7 may be self-propelled on a small two-axle wheeled vehicle or towed by a truck on a two-axle trailer. An upgraded version, the FM-90, is reported to have been developed. The HQ-7 has been deployed to mixed air defense brigades subordinate to group armies.

- *PL-9.* The PL-9 is a short-range, low-altitude SAM reported to be based on Israeli Python-3 technology. It was marketed as part of a ground-based mobile system, the Type 390 Integrated Gun-Missile Air Defense System, integrating the PL-9 with 35-mm or 37-mm AAA guns, such as the Type 90 or JP-113. The missile or the system has not been confirmed in the PLA ground forces.

Air defense systems in the 1999 military parade were represented by the Type 95 quad 25-mm gun/SAM self-propelled system (marked with the letter "L"), the towed Type 90 twin 35-mm anti-aircraft gun (marked by the letter "O"), and the HQ-7 system, both self-propelled and towed (identified by the letter "P"). The Type 95 SP gun/missile system was reported to be from an armored regiment in the Jinan Military Region, indicating its mission to accompany maneuver forces. The towed 35-mm AAA gun was subordinate to a group army in the Nanjing Military Region. Finally, the HQ-7s were identified as belonging to both a group army in the Beijing Military Region, i.e., the 38th Group Army, and a missile regiment of the PLA Air Force. The fact that the HQ-7 was in a mixed formation of ground and air force units implies the system was not widely deployed to the army in 1999. Subsequent photographs of the system in the field, as well as the unit patch for the air defense brigade of the 38th Group Army, confirm that the self-propelled model is used by the ground forces. A naval version of the HQ-7 was also included in the parade (identified by the letter "Q"), along with a naval version of the HQ-61 in the same formation.

Helicopters

The number of helicopters in the PLA ground force is relatively small for such a large force. Most estimates range from about 300 to 400 aircraft of all types. *The Military Balance* lists about 381 while a late 2003 article in *Flight International* gave a total of 394.[29] The various types and numbers of helicopters from these two sources are compared in Table 6.1.

The PLA ground force's one major recent equipment import from Russia has been over 100 Mi-17 helicopters of various sorts. These airframes were added to the older Mi-8s that had been in the inventory for some years. The majority of the European and American helicopters in the force were acquired in the 1980s prior to the Tiananmen massacre. Sanctions imposed on China in June 1989 do not allow the sale of spare parts for the US Blackhawks. Table 6.1 lists numbers of aircraft in the inventory; many older aircraft may no longer be airworthy or nearing the end of their useful life cycle. The Chinese defense industries (AVIC II in particular) produce the Chinese-made helicopters entering the force, identified by the "Z" (for *zhishengji*, helicopter) or "WZ" (for *wuzhuang zhishengji*, armed helicopter) designators. A Z-10 helicopter is under development ("some" are identified by *The Military Balance* as being deployed) and will probably fill the dedicated gunship role for the PLA. A prototype helicopter gunship is reported to have flown in 2003.

Table 6.1 Types and estimated numbers of helicopters

Type	Role	Number: The Military Balance	Number: Flight International
SA316B AlouetteIII	Trainer	8	8
SA342L1 Gazelle	Attack	8	8
AS350B2 Ecureuil	Trainer	0	7
S-70C-2 Blackhawk	Utility	19	19
Z-8A	Transport	7	7
Z-9/Z-9A/B *Haitun*	Utility	61	61
WZ-9 Combat *Haitun*	Attack	31	31
Z-10	Gunship/transport?	"some"	
Z-11	Trainer/utility	53	53
WZ-11 Combat *Songshu*	Attack	0	6
Mi-6A Hook A	Transport	3	3
Mi-8T Hip C	Transport	30	30
Mi-17 Hip H	Transport	47	47
Mi-171 Hip H	Transport	45	45
Mi-17V-5 Hip H	Transport	69	69
Total		381	394

In late 2004, the test flight of an armed Z-11 light helicopter was reported in the Chinese press.[30]

A total of 25 Z-9-series helicopters (10 Z-9 and 15 armed WZ-9) flew over Tiananmen Square in the 1999 military parade. No Russian Mi-17-series helicopters took part.

Unmanned aerial vehicles and battlefield electronics

The PLA has a variety of unmanned aerial vehicles (UAVs), both air- and ground-launched, in its inventory that are used by all services. Several types of air-launched UAVs are employed as target drones for air defense artillery and missiles, and for high-altitude reconnaissance. These include the ASN-7, *Chang Kong* 1 (CK-1), *Chang Hong* 1 (CH), JM-2 simulated cruise missile target, *Gai-1* (G-1) airborne target drone, S-45 target drone, S-70 target drone, S-80 naval target drone, S-100M target drone, S-100W target drone, and S-200W high-speed target drone to simulate cruise missiles.[31] The PLA also acquired a number of *Harpy* UAVs from Israel in the 1990s. This system may be ground- or ship-launched and is designed to detect and destroy radar systems. The deal came to light in late 2004 after some of the UAVs were returned to Israel for technology upgrades.[32] It is not clear which PLA service operates the *Harpy*.

A number of PLA research centers and defense industries are also in the process of developing mini-UAVs, some with wingspans as small as 22, 30, and 60 centimeters. These craft are man-portable and equipped with video and electronic warfare equipment. Other mini-UAVs include the AW-4 "Shark" and AW-12A.[33]

The PLA ground forces have been experimenting with UAVs for a number of years. Both a divisional reconnaissance battalion and a Military Region-level Special Operations unit have been reported training their troops with UAVs.[34] UAVs are also likely found in some Military Region-level electronic counter-measures regiments, organized into a UAV battalion. A number of UAVs are suitable for ground force operations:[35]

- The ASN-104 has a wingspan of 4.3 meters, range of 300 kilometers and endurance time of 2 hours, remote control distance of 60 kilometers, and is equipped with a camera and television system. An ASN-104 system includes six aircraft and a ground control station consisting of a command and control vehicle, a mobile control vehicle, and a photographic processing and intelligence processing vehicle. The UAV is launched using a rocket booster from a launch platform and lands using a parachute retrieval system.
- The ASN-105B has a wingspan of 5 meters, endurance period of 7 hours, and remote control distance of 100 kilometers. The ASN-105B is equipped with a GPS navigation system, camera, and television/infrared imaging system. It also is launched using a rocket booster from a launch platform and lands using a parachute retrieval system.
- The ASN-206 has a wingspan of 6 meters, can operate for 8 hours out to a radius of 150 kilometers, and may be equipped with a low-light camera, infrared line scanner, airborne videorecorder, and laser altimeter. The ASN-206 system consists of six to ten aircraft and a ground station consisting of a command vehicle, mobile control vehicle, launch vehicle, power source vehicle, intelligence processing vehicle, maintenance vehicle, and transport vehicle.
- The ASN-15 (which may also be known as the W-30) has a wingspan of 3 meters, an endurance time of 4 hours with control radius of 10 kilometers, and is equipped with a GPS navigation system and camera and relay system. It is launched by catapult and recovered by parachute. A system is made up of three aircraft, a ground control station with remote control transmitter, video receiver, and real-time video downlink.
- The W-50 has a wingspan of 4.8 meters, with endurance time of 4–6 hours, and control radius of 100 kilometers. It is equipped with advanced data link control technology and GPS navigation, and can be used for reconnaissance, battle-damage assessment, surveillance, communications relay, and electronic jamming.
- The Z-3 unmanned helicopter has a main rotor diameter of 3.425 meters, an endurance period of 4 hours, and remote control, telemetry, and GPS navigation systems. It can be used for surveillance, reconnaissance, radio relay, or electronic jamming.

PLA ground reconnaissance units are also experimenting with battlefield video systems, ground surveillance radars, and night vision devices – their effectiveness enhanced by modern communications and computer systems capable of passing large amounts of data rapidly. Helmet-mounted night vision devices and GPS receivers are becoming more prevalent throughout the force. Counterbattery radars are available to artillery units; air defense and AAA units use a variety of air surveillance and target acquisition radars.

The PLA also has an assortment of electronic jammers, which can operate from the ground or aircraft. Particular attention has been placed on localized jamming of GPS signals to protect point targets from attack by precision-guided munitions that use GPS receivers to achieve their accuracy. While many types of high-technology systems are entering the force, sufficient data is not available to know their exact distribution or the numbers available to PLA units.

Small arms, machine-guns, and mortars

The Type 81 7.62-mm family of squad automatic rifles and light machine-guns is common in the PLA ground forces. The Type 81 family is an improvement of the older Type 56 7.62-mm family of weapons based on the Soviet AK-47-series of weapons. The Type 95 5.8-mm family of weapons is gradually replacing the Type 81 family.[36] Within each family of weapons are several variations, including solid-stock and folding-stock models, assault rifle, and light machine-gun. The Chinese defense industries also produce a 5.56-mm family of weapons for export.

Individual and crew-served automatic grenade launchers are available to the PLA, including a 30-mm crew-served grenade launcher; the newer Type 87 (QLZ 87) 35-mm grenade launcher (its prototype the Type W87 did not enter service);[37] and Type 91 35-mm grenade launcher that can be fired from the shoulder, attached to a rifle, or mounted on a vehicle. The shoulder-fired FHJ 84 twin 62-mm rocket launcher, for use against soft (non-armored) targets, may also be coming into the PLA inventory.

The PLA uses a variety of crew-served heavy machine-guns. Older models include several varieties of 7.62-mm, 12.7-mm, and 14.5-mm machine-guns. The QJY 88 5.8-mm machine-gun is coming into service to replace both 7.62-mm and 12.7-mm guns. The QJY 88 can fire either 5.8-mm machine-gun ammunition or 5.8-mm rifle ammunition, which is standard for the new Type 95 5.8-mm rifles entering the PLA.[38]

PLA ground forces employ several types of 60-mm, 82-mm, 100-mm, and 120-mm mortars at the maneuver company, battalion, and regiment level. The 60-mm and 100-mm mortars are light enough to be man-packed, while some 82-mm and 120-mm mortars have been mounted on APCs to be used as firing platforms. Mortars provide small-unit commanders organic, short-range, indirect firepower under their direct control.

The Chinese defense industries are marketing a Type W99 82-mm mortar and 120-mm mortar-howitzer mounted on a six-wheeled WZ 551 chassis. The Type W99 appears to be derived from the Soviet/Russian 82-mm Vasilek automatic mortar system.[39] The 120-mm mortar-howitzer turret and gun are similar to the Russian 120-mm 2S23 NONA-SVK self-propelled mortar.[40] According to *The Military Balance*, some 100 2S23 NONA-SVK self-propelled mortars are in the PLA.[41] That entry likely applies to the 120-mm mortar-howitzer mounted on the WZ 551 chassis. It is unclear if the W99 82-mm mortar has entered service in the PLA (the 82-mm Vasilek system was deployed to Soviet army units in the late 1970s).

Light vehicles and other equipment

A number of new utility vehicles have entered the PLA in recent years. These vehicles are smaller than trucks and may be modified to serve as troop or supply carriers and armed with a variety of weapons. One version has many physical similarities to the US High Mobility Multipurpose Wheeled Vehicle (HMMWV or Humvee). Another light "strike vehicle" used by airborne troops shares common assemblies with the Beijing 2020 jeep. The "indigenous airborne strike vehicle" can be used as a troop transport and may be armed with 5.8-mm and 12.7-mm machine-guns, 23-mm guns, 35-mm grenade launchers, or recoilless rifles.[42] Some PLA SOF or reconnaissance units also have experimented with "dune buggy"-type vehicles that are lightweight, fast, and maneuverable, but offer no protection to riders.

The PLA has also acquired and developed new vehicles to support command, control, communications, and logistics functions. Many headquarters units (at group army and below) have developed their own mobile command vans, which provide shelter and electricity for commanders and staff in the field. These may be in the form of hardened shelter vans on the back of trucks or expandable platform trucks from which shelters may be unfolded to create a field command post. Mobile command post vehicles come in various sizes depending on the size of the headquarters where they are assigned. Vehicles such as these allow for standardized layouts for the various staff sections in the headquarters as well as facilitating rapid set up of communications links while protecting sensitive equipment from the weather. Communications systems (antennas, cables, radio sets, computers, etc.) and communications stations are mounted in vans on the backs of trucks or in civilian-type four-wheel utility vehicles.

Likewise, new vans on the back of trucks for field repair of equipment have been developed and deployed into army units. These vans carry spare parts and have machinery mounted inside to perform many types of repairs away from garrison locations day or night, in any weather. A new generation of camouflaged repair and supply shelters (tents) has also been developed for operations in the field. New field kitchens are being deployed to combat units. These new kitchens use propane gas, freeing cooks from having to build fires as they did in the past.

PLA logistics units have focused on the use of pallets and containers to organize and transport supplies. Containers may be transported by air, ship, rail, or truck, and techniques have been developed for parachute delivery of containerized supplies. Recognizing that large containers or pallets cannot be loaded and unloaded by hand efficiently, the PLA has shifted to the use of forklifts and cranes in the routine handling of materiel. Bar codes, scanners, and computer tracking and management systems are also being incorporated into normal logistics functions to speed up and make operations more effective. Units have developed platforms for loading and unloading railcars away from permanent railheads, thereby expanding the area where transloading operations may take place, i.e., moving equipment and supplies from trucks onto trains and vice versa.

Fuel handling and delivery has received great attention, particularly pipeline units to supply POL to remote locations. Logistics units have practiced laying pipelines across beaches to ships offshore, both to resupply the ships or receive POL supplies from the ships. Such systems would be useful at embarkation points for amphibious units (to make sure vessels are fully fueled before leaving with troops), as well as on the far beach to supply forces after they have landed.

No attempt has been made in this chapter to evaluate the quality of equipment in the PLA inventory. While it is tempting to compare the weapons of one country versus another in a one-on-one appraisal of technical parameters, that is not how modern war is fought. Rarely will a single soldier, tank, IFV, artillery piece, or helicopter face off against a single enemy of the same type in a duel to the death. Instead, modern war is fought by integrated systems (firepower, mobility, intelligence, etc.) linked by advanced communications. Infantry and tanks support each other and are supported by engineers, helicopters, artillery, and air defense units. Reconnaissance and intelligence assets inform the commander of the location and activities of the enemy so he can assign tasks to subordinate units to maximize their chances of accomplishing the mission. Air and naval forces provide ground forces with fire support, transportation/logistics, reconnaissance, and command, control, and communications support. The army that can coordinate, synchronize, and manage the greatest number of combat elements in the most rapid and flexible manner has the better chance of success on the modern battlefield. Success in this type of war is the result of both classroom study (of friendly doctrine and enemy capabilities) and training in the field where theory is put to practice and refined in an iterative process. Confident, aggressive, and properly prepared leaders at all levels are key to combining systems to create an effect that is the greater than the sum of its individual parts.

The capabilities of modern systems vary according to weather and terrain, and the training, logistics support, doctrine, and morale of the troops employing the weapons. Enemy capabilities and actions also have a major effect on the use of modern equipment. For example, if the enemy has the ability to locate incoming artillery fire and respond rapidly with counterbattery fire, then once a friendly artillery unit has fired a mission, it may be necessary to relocate quickly to another position to avoid enemy counter-fire (this technique is sometimes called "shoot and scoot"). In some terrain, against some enemies, a 1950s vintage tank may be appropriate if it has been properly maintained, its crew is highly trained, and it is adequately equipped and supported for its task. In other instances, it would not survive the first five minutes of battle. On the other hand, the most modern tank with the best crew is useless if it cannot get to the battlefield. These are the types of factors that must be considered in comparing military balances and likelihood of success for particular missions. Mere listing of numbers and types of equipment is only the first step in evaluating military capabilities.

7

HOW DOES THE PLA TRAIN?

The first two decades of PLA modernization (from about 1979 to 1998) set the stage for a new level and intensity in Chinese military training which began after 1999 and continues to this day. In the 1980s and 1990s the PLA occasionally would conduct large-scale training exercises, where more than one full division was in the field at the same time, some of which were publicized by the General Political Department's propaganda apparatus in books and film. But the most advanced training was undertaken by only a part of the large force, with priority given to rapid reaction units, and was often limited in duration, complexity, and realism.[1] Single service training focused at regimental and division level appeared to be the most prevalent "large-scale" form of exercise.[2] Force-on-force (*duikang*, often called "confrontational") exercises, allowing for free play or maneuver by opposing commanders, had been introduced and were gradually expanding throughout the army. Though PLA planners were developing the vision of where they would like to take the Chinese military, limited funding, equipment shortcomings, personnel shortfalls, and lack of experience in contemporary combat methods constrained many aspects of training for the first two decades of their modernization program.

The best efforts of the PLA modernization program up to that time were illustrated over the summer of 1995 and into the following spring when the Chinese military conducted a series of amphibious, naval, and air exercises and demonstrations in and around the Taiwan Strait. These events, which included the launch of several unarmed short-range ballistic missiles, were in response to Taiwan president Lee Teng-hui's visit to the United States and before the first popular election of him as president in March 1996.[3] The Chinese government, party, and military leadership used these drills to underscore the importance they attached to the reunification of Taiwan with the mainland and to display the PLA's resolve to accomplish missions assigned. This show of force was made possible by the work of the previous two decades in preparing the PLA for its role in the new century. While achieving propaganda points on the world stage, the exercises and demonstrations, however, were rudimentary and of relatively small scale compared with those to follow in the coming decade.

In 1999, the Central Military Commission issued a new set of regulations outlining how the PLA would make "preparations for military struggle" and conduct future military operations. The new regulations, which continue to be augmented and expanded, replaced older regulations issued in the 1980s and were based in large part on careful examination of foreign military campaigns of the 1990s. The new regulations incorporate lessons learned about the effectiveness of modern technology on the battlefield, while still emphasizing the importance of man and the support of the Chinese population in future conflicts. Once the regulations were issued, however, actual implementation of the new doctrine would require extensive field training and testing to acquire unit proficiency throughout the force. Chinese military leaders understand that the goal to "train as you fight" is as applicable to the PLA as it is to any modern military.

General Staff Department tasking and unit training plans

PLA training for both active and reserve units is guided by the Military Training and Evaluation Program which sets standards for training and evaluation of all types of units and headquarters elements. The MTEP can be modified over time according to new requirements and acquisition of new capabilities. Annual training tasks, which vary according to Military Region and service, are formulated by the General Staff Department. GSD training guidance includes the minimum total hours of annual training, hours devoted to each subject, hours for command training, and hours for unit drill or exercises.[4] Training content prescribed by the GSD includes political and ideological training, technical and physical training, operational and tactical training, and new equipment training. Training tasks are reviewed in a series of party committee meetings at headquarters at all levels throughout the country each December and January. After studying the national-level guidance, each Military Region issues a "Training Mobilization Order" signed by both the commander and political commissar. This order provides guidance for the length of the training cycle (start and end times), live ammunition exercises, and other exercises for units under command of the Military Region.

Commanders and their headquarters staffs from group army level down then prepare and execute annual training plans. Using the guidance issued by higher headquarters, training plans become increasingly detailed as the size of the unit gets smaller. Based on the local environment, regional missions, and potential enemies, units have some flexibility in developing the specifics of their own annual training schedule. Brigades and regiments formulate annual and periodic (quarterly, monthly, etc.) training plans, training content and form (such as classroom instruction, use of simulators, field exercise, or command post exercise, etc.), and evaluation periods. Battalions mainly arrange for appropriate instructors to be available to lead training, while companies are responsible for developing detailed weekly training plans in accordance with content and time requirements issued by battalion headquarters.[5]

Units often are assigned specific topics for experimental training in order to develop and refine tactical procedures, such as night, high-altitude, or logistics operations. After experimentation, successful lessons learned are studied and, if found to be applicable to other units, disseminated throughout the force. Many training experiments are not successful and later discarded.

The unit training year begins in January and continues through annual evaluations (usually in October or November), often culminating in live fire exercises.[6] Early in the year, individual and unit training is conducted mostly in garrison and at local training areas. Throughout the year, physical fitness training and martial arts skills are common subjects to build individual confidence and increase stamina. Winter training is conducted routinely by units stationed in areas of China that have extreme weather conditions. By April some units begin moving away from their home garrisons to larger training areas, where training continues and becomes more complex. The number of these training areas has increased since the late 1990s and units may be deployed for training for periods of several days to several months. Because only a limited number of large training areas are available and funds for training and ammunition are finite, higher headquarters decide on priorities, lengths of time, and schedules for units to rotate in and out of training areas.

Units conduct "progressive" training in which small unit functions are practiced first, proceeding to larger, more complicated and complex exercises involving multiple arms and services. Individual soldier training skills, like marksmanship, map reading, first aid, etc., also may be practiced in the course of unit training to enhance soldier proficiencies. For example, units conducting amphibious exercises may first train in individual skills such as swimming, driving vehicles, and loading/ unloading transport vessels. Next, platoons and companies conduct movements over water and assault on the beach by small units. Battalion and larger exercises would follow, including fire support (from air, ship, and missile forces), electronic warfare, and integration of logistics support. Live fire drills frequently are the final element of the exercise cycle. Since about 2001, exercise periods often extend for two to three months in the late spring through early fall. Approximately one-quarter of training time is scheduled for night operations.

Performance evaluations are made on individuals and units up to division level using a combination of a "two-grade system" (pass, fail) and a "four-grade system" (outstanding, good, pass, fail). Individual performance on training subjects, tactical training from squad to division level, and command organs (headquarters units) use both the "two-grade" and "four-grade" system. However, overall annual training evaluations for both individuals and units use the "four-grade system."[7]

Joint training

The 1979 campaign into Vietnam was fought exclusively by ground forces supported by militia without PLA Air Force or Navy participation in combat operations. As a result of the PLA's inability to execute large-scale joint campaigns, joint service exercises quickly became an important focus of PLA modernization. The first highly publicized large-scale exercise integrating forces from more than one service occurred northwest of Beijing near Zhangjiakou in 1981. Over the next two decades, similar large-scale exercises were held occasionally with varying degrees of complexity and competence. But instead of actually integrating and coordinating operations in a single unified effort, various forces often merely conducted separate tasks in proximity of each other.[8] As time went on and PLA units became more capable and better able to communicate among themselves, exercises became more truly joint, in which a single headquarters actually controls and synchronizes the simultaneous activities of units from many arms and services.

By the middle of the first decade of the twenty-first century, joint and combined arms training exercises conducted over extended periods away from garrison locations had become common for ground force units in all Military Regions. As the PLA's electronics and communications capabilities increased, information operations by units that had been upgraded with information technologies were incorporated into most training scenarios. Information operations commonly reported in exercises include rapid, secure transmission of orders and data among friendly forces; intelligence collection using various technical means, such as UAVs, battlefield radars, and tactical imaging systems; protection from enemy attacks on friendly command and communications systems; use of information to influence the enemy through propaganda and psychological warfare; and the offensive and defensive employment of electronic warfare against enemy systems.

Although PLA amphibious exercises received the most foreign attention from 1996 onwards, Chinese ground forces were involved in a wide range of training activities in every corner of the country.[9] Units prepared for missions appropriate to their local situations (coastal, interior, desert, mountain, etc.), which included defense from external threats, anti-terrorist exercises, and disaster relief operations. Throughout the PLA ground forces, many tasks are highlighted during field deployments, but nearly every major exercise includes:

- *Rapid mobilization and deployment from base.* These "rapid reaction" functions are practiced by active forces, as well as reserve units and militia forces. Many units have experimented with new forms of communications, such as beepers, cell phones, and email, to decrease the amount of time necessary to assemble and prepare for departure from garrison locations. Over the 1990s and into the new century, units were issued more trucks and modern logistics equipment and technologies, such as forklifts, containers, and bar codes and scanners, to more quickly organize and upload gear for deployment. While rail and road transportation remain the mainstay for ground force deployments, increasingly aircraft and helicopters are used to move troops and equipment, especially headquarters units, to distant locations. Units routinely travel hundreds of kilometers over periods of several days to exercise areas. Such long movements require both organic and reinforcing support units to provide logistics support (food, water, POL, repair, etc.) and are often augmented by civilian assets. Significantly, the Chinese press has also reported on movements of troops across Military Region boundaries to participate in training exercises. (In previous decades, nearly all training was conducted only in the Military Region where units were assigned.) Basic actions like assembly and deployment may appear to be routine, simple activities, but they become more complex as PLA equipment becomes more technologically advanced and must be practiced as new soldiers enter units and old soldiers leave. As the PLA NCO corps matures, small-unit leadership abilities should improve and fundamental tasks such as these should become more efficient over time.

- *Defensive measures to protect from long-range enemy air or missile attack.* Air defense is probably the task most frequently practiced by all PLA units, whether in the active force or reserves, and militia. Under the rubric of the new "three attacks, three defenses" (strike at stealth aircraft, strike at cruise missiles, strike at helicopter gunships; defense against precision strikes, defense against electronic jamming, defense against reconnaissance and surveillance), air defense training includes both active and passive measures.[10] Active measures include use of anti-aircraft machine-guns, artillery, and missiles deployed in air defense zones to shoot down enemy aircraft and missiles. Air defense units are increasingly becoming linked by modern communications and integrating fire control and warnings from radars found in all services. Electronic jamming techniques are incorporated into many exercises to interfere with enemy communications, GPS guidance, and homing/targeting instrumentation on aircraft and munitions. Passive measures include frequent movements, the extensive use of camouflage to conceal positions, construction of decoy positions with dummy equipment, employment of radar reflectors to create false images, and use of smoke to conceal friendly positions and blind enemy weapons as they approach their targets. PLA AAA and air defense units are reported to train with PLA Air Force flight units to improve their aircraft recognition, tracking, and target acquisition skills. Live fire practices are directed at a variety of targets such as balloons, model aircraft, and unmanned aerial vehicles. These targets provide a modicum of realism in training, but are unlikely to simulate accurately the flight characteristics and defensive measures used by many modern cruise missiles, attack helicopters, or fixed-wing fighter aircraft. Exercises frequently employ AAA and air defense assets organic to maneuver divisions and brigades reinforced by units from higher headquarters (such as AAA or air defense brigades found at group army) and reserve and militia forces. In addition to combined arms exercises with maneuver forces, AAA and air defense units routinely conduct specialized training on their own. Active, reserve, and militia anti-aircraft units train together stressing defense of China's urban areas. A major mission of the urban militia is local air defense and restoration of infrastructure, such as electricity generating facilities, bridges, and railroads, after enemy attack.[11] Exercises also frequently include training on the old "three defenses" (defense against atomic bombs, defense against chemical weapons, defense against air raids), which now emphasizes protection from chemical and biological warfare weapons delivered by conventional means (bombs, missiles, etc.) or by terrorists.[12] Chemical defense units found throughout the PLA are used for reconnaissance of contaminated areas and to decontaminate personnel, equipment, and small areas. Response to the enemy's use of chemical or biological weapons is often practiced, but the Chinese press has not publicized any scenarios in which the PLA uses chemical or biological weapons, even in retaliation to the first use of weapons of mass destruction by the enemy.[13]

Mobilization and deployment exercises are often the first phases of an exercise cycle that takes regimental and higher units to regional combined arms training bases. Combined arms training bases have been created in each Military Region found near:

- Zhaonan, Jilin, for the Shenyang Military Region;
- Juhr (also known as Zhurihe and sometimes referred to as "beyond the Great Wall"), Inner Mongolia, for the Beijing Military Region, the PLA's largest combined arms training base;
- Yongning County (Helanshan), Ningxia, for the Lanzhou Military Region, established in 2000;
- Queshan, Henan, for the Jinan Military Region;
- Sanjie, Anhui (often referred to as located "in eastern Anhui"), for the Nanjing Military Region and the PLA's first combined arms training center established in 1986;
- Luzhai in Lusai County, Guangxi, for the Guangdong Military Region
- Xichang, Sichuan, for the Chengdu Military Region.[14]

Each combined arms training base has been equipped to varying degrees with modern communications, monitoring, and mapping technologies to follow the course of mock battles conducted between friendly "Red" and enemy "Blue" units. Umpires, or coordinators, follow units at company and battalion level to control the exercises and render objective evaluations of operations.[15] Laser technology is available to measure weapons' firing accuracy during force-on-force maneuvers, and live fire exercises or competitions between units are also incorporated during the training cycle to measure individual and unit proficiencies. Training may also include participation by air force and helicopter units. Some units have created permanent "Blue" forces, which are organized, equipped, and trained to simulate the tactics of foreign armies. Often the "Blue" force defeats the "Red" force, allowing the PLA unit to better understand its own training, leadership, and equipment shortfalls. One training base commander revealed that after each exercise a 40-page assessment is written, of which "only 10 percent deals with the strong points, while the other 90 percent discusses existing problems."[16]

In addition to combined arms training bases, regional training areas and live fire ranges for armored and artillery training are also found throughout the country. Individual divisions, brigades, and regiments have their own local training areas and firing ranges, which often include facilities for amphibious operations even when located away from the coast. Nonetheless, as the PLA ground force modernizes, the need for more training areas where all aspects of joint operations can be practiced will continue. A variety of training areas available to a unit permits it to conduct preliminary training in one area and later be evaluated during a separate exercise in different terrain.

Joint operations training received a great deal of attention in the first decades of reform, and, in fact, some exercises were indeed joint training experiences incorporating units from ground, naval, air, and missile forces acting in concert. Elements of joint operations are apparent in the examples of basic deployment and air defense exercises cited earlier. Nevertheless, for many years some joint exercises were not as "joint" as they theoretically should have been. As a result, in 2004 the term "integrated joint operations" found its way into the vocabulary of PLA leaders and the Chinese media.

"Integrated joint operations"

In order to highlight the need for true joint operations, the PLA has stressed the notion of "integrated joint operations" (*yitihua lianhe zuozhan*). Use of this new term suggests official acknowledgement of shortfalls in previous training. To the Chinese, the concept of "integrated joint operations" generally means incorporating many types of units (ground, naval, air, missile, logistics, and armament support) and battlefield systems (intelligence, reconnaissance, communications, electronic warfare, fire support, etc.) into operations while treating each element equally in planning and execution.[17] Improved communications (resulting from "informationalization" of the force"), which allows units from all services to pass information to each other, is a central component of "integrated joint operations."

"Integrated joint exercises" are practiced in several "coordination zones" throughout the country, in addition to previously established combined arms tactical training bases and amphibious training areas. "Coordination zones" are large areas in which forces from the various services may interact during training. Along with active duty PLA forces, "integrated joint operations" will also employ PLA reserve units, militia forces, PAP units, civilian police, and civilian support assets especially to perform logistics and rear area security functions.

In many ways, this new emphasis is a concrete example of the shift in focus of attention away from the PLA's traditional ground force orientation to the other services and support units. "Integrated joint operations" acknowledge both the change in the PLA's most likely potential enemies (by recognizing the need for air and naval operations to often take the lead in military campaigns) and the importance of high-technology weapons and equipment. These trends had been apparent since the mid-1990s, but several years after the turn of the century the PLA leadership evidently saw the need for a course correction in training. By utilizing this new terminology, unit commanders are reminded true joint operations involve the combination of all units and battlefield systems now available to the newly modernized PLA. Focus on "integrated joint operations," or some other new slogan in the future, reflects the PLA's constant self-examination and calibration of its training methods and performance standards. PLA exercises can be expected to become increasingly more complex and realistic as the force becomes technologically sophisticated and officers and NCOs become more familiar with new doctrine and operational techniques.

Amphibious operations

Amphibious operations are among the most complex missions any military can undertake. Though amphibious operations were recognized as a necessary element in PLA training in the 1980s and early 1990s, as late as 1995 they were not included specifically as a high priority among guidelines for military training.[18] By the end of the 1990s, however, the PLA had shifted focus towards amphibious operations for a significant part of the ground forces. At an "All-Army" training meeting held in Beijing in April 2000 concerned with understanding China's security situation, especially attempts at "Taiwan independence," PLA leaders acknowledged that realistic training reflects the combat missions assigned the forces. Accordingly, the Nanjing and Guangzhou Military Regions had concentrated on amphibious operations; the Shenyang, Beijing, and Jinan Military Regions had increased long-range mobility and rapid reaction exercises; while the Lanzhou and Chengdu Military Regions explored operations at high altitudes.[19] This priority list is consistent with exercises reported and observed in the following years where army units from the Nanjing and Guangzhou Military Regions, which would comprise the first echelon of amphibious assault forces, received the majority of amphibious training. Units from the Shenyang, Beijing, and Jinan Military Regions, which would provide follow-on and support forces in amphibious campaigns, had fewer units involved in this type of training. The Chinese leadership apparently assumes that the PLA's extensive amphibious exercises serve the dual purposes of (1) preparing the force for potential contingencies, while (2) helping to deter Taiwan from moving toward independence through the propaganda value of high profile domestic and foreign media coverage.

Large-scale amphibious operations require specialized equipment and skills that were not a major emphasis in the first decade and a half of the PLA's modernization program that began in the late 1970s. During the 500,000-man reduction from 1997 to 2000, one ground force division in the Guangzhou Military Region (the former 164th Division) was transferred to the PLA Navy to become the second marine brigade. Starting in about the year 2000, the 1st Motorized Infantry Division in the Nanjing Military Region and 124th Infantry Division of the Guangzhou Military Region were issued new equipment and transformed into amphibious mechanized divisions. Since 2001, these two amphibious mechanized divisions have been given priority for training and, along with other regional units, have deployed to amphibious training areas for extended periods of time from the late spring to early fall.[20]

Joint amphibious training areas have been established in the Nanjing and Guangzhou Military Regions at Dongshan and Pingtan islands in Fujian province, Zhoushan island in Zhejiang province, and Shanwei near Shantou, Guangdong province.[21] Dongshan island is at the southern end of Fujian province, just north of the border with Guangdong, thus making it easily accessible to units from both the Nanjing and Guangzhou Military Regions. (PLA Navy marine brigades also practice amphibious operations on the Leizhou peninsula in Guangdong near their bases at Zhanjiang.)

Entire brigades and divisions have deployed to these training areas for up to three months to conduct training from small-unit level up to joint army–navy–air force amphibious landing operations controlled by group army or Military Region headquarters. Infantry and armored brigades and divisions are often joined in training by group army and Military Region assets, such as artillery, air defense, AAA, helicopter, engineer, chemical defense, electronic warfare, logistics, and armament support units. Exercises along the coast also incorporate reserve, militia, and civilian augmentation forces and have been used to test and improve real-world logistics and armament support to deployed forces. In many cases, only *elements* of larger units, such as one or two regiments of a division or a single division in a group army, are involved in an exercise controlled by the higher headquarters mentioned in press accounts. Therefore, the exact size of units actually participating in amphibious (or other) exercises is often difficult to ascertain from Chinese media reports which may use vague, round numbers.

In reporting amphibious exercises to be held in the summer of 2004, the Chinese media reviewed the large-scale exercise held at Dongshan island in 2001, said to be the largest tri-service (joint) exercise the PLA had ever conducted.[22] The 2001 exercise cycle, called "Liberation 1" (*jiefang yihao*), lasted for four months and involved nearly 100,000 troops of all services using the PLA's most advanced equipment. Dongshan was selected as a training site because its terrain "closely resembles the west coast of Taiwan." *People's Daily* acknowledged that the series of Dongshan exercises began in 1996 and had been conducted eight times (through 2004). As in previous exercises, army units from the Nanjing and Guangzhou Military Regions formed the bulk of the ground force, but in 2001, unlike earlier iterations, they were augmented by elements of group armies from the Beijing and Jinan Military Regions. Notably a rapid reaction unit from a Beijing Military Region group army was flown into the theater of operations by PLAAF Il-76 transport aircraft.[23] Additionally, PLA Navy units from all three fleets, PLA naval aviation and units from four PLAAF air armies (or corps), Second Artillery units, and reserve forces were reported to be among the 100,000 participants.

The number of troops involved in the 2001 exercise (as reported in 2004) *suggests* the participation of several (more than three) divisions and brigades from at least two group armies from the two southeast Military Regions (along with elements of at least two other group armies deployed from out of region). These forces were supported by additional Military Region ground assets as well as several thousand naval, air force, and Second Artillery personnel in various sorts of units – all focused in the vicinity of Dongshan island. The Chinese media's 2004 description of the exercise is somewhat at variance, however, with contemporaneous reporting of amphibious training by the Guangzhou Military Region's own newspaper in

October 2001. The discrepancy between the 2001 and 2004 reports illustrates the difficulties in judging the true extent of PLA exercise activity based solely on newspaper reporting.

In a summary article published in the fall of 2001, the Guangzhou Military Region newspaper reported that beginning in mid-May of that year, and continuing for several months, close to 100,000 troops from two group armies in the region and elements of the South Sea Fleet and Military Region air force trained in the coastal areas of Guangdong and Guangxi.[24] As stated, this summary of training does *not* appear to include training conducted at Dongshan island (in the Nanjing Military Region) by Guangzhou Military Region forces. Instead, this large-scale exercise was conducted using only Guangzhou Military Region forces in training areas within the region itself, such as at Shanwei or on the Leizhou peninsula. Whether or not this report reflects the same training as described in the 2004 articles, the summer of 2001 saw amphibious exercises of a scale unlike any conducted by the PLA in previous years. As outlined on pp. 154–55, in a synopsis of amphibious exercise activity from 2001 to 2004, a total of perhaps eight PLA maneuver divisions and two brigades, plus support troops, in both the Guangzhou and Nanjing Military Regions conducted amphibious training throughout the summer of 2001; the aggregate of all troops involved probably amounted to well over 100,000 personnel, possibly nearly twice that number. The 2004 reports of this exercise activity, however, emphasized specific elements the Chinese government wished to stress at that particular time and contained details that usually are not included in reports of training activity.

For example, the 2004 Chinese media reports explicitly identified the three phases of a potential military campaign against Taiwan and highlighted three purposes for the Dongshan exercises. The three operational phases are consistent with PLA doctrine as described in Chapter 5:

- Phase 1, the "information war, with the focus on electronic countermeasures and paralyzing the enemy's communications and command systems."
- Phase 2, tri-service (joint) Navy, Army, and Air Force sea crossing and amphibious landing operation, involving "missile attacks, air raids, a nighttime airborne landing, an Army–Navy island landing assault, special forces units attacking ports and airfields . . ."
- Phase 3, "counterattack against enemy reinforcements," directed primarily against "intervention by the U.S. Pacific Fleet." These operations would rely upon the capabilities of the PLA Navy's most modern surface and submarine forces, PLAAF and PLA naval aviation long-range attack assets (including Su-27 and Su-30 fighter aircraft) with air-launched anti-ship cruise missiles, and "counterattacks by land-based missiles and nuclear submarine-launched missiles" to destroy "enemy combat groups on the surface of the sea."[25] PLA ground forces would have minimal impact on this phase of operations.

The three purposes of conducting the Dongshan exercises over the eight year period were defined as:

- to improve the army's joint combat capabilities under modernized conditions, and to examine the achievements in the training of the PLA;
- to declare to the 'Taiwan Independence' elements, should they remain impenitent and dare to disintegrate the country someday, that the PLA is capable and confident in settling the Taiwan Issue by military force;
- to declare to the whole world that it is China's internal affair to settle the Taiwan issue and will tolerate no foreign country to poke its nose into the matter.[26]

Unlike previous amphibious exercises, the 2004 Dongshan exercises were billed by the Chinese press to have "seizing air superiority over Taiwan" as their focal point. In particular:

> This change not only shows a major transformation in the PLA's ideology [*sic*] for the buildup of its armed forces, it also shows that our Army is becoming increasingly aware that "air superiority" is the paramount ideology [*sic*] in modern warfare, and that the PLA is emphasizing the development of its air forces. The PLA Air Force is gradually orienting itself on compressing the Taiwan air force's air superiority over the Taiwan Strait, thereby forcing the scope of the Taiwan air force's activities toward the island of Taiwan itself, restricting the airspace in which the Taiwan air force can operate, and ultimately imposing the PLA's air superiority over the whole of the Taiwan Strait.[27]

With this stated emphasis in 2004, it is significant to note that only 18,000 troops were to be involved in the one-week exercise, with the PLAAF taking the "major role" along with "army missile troops and Second Artillery" participation. As in previous years, this particular exercise received the bulk of foreign media attention; however, it was only a small part of the many other PLA exercises conducted during the same peak period of amphibious training time.

The foreign press usually picks up on only a few examples of the large number of PLA training events held throughout the year. The numerous newspapers and magazines controlled by the General Political Department system, however, chronicle many more training exercises to build morale and pass on lessons learned through these experiences. Based on analysis of Chinese press articles from May to September from 2001 to 2004, PLA amphibious exercises along the coast involved multiple brigades, divisions, and group armies training in a variety of areas each year. Because of the limitations of this database, the following summary does not profess to be a complete listing of all amphibious training activity, but rather provides an idea of the scale of this type of training since the turn of the new century:[28]

- In 2001, it is likely that at least two infantry divisions, two armored divisions, and an infantry brigade from the three group armies in the Nanjing Military Region, and four divisions and an armored brigade from the two group armies in Guangzhou Military Region, conducted amphibious training throughout the summer. Group army artillery and AAA assets supported many of these exercises. An armored division and a motorized infantry division in the Jinan Military Region also conducted training along the coast and an armored division in the Shenyang Military Region trained at an inland reservoir.

• In 2002, three infantry divisions, two armored divisions, and a motorized infantry brigade in the Nanjing Military Region, and three infantry divisions from the Guangzhou Military Region, were identified in amphibious training. Beijing Military Region engineer units also participated in competition to support amphibious operations.

• Training in 2003 was delayed because of the severe acute respiratory syndrome (SARS) outbreak in China. After training commenced, a total of at least two infantry divisions, an armored division, a motorized infantry brigade, and an artillery brigade conducted amphibious training in the Nanjing Military Region. In the Guangzhou Military Region, two or three divisions plus an armored brigade were identified. In both Jinan and Shenyang Military Regions, motorized infantry brigades also conducted amphibious training. Because of the SARS impact, fewer units than might have originally been scheduled for training probably deployed in 2003.

• In 2004, though the 18,000-man exercise at Dongshan island described above received the most foreign attention, throughout the Nanjing Military Region elements of two infantry divisions, a motorized infantry brigade, an armored division, and an armored brigade, supported by artillery and air defense brigades, were mentioned in the Chinese press conducting amphibious training. Additionally, a smaller exercise integrating PLA, PAP, and militia forces was conducted at Zhangzhou (see "Reserve and militia training," pp. 167–68). In the Guangzhou Military Region, two infantry divisions, an armored brigade, and air defense and AAA brigades trained along the coast. An armored division and a motorized infantry brigade conducted amphibious training in the Jinan Military Region, and an armored division, motorized infantry brigade, and AAA unit actively participated in amphibious training in the Shenyang Military Region. Thus, throughout the PLA a much larger number of units actually practiced the various phases of amphibious operations than just the ones engaged in the relatively small-scale exercise which received the attention of the international press.

Over each summer since their establishment, the two new amphibious mechanized divisions from the Nanjing and Guangzhou Military Regions have focused on landing operations. By the numbers reckoned above, it is likely that roughly another 20 infantry and armored divisions or brigades, or about one-quarter of all PLA maneuver units, plus several artillery, AAA, and air defense brigades, have trained *to some extent* for amphibious operations. Many of these other units may not train for amphibious operations as frequently or as intensively as the two amphibious mechanized divisions, but a significant portion of the ground force in north and east China has been exposed to the complexities of landing operations. The units involved in the amphibious training outlined above were in the field, staggered over a five-month period each year, in a series of individual exercises controlled by many different headquarters at various organizational levels. These numbers *do not* necessarily represent the size of a force the PLA could put together at one time to conduct an amphibious campaign.

The potential size of PLA amphibious operations is limited by support available on the ground (including communications and transportation assets) and the number of military and civilian vessels available to transport troops over the water, though the number of PLA Navy amphibious ships and craft has increased in recent years. Since about 2002, the Chinese defense industrial shipbuilding sector has built a notable number of amphibious ships. According to a reliable foreign source, from 2002 to 2004 the number of Tank Landing Ships (LST) increased from 16 to 23 and Medium Landing Ships (LSM) increased to about 42 (from about 37).[29] Additionally, dozens of smaller amphibious craft are in the inventory, including a small number of air-cushioned vessels, and an unknown number of civilian ships and vessels could be used to augment the fleet.

Based only on media reports, it is not possible to predict with any degree of confidence the size of amphibious operations the PLA may be able to conduct, nor the level of proficiency these units have attained. The total number of ground force units trained to some degree in amphibious operations is certainly much larger than could be transported by military and civilian vessels in any single operation. Still, properly trained brigades and divisions will be the building blocks upon which larger operations are constructed. While no specific conclusions can be drawn, as judged by the number of units trained and equipment available to them, the PLA's capability to conduct amphibious operations increased tremendously over the ten-year period starting from 1996 to the middle of the first decade of the twenty-first century.

Though amphibious exercises most often receive international attention, a wide variety of other ground force training is also conducted throughout the same time period each year. The scope and type of training reveals a ground force in the process of preparing for many different tasks to accomplish a variety of missions assigned by their political leadership.

Anti-terrorist operations

After 11 September 2001, anti-terrorism training was elevated in priority for the PLA, PAP, militia, and civilian police forces. Anti-terrorism training is conducted in all parts of the country, but especially in China's western regions, including Xinjiang and Tibet, and the major cities. Dozens of small anti-terrorist emergency units (*fendui*) have been established in PLA and PAP units throughout the country, and special training courses have been conducted to introduce commanders to terrorist techniques and countermeasures.[30] All elements of the uniformed armed forces (the PLA, PAP, and militia) train with the civilian police force in anti-terrorist operations. Police and PAP units have been issued special armored vehicles for this mission, as well as for use in anti-riot contingencies. (These vehicles are marked with either PAP or police insignia and are often painted white, distinguishing them from PLA armored vehicles.)

Training scenarios frequently include hostage rescue, anti-hijack, bomb detection and disposal, and chemical, biological, and radiological ("dirty bomb") situations. Special equipment and operational methods are employed in these missions, which are usually executed by small teams of highly trained individuals. Police and militia units control the perimeter of the scene, while PLA or PAP anti-terror units conduct surveillance and make the final assault. Often the "enemy" force is portrayed as a small group of international terrorists, who eventually must be eliminated from their hideout after Chinese forces track them down using high-technology reconnaissance and human sources of information. To deal with terrorist strongholds, exercises may include the use of tanks, armored personnel carriers, artillery, and helicopters to overcome the opposition. Still, the size of forces used to fight terrorists is generally small compared to other conventional operations. Some exercises are conducted over only a period of a few hours, while other anti-terrorist scenarios are incorporated into longer and larger exercises.[31] The PLA has also conducted several anti-terrorist exercises with military forces from neighboring countries (see "International cooperation and transparency," pp. 168–69).

Anti-terrorism exercises provide opportunities to integrate civilian and military leadership operating out of joint military–civilian command centers. The Ningxia newspaper reported a typical anti-terrorist exercise that took place on 12 August 2004, called "Helanshan 2004."[32] According to the newspaper, over 1,000 PLA, PAP, public security police, and medical personnel took part in a single day exercise held at a training area in Yinchuan city. After demonstrating their ability to deploy rapidly from their home bases to a training area, the forces contended with four situations: chemical and biological terrorist incidents, multiple bomb explosions, attacks on important targets, and hostage taking. The drills were observed by the Lanzhou Military Region deputy commander and civilian leaders from the Ningxia Autonomous Region and involved three levels of command (presumably, Military Region, Military District, and local garrison or Military Subdistrict). As with many newspaper reports about military training, specific details of the exercise were sparse. Because of the high-level observers present and the short time-frame, it is likely these events were more of rehearsed demonstrations to illustrate technical proficiency than interactive, free-play exercises which test the decision-making abilities of commanders and staff. As the various security elements throughout the country continue to practice anti-terrorist skills, exercises will become longer, more complex, and more realistic.

Despite the tendency to lump the two missions together as "special operations," anti-terrorist tactics and techniques practiced by PLA and PAP units against armed insurgents are quite different from anti-riot or domestic stability operations used to control unarmed civilians. When possible, anti-terrorist operations use high-technology reconnaissance to gather information about the target and then seek to eliminate the terrorists quickly using speed, stealth, and violence while protecting the lives of any hostages or innocent civilians in the area. Many types of deadly force are employed to subdue an armed terrorist enemy, especially long-range snipers and forced entry by small, heavily armed assault teams. In contrast, anti-riot procedures require much larger formations of troops or police to intimidate rioters or demonstrators overtly by their mass and discipline, preferably without using deadly force. Anti-riot forces are also provided with different equipment than anti-terrorist units, such as riot shields, helmets, batons, water cannon, non-lethal weapons and chemicals, and pyrotechnics. Both types of forces, however, may be equipped with armored personnel carriers, and both anti-terrorist and anti-riot operations require close coordination between local civilian leadership and the units from the Chinese armed forces involved in the incident. PLA Special Operations Forces are likely to be tasked with anti-terrorist missions, and occasionally may be involved in anti-riot operations, if requested by civilian authorities in accordance to the law. (For discussion of PLA support to domestic security operations, see Chapter 8.)

Special Operations Forces and helicopter operations

Special Operations units have had only a short history in the PLA. In the first ten years of their existence, their greatest focus was on organizing themselves and enhancing the specialized individual and team skills needed for the missions assigned. As such, most reporting about SOF training emphasizes their physical toughness and marksmanship abilities, as well as techniques used to infiltrate behind enemy lines, live off the land in extreme conditions, and conduct strike missions. Many reports and photographs can be found demonstrating insertion by maneuverable or powered parachutes from both fixed-wing aircraft and helicopters. SOF units also train to swim ashore using scuba gear, or be delivered by small boats. Once behind the enemy lines, Chinese SOF soldiers are trained to drive many types of vehicles, fire advanced weapons, and operate sophisticated navigation and communications gear, such as man-packed satellite communications.[33] Training in foreign languages and computers is also part of the special forces' skill-set. SOF units have built special training facilities to practice skills like rappeling, demolitions, and close-quarter assault to rescue hostages held in buildings or airplanes.

SOF missions and tasks include prisoner snatch operations; raids on enemy missile sites, command posts, and communications facilities; harassment and interdiction operations to prevent or delay enemy movements; strategic reconnaissance; and anti-terrorist operations.[34] SOF units may also be involved in information operations, such as computer network attacks and psychological operations. There is little Chinese media reporting to suggest PLA SOF units are assigned to conduct covert training of foreign militaries, or to organize and lead guerrilla bands to conduct unconventional operations in enemy rear areas.

Chinese SOF and reconnaissance units study the techniques of other special forces throughout the world and have had some degree of contact with similar foreign forces. Since 1998, PLA reconnaissance and special operations units have sent teams to participate in the annual ERNA international military reconnaissance competitions held in Estonia. Events for the four-man teams usually include landing on a beach in small boats, infiltration and navigation behind enemy lines, escape and evasion, day and night marksmanship, grenade throwing, combat first aid, crossing minefields, etc.[35] In 2002, Chinese teams placed first and second in the competition.

The 2004 emphasis on "integrated joint operations" implies that special operations are one of the capabilities not yet adequately included in many joint PLA exercises. This situation would not be unexpected for a new force in the process of developing its capabilities, especially if conventional ground force commanders are unfamiliar with modern special forces and are not accustomed to planning for and utilizing the capabilities of these small, highly skilled units.[36] In some cases, friction may arise when SOF and reconnaissance units compete for scarce helicopter and other resources available to army commanders. While SOF units very likely have a high training tempo to achieve individual and small unit competence, the integration of their capabilities into large-scale, live conventional campaign training scenarios is still probably in the experimental, exploratory phase.

PLA ground force helicopter units have expanded in size since the mid-1990s, but are still relatively small in number for such a large army. In recent years the Chinese press has highlighted the trend for helicopter units to develop attack capabilities in addition to their more traditional transport role.[37] While still lacking a helicopter gunship designed and dedicated only for the attack mission, PLA aviation units are capable of mounting machine-gun, rockets, and anti-tank missiles on utility helicopters, such as the Mi-17-series from Russia or the domestically produced Z-9 or Z-11. Helicopters are also used in electronic warfare, mine laying, propaganda leaflet drop, medical evacuation, command and control, and reconnaissance missions.

Helicopter pilot proficiency training includes night flights, low level (nap-of-the-earth) operations, over-water flights, and long-distance navigation exercises. Much of this advanced training, however, only began in about 2004. New technologies available to the PLA, such as night vision goggles and advanced avionics, have enhanced the PLA's capabilities in helicopter operations, but also require additional training time and money. Transport and logistics support operations have been improved by practicing slingloading vehicles and equipment underneath Mi-17-series and S-70C-2 Blackhawk helicopters.

Ground force aviation units are frequently seen transporting airborne, SOF, and infantry units into simulated combat situations. Based on photographs in the Chinese press and the distribution of helicopter units throughout the force, the size of these lift operations, however, rarely seems to involve more than a dozen aircraft in flight at one time – if that many. Depending on the type of the helicopter, this means that most exercises probably transport a company or less of infantry soldiers in a single lift, or even smaller numbers of SOF troops. The size of airmobile operations, of course, can be increased through the use of multiple lifts. Some airmobile exercises appear to be supported by helicopters in attack roles to suppress enemy defenses. Multiple lifts and multiple functions, such as attack, transport, command and control, etc., over longer distances greatly complicate planning and logistics factors for headquarters staffs controlling these operations. Nevertheless, PLA helicopter unit capabilities appear to be maturing gradually as more aircraft enter the force and more units are trained in the basics of airmobile operations.

Airborne operations

The PLA Air Force's 15th Airborne Army unquestionably is one of the best-trained units in the PLA. Like other components of the force, it has benefited from new equipment and increased training opportunities made available in recent years. Many media stories, including television segments, depict training with new parachutes and personal equipment, jumping from new aircraft such as the Il-76 transport, and dropping new airborne assault vehicles and containerized or palletized equipment. The size of airborne operations also appears to have grown to include more battalion and regimental exercises, ranging from several hundred to well over a thousand paratroopers, in addition to the numerous company size drops of 100 to 200 personnel. Most missions appear to be raids or seizure of key terrain behind enemy lines, such as ports or airfields, followed shortly by withdrawal or link-up by ground forces.[38]

In order to advance its own "integrated joint operations" capabilities, training now routinely includes the employment of the airborne's own special operations, communications, and logistics forces along with its infantry and artillery units. Airborne forces also train to receive fire support from aircraft and helicopters, as well as missile units. In the mid-1990s, airborne operations were limited by insufficient capability within the PLA Air Force for the heavy drop of equipment and supplies.[39] As late as February 2001, inadequate logistics support was blamed for the defeat of two airborne regiments in a six-day exercise in the hills of northern Hubei province.[40] Since that time, however, the Chinese defense industries and PLA Air Force have both worked to overcome this shortfall. New equipment has been introduced into the force so cargoes in containers or on pallets, along with vehicles, can now be dropped from multiple types of transport aircraft.[41]

One of the PLA's largest and most important airborne exercises took place on 12 July 2004 and received a great deal of attention in the Chinese media. The exercise was called "unprecedented in the history of airborne troops" and demonstrated progress from several years of work.[42] Starting at 8 a.m., PLA aircraft conducted a "firepower assault," including the use of airborne electronic jamming, on enemy units in the vicinity of a drop zone in the Gobi Desert. After the fire preparation, PLA Air Force transport aircraft dropped "several-hundred parachute troops" and dozens of vehicles and equipment.[43] The numbers and types of equipment described by the Chinese press suggest an airborne infantry battalion reinforced with artillery, air defense, engineer, chemical defense, communications, and logistics units. (Most of the support troops would probably be found at regimental or division level.) Once on the ground, the paratroopers mounted airborne assault vehicles and, supported by artillery, electronic jamming, a ground missile unit, and armed helicopters, proceeded to seize the objective of an enemy airfield.[44] The "Red" airborne force was opposed by a motorized infantry "Blue" force which launched counterattacks against the drop zone and defended the airfield. The airborne commander employed all elements of his force, including air support, to repel the "Blue" force counterattacks. After an hour of simulated combat, frontline troops were resupplied by trucks with ammunition that had been dropped earlier. Live fire exercises were also incorporated into the scenario to add realism and difficulty. Though other airborne exercises have delivered more paratroopers, and the heavy drop of dozens of supply containers had been demonstrated previously, the July 2004 drill integrated more disparate, but essential, tasks than ever before in a single tactical airborne problem. Despite being conducted in daylight and lasting only one day, it was a significant event illustrating the complexity of the "integrated joint operations" the airborne and the rest of the PLA are seeking to achieve. Much of the equipment and many capabilities on display in the Gobi Desert simply did not exist in the PLA in 1995 and 1996.

PLA airborne operations, however, are still limited in size due to the number of air force transport aircraft available to support them. According to *The Military Balance*, the PLAAF has slightly more than 500 transport aircraft, but the majority of them, some 300, are Y-5 (An-2) biplanes with a capacity of 10 to 14 passengers. Larger aircraft include about 20 Il-76MD, 49 Y-8 (An-12), 93 Y-7 (An-24/An-26), 15 Y-11, 8 Y-12, and 15 Tu-154M.[45] (China may be in negotiation to purchase additional Il-76s to more than double the number of these aircraft currently in the force, but deliveries have not yet been verified.[46]) If *all* transport aircraft were operational and rigged for paradrop, and *all* were dedicated to that task, the PLA's large transports could deliver about 11,000 parachutists in a single lift depending on how much equipment is carried. That number could be augmented by about 3,000 more troops carried in the old Y-5s, which, while slow, have a small radar cross-section making them hard to detect.[47] The transport aircraft would then be required to make multiple sorties to reinforce and sustain an airborne landing with follow-on troops and more equipment. The limited PLA Air Force transport fleet would have many competing demands in a major military campaign, thus lowering the likelihood that all transport assets could be dedicated to a division size airborne operation (10,000 men plus equipment). The early stages of a campaign would more likely see one or two regimental or smaller drops, supported by numerous SOF insertions, followed by reinforcing waves delivered to the same or nearby drop zones, or airlanded on an airfield captured in the initial assault.

One of the few public candid foreign assessments of PLA capabilities was made by the commander of Russian airborne forces after a visit to the 15th Airborne Army in 2000. General Georgy Shpak told *Itar-Tass*: "China is capable of conducting large-scale airborne operations" (though he did not specifically define what "large-scale" was). Shpak went on, however, "Chinese paratroopers 'are somewhat inferior' to Russian airborne troops in weaponry, supplies, including in airborne large-size cargoes," but they demonstrated "very good training of soldiers, especially individual drilling."[48] Shpak's observation of the skill, discipline, and toughness of the individual Chinese soldier is a judgment commonly made by foreigners who have the opportunity to see PLA units in training.[49] As demonstrated by the July 2004 exercise, in the years since Russian airborne commander's visit, PLA airborne capabilities have improved and progress has been made in overcoming many of the deficiencies he observed.

Training in the interior and cost-saving techniques

While amphibious exercises, special operations, and airborne training sometimes attract the attention of the foreign media, more mundane PLA training conducted in the interior of the country is mostly overlooked. PLA units stationed in inland provinces and regions routinely train in the mountains, jungles, open plains, and deserts throughout China in all seasons. In all Military Regions, upgraded and reorganized divisions, along with newly transformed brigades, participate in longer, more complex field training exercises covering a variety of offensive and defensive missions tailored to local requirements. Training includes the gamut of infantry, armor, artillery, air defense, engineer, and logistics operations. Winter training and high-altitude exercises are a major focus because of the demands extreme conditions place on troops and equipment.[50] These deployments often begin with rapid mobilization followed by long-distance maneuver emphasizing new "three attacks, three defenses" training (as described – see p. 148). "Red" versus "Blue" force training may occur en route to or after units have arrived at designated training areas. Border defense operations against a conventional foe are practiced, as well as reaction to cross-border attacks by international terrorists. As time goes on, cross-regional deployments are likely to become more frequent as units are assigned new missions based on their enhanced capabilities.

Despite its smaller size than a decade before, as the ground force becomes more modernized and mechanized, the cost of training inevitably increases over time. Compared to the 1990s, training is considerably more expensive for many reasons, including:

- a higher tempo of training at more numerous, better-equipped training areas;
- greater consumption of POL by more mechanized forces;
- higher costs of live ammunition for new weapons systems; and
- increased wear and tear on more technologically advanced equipment used for longer periods of time, often in adverse weather conditions.

As a result, many training techniques have been implemented to save money, better utilize funds available, protect equipment from excessive usage, and prepare troops and headquarters staff to achieve better results when they do go to the field.

The PLA makes widespread use of sand table exercises, computer war games, and command post exercises (focusing on decision-making, staff procedures, and communications training). Commanders and headquarters staffs in different units fight mock battles against each other using Internet connectivity to test their ability to plan and execute new doctrine. Additionally, PLA units use an extensive array of mechanical simulators for driving, firing, and maintenance training, especially for new soldiers. Many simulators are developed by the units themselves to enhance training capabilities while in garrison. In recent years, "training halls," which incorporate simulators, computers, and video monitors, have been built in many unit barracks.[51] While many simulators and computerized war games are elementary, gradually they are becoming more sophisticated and complex as new technologies become available to the PLA.

Throughout the country, headquarters routinely hold competitive training events among same type units (e.g., SOF, reconnaissance, tank, artillery, engineer, chemical defense, etc.) to increase skills and build morale. Each year a number of individuals and units from each service and Military Region are selected for excellence in training.

In summary, though the quality of training is difficult to judge from media reports, a comprehensive military training program undertaken by all, or nearly all, ground force units is apparent from the level of training described by the Chinese press. While amphibious training is at the forefront, all ground force missions are addressed in all parts of the country. The training outlined above is directed by the General Staff Department and executed by the training sections in headquarters from Military Region down. Moreover, political, logistics, and equipment training regimes are increasingly being incorporated into exercise scenarios to produce "integrated joint operations" training.

General political department-related training

Even with the focus on military training, political and ideological instruction continues apace both in garrison and in the field. Following decades of PLA tradition, the purpose of political training is to disseminate official party and military guidance, promote good morale, and to ensure discipline among the troops. Political sessions also provide a means for feedback from bottom to top of the chain of command. Ideology and political work is always placed high on the task list for PLA headquarters and units.[52]

The ability to perform political work is one of the "Four Can Do's" all NCOs strive to achieve (see Chapter 3). As part of political work and in order to maintain combat readiness, PLA units attempt to assist new recruits to learn their functions quickly and acclimatize to military life. Experiments are underway with psychological testing and counseling to lessen the shock of entering the military or weed out those unsuitable for service.[53]

As PLA units spend more time in field training exercises, political officers are portrayed as being involved in military training in order to improve morale.[54] Frequently political officers are shown displaying or improving their own tactical and technical proficiencies to better relate to the average soldier. Following PLA tradition, political officers seek to "learn from the troops."

The work of the political officer system is also incorporated into the "integrated joint training" regimen through practice of the "three war" operations, defined as media (or public opinion) war, psychological war, and legal war. These efforts fall under the umbrella of information operations and are officially considered among the "combat patterns" of the PLA. "Three war" operations include:

- publicity campaigns using the modern electronic media to mobilize the Chinese population and demoralize the enemy;
- traditional use of propaganda leaflets and loudspeakers on the battlefield to encourage defections or surrender;
- the education of Chinese forces to minimize civilian casualties, to avoid collateral damage to cultural treasures, and to respect the laws of war, as in treatment of prisoners and non-combatants.[55]

In particular, legal war seeks to legitimize Chinese policies while undercutting the authority or justification of enemy actions.

The goal of the "three wars" is to seize the political initiative and contribute to the success of military campaigns.[56] These operations are envisioned as being integrated not only into military campaigns but also into China's larger national strategy employing all forms of power, including political, diplomatic, social, and economic means. The "three wars" may be conducted before, during, or after a military campaign, with true success being achieved in political victory without battle.

General Logistics Department and General Armaments Department-related training

In order to "prepare for military struggle," PLA leaders use the term "two capabilities," defined as combat and technical support, to encourage the development of a comprehensive fighting force.[57] Combat training is overseen primarily by the General Staff Department system, while technical support training includes logistics and armament functions supervised by the General Logistics Department and the General Armaments Department systems. Logistics and armament support units are routinely integrated into larger joint exercises; these units also conduct an array of functional exercises on their own to hone the skills necessary to support the combat forces. Proficiency in technical support operations is tested in every training exercise simply by moving, feeding, and sustaining troops in the field.

As part of its efforts to cut costs and increase efficiency, the PLA has turned to the civilian sector to augment many aspects of its technical support capabilities. As an example, the Chinese government issued "Regulations on National Defense Mobilization of Civil Transportation" in late 2003 to formalize procedures for military use of civilian vehicles and related facilities. The regulations cover compensation to owners for injury or loss, but not necessarily reimbursement for time lost from business activities while in service to the military.[58] Other legal frameworks for civilian support to military operations are expected to be approved in the future. The "National Defense Mobilization Law" and "State of Emergency Law," which were reported in 2005 to be under consideration by the National People's Congress, will address other requirements for civilian support to military and emergency situations.[59]

PLA logistics units have benefited from an influx of new equipment and training opportunities, with improvements seen across the entire spectrum of logistics functions. As mentioned earlier, transportation capabilities are put to the test in nearly every deployment exercise, while real-world requirements to support forces in Tibet and other distant border regions provide the opportunity to evaluate transportation capabilities in all-season conditions.

Supply or quartermaster capabilities have been enhanced by many technological advances, such as:

• the distribution of computers and bar code and scanner technology throughout the logistics system to monitor inventory and track shipments;
• improvements in communications for units in garrison and in the field;
• the experimentation with smart cards for individual and unit use to requisition and pay for materials.[60]

Warehouse capacities have been expanded physically and their capabilities improved by modern management techniques and the introduction of forklifts and containers to move material. New tents, shelters, and camouflage are being issued for setting up field depots. Logistics personnel practice new supply techniques daily as they support forces at their homes bases and when warehouse units deploy to forward locations to sustain extended field training exercises.

Food service operations have been improved in garrison and in the field. Many mess halls have "outsourced" food preparation to local civilian companies, mess management procedures have been standardized, cafeteria-style (buffet) dining has expanded, and food ration subsidies have increased several times.[61] New mobile, propane-fired field kitchens and refrigerator trucks have been sent to units. A variety of individual field rations and beverages are now in use. Vacuum-packed, light-weight, long-lasting, portable meals, some of which include self-heating devices, have been developed and distributed to troops all over the country. As a result, the number of trucks needed to support mess operations may decrease while the culinary options available to soldiers increase. A single box of "convenient dishes" can supply 100 personnel for a day, and a single refrigerator truck reportedly can store enough meat for a reinforced battalion to last for 30 days.[62] These developments have been highly publicized by the PLA media and many pictures of happy troops enthusiastically eating good food are intended to increase morale.

Many new types of fuel vehicles and refueling methods have also been developed. New fuel trucks and portable bladders have been issued and rapid refueling of columns of vehicles is practiced often. Some fuel bladders can be dropped from helicopters and others can float. Mobile pipeline units extend the reach of POL supply operations beyond permanent or fixed facilities. Procedures for transferring

POL from ship-to-shore and from shore-to-ship are used to support amphibious training. Researchers at the General Logistics Department's POL Equipment Research Office of the POL Research Institute have paid attention to many details, such as hose nozzles and quality control testing, to ensure all facets of POL supply have been upgraded.[63] Additional efficiencies have been achieved through the merger of many separate service POL facilities under the Joint Logistics Departments at Military Region level.[64]

Forward medical support has been improved by the development of portable, modular field hospitals and lightweight equipment, including air-droppable medical support packages.[65] Field treatment now includes the use of long-distance video consultation made possible by widespread distribution of computers and satellite or Internet communications.[66] Personnel from PLA hospitals, in addition to medical personnel assigned to operational units or logistics subdepartments, frequently deploy to field training exercises to practice in austere conditions.

Military Region logistics subdepartments and group armies form "emergency support units" from the menu of units assigned to them to provide forward-based, reinforcing support to lower-level units. The size and composition of "emergency support units" varies according to the needs of the unit supported, the mission, and terrain. Lower down the organizational chain, "emergency support units" and unit field service centers also incorporate units from the armaments system to perform ammunition supply and maintenance and repair functions.

The General Armaments Department system, responsible for repair, maintenance, ammunition, and specialized supply, has benefited from many of the same developments found in the logistics systems. Examples include greater availability of material handling machinery (fork-lifts, cranes, containers, etc.) and better communications support, allowing for long-distance consultation on repair and maintenance and faster replacement of inventory. In addition, many mobile repair vans and shelters, complete with spare parts and heavy machinery, have been produced to permit all-weather repair in remote areas. Armament units conduct their own exercises to improve skills in the field and also deploy to support maneuver units during extended training exercises.[67] In addition to these tasks, "new equipment training" to instruct soldiers how to operate and maintain the new and upgraded equipment is a major responsibility of the GAD system.

"New equipment training" is mainly conducted in garrison, but is also practiced in the field during exercises. Armament officers, NCOs, and technicians are responsible to teach other soldiers proper techniques for the daily maintenance and operation of weapons and equipment. Often before equipment is issued to a unit, higher headquarters, service schools/academies, or weapons factories send training teams to units to prepare them to receive new gear. Units may also send their own personnel to schools, to other units that already have similar equipment, or to the producing factories to receive pre-deployment training. Equipment simulators also are used to familiarize soldiers with new equipment prior to and after its arrival. Whenever possible, efforts are made to provide units with instructional material for new equipment along with the equipment itself. The PLA recognizes it may take several months, even up to a year, to train personnel fully and integrate new equipment into the unit. In recent years, there have been fewer reports of soldiers "being afraid" of new equipment than when the influx of modern equipment began in the 1990s.[68]

For over a decade, officers at all levels from the chairman of the Central Military Commission on down have emphasized the importance of equipment training for the PLA to "leapfrog" into a new era of military capabilities. The accentuation of this element of modernization has resulted in many units achieving combat readiness earlier than expected after new equipment has been received. Similarly, a *PLA Daily* article highlighted the significance of maintenance and equipment reliability by describing how "a tiny screw falling off from a radar system brought a [brigade] field exercise to a standstill."[69] The lesson of this modern parable was that even "minor specialized elements," such as a repair unit, can play a major role in overall unit capabilities. Without proper equipment training it will be impossible for the PLA to take advantage of new technologies and transform the force.

Reserve and militia training

As reserve and militia units underwent structural reforms following 1998, like the active PLA they too increased their training tempo to prepare for new missions assigned. In addition to conducting independent training to develop functional proficiencies, PLA reserve units and militia forces are frequently mixed into active duty field training exercises, along with civilian support.

Because the reserve force is composed largely of civilians, who serve only part-time as soldiers, many exercises begin with rapid call-up, mobilization, and deployment from dispersed locations within a province. Training then proceeds to include infantry, artillery, air defense, and engineer exercises up to regimental and division level, supported by logistics forces. Reserve and militia units along the coast now conduct amphibious and river crossing training on their own.[70] Air defense and chemical defense operations are practiced frequently within the reserve force. The reserve logistics support brigades in each Military Region are among the busiest units as they support both reserve and active forces. Militia forces, in particular, are important components of active force rear area security planning.[71]

Considering that the force was created in 1983, the integration of reserve units into training with active PLA units was publicized much later than might have been expected. In what was called the "first drill with reservists joining active service-men," in September 2002 *Xinhua* reported a reserve regiment from the Beijing Military Region mobilizing to link up with an active duty unit for a "confrontation exercise" against a "Blue Army." More than 1,500 officers and men assembled from five counties and cities and deployed by road over 730 kilometers across three provinces. This 20-day exercise was said to explore "the approach for joint operation and training between reservist units and active-service units through-out the Army."[72] Since that time, reports of active-reserve training have become more frequent.

A good example of integrated PLA–PAP–militia training occurred over the weekend of 24–25 July 2004, at about the same time as the more highly publicized 18,000-man exercise conducted at Dongshan island. Just up the coast from Dongshan, the Zhangzhou city National Defense Mobilization Committee ordered the mobilization of citizens and militia units to provide transportation, fuel resupply, maintenance, medical, communications, and air defense support to a PLA unit, probably a regiment of the motorized infantry division stationed in the city. In total, approximately 3,000 PLA, People's Armed Police, and militia personnel participated in a series of demonstrations to highlight local support to PLA amphibious operations. The Nanjing Military Region commander, who observed the demonstrations, summarized what he saw, stating: "People's War is the heir-loom of our Party and our army. People's War is able to help us win fights in the future. People's War can help us finish the great cause of reunification."[73]

International cooperation and transparency

For many decades, the PLA did not conduct joint (or combined) exercises with foreign militaries or allow outsiders to observe its own military training. In 2002, however, in a major change of policy, the PLA conducted its first multilateral military exercise with foreign military forces. In 2003, it began to allow foreign visitors to observe a few of its own unilateral military exercises.[74] By conducting training with the militaries of other countries, the PLA provides a glimpse into its operational capabilities and permits its soldiers to interact with foreigners in a manner heretofore not possible.

In October 2002, PLA forces from the Xinjiang Military District and the armed forces of Kyrgyzstan held a small joint anti-terrorist exercise on the border of the two countries. This was the first bilateral anti-terrorist exercise conducted by members of the Shanghai Cooperation Organization (SCO). It was followed in August 2003 by the first combined anti-terrorist exercise involving units from all five members of the SCO. "Coalition 2003" was a week-long exercise with participating forces from China, Kazakhstan, Kyrgyzstan, Russia, and Tajikistan. In August 2004, PLA troops and Pakistani forces held an anti-terrorist exercise on the border with Pakistan, and later in the month PLA and Indian frontier forces held mountaineering training in Tibet. Bilateral combined training exercises with PLA and Russian forces have been suggested for the latter half of 2005 or after. In addition to ground force training, the PLA Navy conducted search and rescue exercises with Pakistani naval forces in October 2003 and Indian naval forces in November 2003, and maritime exercises in Chinese waters with French forces in March 2004, Great Britain in June 2004, and Australia in October 2004.[75]

In another major effort at transparency, since the middle of 2003 the PLA has opened a number of its training exercises to observation by outsiders. Previously, foreigners were allowed to see only small-scale, highly scripted demonstrations by showcase units. The exercises the PLA recently has allowed foreign guests to attend have included large-scale exercises of some the PLA's most advanced units conducting high-interest military operations in areas usually off limits to non-Chinese. In August 2003, the PLA allowed foreign observers to attend an armored brigade exercise (*beijian* 0308, Northern Sword 0308) at the combined arms training base in Juhr, Inner Mongolia.[76] In early September 2004, foreign observers watched a marine brigade conduct amphibious operations at Shanwei, Guangdong in Exercise Dragon 2004 (*jiaolong* 2004). Later that month, a different group of guests was invited to view the 127th Light Mechanized Division execute joint training in Exercise Iron Fist 2004 (*tiequan* 2004) at the Queshan combined arms training base in Henan.[77] In November 2004, the PLA invited diplomats from the Security Policy Conference of the ASEAN Regional Forum (ARF) held in Beijing to a hostage-rescue demonstration conducted by the Beijing Military Region's Special Operations unit at its garrison south of the capital city.[78] All of these exercises received considerable attention in the Chinese media, with many articles and photographs reflecting what the foreigners saw first-hand. Despite the local coverage of these events, little, if any, notice was made by the foreign press of these Chinese efforts to make their military modernization program more "transparent" to outsiders.

A few notes of caution

Not every development outlined above can be applied to every unit in the PLA, but evidence points toward the continuation of these trends and an increase in the number of combat-ready units that can perform a variety of missions. Unit readiness will fluctuate as new personnel and equipment are assigned. Therefore, despite having proved effective in one training cycle, units will be required to repeat training tasks to maintain proficiency. Over time, as new missions are added, more training and evaluation is required. As training becomes more complex and realistic, and more officers and NCOs have first-hand experience in planning and executing "integrated joint operations," the ground forces will provide their leaders with more options to consider as they make strategic calculations and decisions.

Though ground force capabilities are obviously improving, Chinese newspaper articles are not the best method for judging the degree of change. Many reports of the time it takes to accomplish certain military operations, such as 3 minutes to rescue hostages or 30 minutes to load an armored unit on a train, should be evaluated with caution. Reports of such accomplishments likely only include certain portions of a complex exercise, or start the clock only after all preparations have been completed and the forces are lined up and waiting to go. Likewise, reports of "first ever" or "largest in history" training events must be read carefully to determine exactly what is meant by these modifiers and whether the description applies to a single unit, or region, or the PLA as a whole. Often the most revealing insights of the actual status of PLA tactical proficiency can be gained from a few short paragraphs of criticism buried among much descriptive prose and glowing praise. Finally, on a few occasions PLA writers, who describe *foreign* doctrine or training exercises they have observed outside of China, may highlight particular points of other countries' military operations which also reflect on the state of PLA competence.

Good military training will never be easy, nor will it get any cheaper for the PLA. Additionally, other demands on the force may detract from training and "preparations for military struggle." Non-training activities often involve the PLA's relationship to the rest of Chinese society. These real-world requirements, however, may help contribute to and test the PLA's operational abilities.

8
WHAT IS THE ROLE OF THE PLA IN CHINESE SOCIETY?

The actions ordered by the senior leadership of the Chinese Communist Party and executed by units of the People's Liberation Army and People's Armed Police in June 1989 undercut much of the good will the Chinese army had established with the people of China over the previous half century. To reestablish the supportive relationship between the population and the PLA throughout the 1990s and into the new century, the PLA undertook many tasks to rebuild its ties between the military and society, restore the army's reputation, and truly "serve the people" once again. These tasks include PLA efforts in support of society, in disaster relief operations, in domestic security operations, and in support of United Nations (UN) peacekeeping operations (PKO), all of which are aimed to portray the PLA in good light to both the Chinese people and to the outside world. Even if there had been no 4 June, changes in China's international status and the traditional roots of the PLA would have motivated it to perform many, if not all, of these same actions.

The obvious propaganda intent by the PLA in reporting these tasks is acknowledged from the outset. From the PLA's perspective, however, in order to accomplish its deterrence and warfighting missions the army still needs the support of the people. In attaining that support, the PLA must be a servant of two masters – the Chinese Communist Party and the people of China.[1]

PLA actions in support of society

The reciprocal relationship between the Chinese people and the PLA falls under the banner of "Double Support Work" (or "Mutual Support," *shuang yong*), defined as requiring "civilian work units to support the military and to provide favored treatment terms to families of military professionals in service and . . . military work units to support the civilian government and to love civilian people."[2] Both the Ministry of Civil Affairs and the PLA General Political Department act in conjunction to orchestrate this program. Peaks of activity occur around New Year's Day (1 January), during the Chinese New Year (Spring Festival), and on Army Day (1 August). These efforts are aimed at creating a "well-off society" and further developing "socialism with Chinese characteristics." In 1991 (two years after Tiananmen), a national conference on "Double Support Work" kicked the program into high gear, and in 2004 a staff commentator article in the *People's Daily* urged party committees, governments, and military leading institutions at all levels to regard "Double Support Work" as a "strategic task."[3]

From the civilian side, "Double Support Work" primarily involves giving preferential treatment to families of service members, helping to reintegrate demobilized soldiers back into society by finding them jobs and housing (or providing monetary stipends[4]), and making available various types of support to military units stationed in the area (from construction work to the provision of electricity and other local subsidies). Central to the program's success is the close coordination of party, government, and military officials at all levels. The system of National Defense Mobilization Committees is a major component of contemporary civil–military relations and for "Double Support Work." Local provision of goods, services, and money to PLA units and demobilized personnel helps reduce the amount of central funding required for the military and is part of the overall extrabudgetary sources of income available to the PLA. (See discussion on the announced military budget in Chapter 1.)

The Chinese armed forces "love the people" in various ways. For many years the PLA has supported national economic construction by participating in a variety of infrastructure construction projects throughout the country.[5] The General Staff Department and the General Political Department have directed each member of PLA units to devote not less than eight days a year to national defense construction work.[6] PLA engineer units (of all services, along with PAP construction units) have contributed heavy machinery (such as cranes, road graders, dump trucks, etc.) and technical expertise (including engineering and architectural designs), while other units have provided manpower and vehicles for labor-intensive work. Projects include construction of innumerable buildings, highways, bridges, airports, ports, pipelines, and railroads, and laying many miles of optical fiber cable, often through remote areas.[7] Many, if not most, of these projects also have military applications in wartime, such as highway landing strips and dual-use seaports and airports. In addition to their military and social value, some of these projects increase the expertise of the PLA units involved by requiring them to organize and actually accomplish construction missions they might be assigned in wartime. On the other hand, many projects require little more than an organizational structure, strong backs, and vehicles for transportation. Much of the PLA effort in this regard is directed toward the western provinces and autonomous regions and the northeast "rust belt," in conjunction with larger government efforts to develop the regions away from the eastern seaboard.

PLA doctors, nurses, and hospitals are actively engaged in supporting the local populace, particularly in remote and impoverished areas. In 2001, the PLA General Logistics Department and the Ministry of Health issued a "Notice on Military Hospitals Supporting Civilian Hospitals in Western Provinces (Municipalities, Autonomous Regions)."[8] This program requires PLA hospitals to render support to civilian hospitals in both manpower and technology. As with all good campaigns, meetings and exchanges are routinely held to promote the effort and allow others to learn from practical experience. Photographs and reports of PLA medical personnel treating local civilians or soldiers donating blood are common in Chinese military newspapers. The 2004 Defense White Paper states "more than 100 military hospitals" have provided support to civilian hospitals in "remote and less developed areas."[9]

An excellent example of the best and worst of the PLA's role in society can be seen in the severe acute respiratory syndrome crisis of 2002–03.[10] Like the rest of the government, the PLA publicly downplayed the severity of the SARS problem for many months, even while its hospitals were treating increasing numbers of SARS patients. Also like other health officials, the PLA did not accurately report the number of SARS cases in its hospitals, and was blamed for the disease getting out of control by the chief of the Chinese Center for Disease Control. The cover-up was exposed on 9 April 2003 by PLA doctor Jiang Yanyong who contradicted the minister of health's admission of a small number of SARS cases. After Dr Jiang's revelation the government shifted into action, firing the minister of health and the mayor of Beijing and initiated actions that should have been taken months earlier. The PLA then played a significant role in the campaign to combat the disease. Once the political decision had been made to confront SARS directly, the General Political Department lost no opportunity to highlight the PLA's contributions to the campaign. Military headquarters and hospitals throughout the country implemented policies to manage and treat the disease and conducted research to control it. The most visible example of the SARS struggle was the PLA's building and manning a new hospital outside of Beijing at Xiaotangshan in a matter of days to care for SARS patients. The SARS experience demonstrates on one hand how the PLA can participate in "Big Lie" tactics still employed by the party, but on the other how it can contribute positively to society through its mobilization and active involvement in medical support to the public. The 2004 Defense White Paper described the PLA's contribution as follows:

In 2003, the PLA and PAPF [People's Armed Police Force] offered all-out support to governments at all levels in the fight against SARS by sending 37,000 officers and men to help control the spread of the disease and sterilize on a large scale key places, sites and areas with a high incidence of SARS. Eighteen military hospitals provided meticulous medical treatment to 420 SARS patients. The Military Academy of Medical Science was the first to separate the SARS pathogen in China and develop a rapid-diagnosis reagent for SARS. A total of 1,383 medical personnel from different PLA units worked hard continually at the Beijing Xiaotangshan Hospital for more than 50 days to give meticulous treatment to 680 SARS sufferers.[11]

The transfer to local government control of the former First Military Medical University, the Chengdu Medical Institute of the Third Military Medical University, the Jilin Medical College of the Fourth Military Medical University, and the Quartermaster University during the summer of 2004 (see Chapter 3) is another example of support to the civilian population while eliminating excessive infra-structure within the PLA's own ranks. The shift of these schools to local government subordination is an element of a decades-long "defense conversion" process in which excess military capacity is transferred from the PLA or the civilian defense industrial sector to provide the national and local economies with the benefits of redundant defense facilities.[12]

The PLA has an active environmental protection effort. The PLA has created an Environmental and Afforestation Committee in the General Logistics Department to manage the military's "green" program with the GLD Director as chairman of the committee.[13] For many years the PLA has participated in the country's larger reforestation efforts. Every spring around 1 April, PLA officers and men take part in tree-planting ceremonies throughout the country in symbolic representation of this campaign. Units routinely plant trees around their barracks for both ecological and aesthetic reasons. Units in north, northeast, and northwest China, in Inner Mongolia in particular, plant large acreages of trees to prevent loss of grasslands to the desert. New regulations for environmental protection were issued in September 2004 and include measures to "protect and improve the environment of military facilities; protect natural resources; prevent and [remediate] pollution caused by military activities, military installations, and high-risk materials and articles; and protect the environment of the country's major environmental protection zones."[14] As China's urban areas expand into the surrounding countryside, pressure is being placed on PLA units, formerly located outside of city limits, to be good neighbors in cleaning up their waste and limiting pollution.[15] Delegates from 54 countries, including the United States, Germany, France, Japan, and India, attended an environmental protection conference in Beijing in October 2004 to "promote both Chinese and global military environmental protection and construction."[16]

Some units approach their relationship with local governments and the population in a very methodical fashion. For example, since April 2002 the Tianjin Garrison has required active PLA units, local People's Armed Forces Departments, reserve, and militia units to implement an "Eight Task Program." Every garrison unit at and above the regimental level was tasked to:

- develop an enterprise;
- help a village develop;
- support a key project;
- run a student aid center to support education;
- build a model unit to demonstrate joint efforts by the army and the public in the construction of spiritual civilization;
- run a national defense education base;
- launch an aid-the-poor project;
- build a contingent detachment that is competent in all areas.[17]

This program was framed in the language of the "Three Represents," demonstrating party control of the armed forces in order to promote "the coordinated development of national defense and economic construction," as well as social development. Such work likely would be quite time and labor intensive and overseen primarily by unit political officers. The General Political Department wastes no chance to publicize these and many other ancillary areas in which the Chinese armed forces provide support to the general population or create pride in the Chinese people. Typical reports range from helping peasants with the harvest, to saving pandas, to congratulating PLA Olympic medal winners.

PLA actions in disaster relief operations

Every year all elements of the Chinese armed forces – the PLA, PAP, and militia – are involved in numerous relief operations in response to natural disasters such as floods, hurricanes, earthquakes, and forest fires. Manpower, equipment, and materiel assets dedicated to these efforts vary from year to year, but usually range from tens of thousands of personnel up to hundreds of thousands with accompanying vehicles, helicopters, boats, and aircraft. The 1998 flood relief efforts are usually regarded as the largest of these efforts. More than 300,000 personnel, 12,500 vehicles, 1,170 boats and ships, and over 200 aircraft rescued or evacuated more than three million citizens in the Changjiang (Yangtze), Nenjiang, and Songhua river areas.[18] According to the 2004 White Paper on National Defense, in the years 2003 and 2004 PLA and PAP units were mobilized to conduct disaster relief operations on 120 occasions. The PAP alone deployed some 240,000 troops, rescued over 230,000 civilians, and transported more than 2.6 million tons of relief supplies.[19] Military participation in these activities has the dual benefits of improving the PLA's image in the eyes of the average Chinese citizen while exercising the force's rapid response capabilities for mobilization and transportation. Disaster relief operations also test command and control (especially small unit leadership abilities), and the logistics systems, under real-life, stressful conditions.

Recognizing that disaster relief will be a continuing responsibility, the PLA has established specific forces for the mission and incorporated emergency training into the Military Training and Evaluation Program. In 2002, 19 special units were formed to perform flood-fighting operations.[20] Though nearly any unit may be called upon to act as a "shock brigade" in time of emergency, each group army is likely to have designated some of its engineering assets as disaster relief emergency response units. Specifically, a number of engineering brigades and regiments (especially pontoon bridge units, which have many small boats as well as bridging equipment and material) have been chosen to be an "all-army specialized contingency force to combat floods and deal with emergencies." Several "regulatory documents," including the "10th Five-Year Plan for Building Army Units to Combat Floods and Deal With Emergencies" and "Views on Building Flood-Fighting Specialized Contingency Units by the Military and the Civilian Sectors," have been issued to guide planning, with emphasis on civil–military coordination.[21] The 2004 Defense White Paper confirms that "in rescue and relief operations," PLA and PAP forces "receive orders from the joint military–civilian headquarters."[22]

In 2002, rescue and disaster relief training was incorporated for the first time into the army's military training plan.[23] Units from all over the country now routinely prepare to participate in these operations and have a guideline for training and evaluation. To better accomplish this mandatory training, in 2004 a pontoon bridge regiment in the Shenyang Military Region set up a specific training area for disaster relief and flood-fighting operations.[24] The training area has replicas of dykes and dams and special equipment available necessary for fighting high waters, such as sandbags, pipes, and reinforcement material. Another pontoon bridge regiment in the Guangzhou Military Region has been cited several times for its meritorious service in flood relief and has integrated new equipment into its inventory. Significantly, this regiment has established an electronic database on "on rivers, hydrology, roads, bridges, culverts and landforms" in the area.[25] Other units throughout the country undoubtedly have taken similar steps to facilitate disaster relief preparation.

These examples indicate that the PLA is applying funds, resources, and intellectual capital to a civil–military mission they expect to continue into the future. In this case, a relatively small amount of spending can result in a much larger amount of good will on the part of the people assisted by PLA disaster relief operations.

PLA actions in support of domestic security

The "conventional wisdom" among many people outside China is that the PLA has been responsible to control domestic disturbances throughout the country, such as riots and political protests, in the years following the Tiananmen massacre.[26] Although such a belief may be widespread, there is little evidence to support this claim. While there is no question the PLA has *the potential* to be used to suppress civilian dissent and demonstrations as it was in 1989, it is an exaggeration to assert that the PLA is *actively* involved in controlling domestic unrest on a routine or recurring basis. Nevertheless, the PLA is the Chinese Communist Party's final insurance policy to maintain public order, *if* the civilian Ministry of Public Security police and the paramilitary People's Armed Police fail in their primary missions to maintain domestic stability.

The US State Department defines the Chinese *security apparatus* as composed of "the Ministries of State Security and Public Security, the People's Armed Police, the People's Liberation Army, and the state judicial, procuratorial, and penal systems." (See Chapter 2 for discussion of the Chinese security apparatus, including the primary and secondary missions for the police, PAP, and PLA.) The State Department's 2005 Report on Human Rights in China goes on to say: "Civilian authorities generally maintained effective control of the security forces. Security policy and personnel were responsible for numerous human rights abuses."[27] While government "policy and security personnel" were no doubt involved in human rights abuses of concern to the US government and non-governmental organizations which monitor human rights, there is no specific mention of PLA use or abuse in any of the State Department reports from 1999 forward.[28] Omission of direct reference to PLA routine involvement in the control of public disturbances strongly suggests that the conventional wisdom is wrong in this case.

On the other hand, over the years since 1989 there have been many reports of the PAP being used in this role. Unfortunately, PAP units are sometimes misidentified as PLA or their role confused by terminology when PAP forces are referred to as "military police."[29] As both civilian police and PAP forces build their own anti-riot units, it is also understandable that some people may confuse these units with PLA forces.[30] A 2004 report of the detention of a Buddhist leader in Inner Mongolia illustrates the misidentification problem. In August 2004, local authorities in Kulun county cut power and water service to a Buddhist temple and "military police" forced about 70 monks into buses and drove them away.[31] The context of the article, which speaks about local authorities and police, makes it very likely that the "military police" reported were PAP and not PLA soldiers. PAP units are often used to support civilian police by providing manpower (and muscle) while the police make arrests. Just weeks before the arrests in Inner Mongolia, between 500 and 1,000 "riot police" with "50 armored vehicles" were used in Shijiahe village in Henan province to control farmers who threatened to protest in the provincial capital of Zhengzhou. Interestingly, the article concludes, "There have been relatively few cases of Chinese police shooting at unarmed crowds, even with rubber bullets, in recent years," with no mention of any PLA involvement in domestic security situations.[32]

The example most frequently cited to support PLA participation in domestic security operations is an incident in the city of Yangjiazhangzi, near Huludao in Liaoning province, where molybdenum miners confronted Chinese security forces in late February 2000.[33] According to *The Washington Post*, "police and soldiers" battled the miners and their families. The article was based on Chinese eye witnesses, who alleged the PLA's involvement. Though the reporter who wrote the article knows the difference between the PLA and the PAP, many Chinese and foreigners do not.

What *was not* reported with regard to the Yangjiazhangzi incident is the fact that a People's Armed Police unit, the former 120th Division of the 40th Group Army that had been transferred from the PLA to the PAP during the 1997 500,000-man reduction, was stationed about 23 kilometers south of the Huludao peninsula at Xingcheng.[34] This PAP unit, identified by designation "8620 unit," most likely provided the "soldiers" who eventually were called in to control the miners. Though the PLA 40th Group Army is headquartered in Jinzhou, about 40 kilometers north of Huludao, its combat forces are garrisoned considerably farther to the north, leaving the PAP 8620 unit the closest force to the disturbances at Yangjiazhangzi. To locals who knew the former PLA unit as "soldiers," when these same troops came from the same barracks wearing green uniforms, they easily could have been mistaken for PLA. While there is a possibility that the PLA was involved in the Yangjiazhangzi incident, the proximity and purpose of the 8620 unit makes it more likely that the PAP was involved.

For definitional purposes, it is important to distinguish between domestic disturbances, such as riots and peaceful demonstrations over corruption, factory closings, unemployment, religious persecution, etc., and the fight against "terrorism, separatism, and extremism," focused primarily in China's western regions. In cases of armed uprising against the government, the military (i.e., the PLA) has a legitimate role in responding to or preventing terrorism and violence within China's borders. In many cases, the PLA and PAP will cooperate with each other in such operations.

The PLA leadership appears to have learned the lesson from 1989 that it is not good policy or public relations (either internally or internationally) for heavily armed soldiers to act as police to control unarmed demonstrators or rioters. While it accepts domestic security as a secondary mission, the PLA currently is more focused on its military modernization program to defend China from external foes and protect China's sovereignty. As the PLA ground force gets smaller, more mechanized, and more focused on the Taiwan contingency, it will have less time to spend training for domestic security roles. Training for the secondary mission of domestic security is probably considered by many Chinese military officers to be a distraction from the PLA's main mission of preparing to fight Local Wars on China's periphery. As the PLA continues to downsize and restructure, some of the lower priority infantry units, which would have been best suited for internal security missions but who do not train as much nor have as advanced equipment as higher priority units, may be cut from the force and no longer be available for domestic security missions. As they modernize, more technologically advanced ground force units will find themselves less suitable for domestic security roles. The new tanks, infantry fighting vehicles, artillery, and air defense missiles now found in larger numbers in units throughout the country simply are not appropriate for police actions, though they could, of course, be deployed for such operations. Concurrently, PAP and local police forces continue to be strengthened with new equipment and provided with new tactics and training for their primary role in domestic security. The reality on the ground today for the PLA is quite different than the images held by many outsiders based on conditions of 15 or 50 years ago.

PLA actions in support of UN peacekeeping operations

China's participation in UN PKO missions began in the early 1990s with military observers going to the Middle East, Western Sahara, and the Iraq–Kuwait border, as well as PLA engineers operating as part of the UN Transitional Authority in Cambodia (UNTAC) from 1991–93. Chinese participation expanded over the 1990s to the point where China contributes more peacekeepers to more UN missions than any of the other Permanent Members of the Security Council. As of early 2005, UN statistics show China had deployed 1,036 military and civilian personnel in 11 UN missions, followed by France with 606 personnel in ten missions, the United Kingdom with 423 personnel in six missions, the United States with 371 personnel in seven missions, and Russia with 361 personnel in 11 missions.[35] In overall ranking, China is a mid-level contributor (at about number 15), with Pakistan and Bangladesh leading (with 9,860 and 8,054 personnel, respectively), followed by

India, Ethiopia, Nepal, Ghana, and Nigeria (each with 3,000 or more personnel deployed in February 2005).[36]

In early 2005, PLA personnel were participating in the eight UN missions identified in Table 8.1, with Chinese civilian police only in an additional three. China also sent personnel to Mozambique (ONUMOZ from 1993 to 1994), Bosnia (UNMIBH, civilian police from 2001), and Afghanistan (UNAMA, civilian police from 2003 to 2004).

The PLA has taken its role in UN PKO seriously by committing itself to provide "one UN standard engineering battalion, one UN standard medical team, and two UN standard transportation companies."[37] It has designated an engineering brigade in the Beijing Military Region as its primary PKO force to be augmented by units from other parts of the country. The engineering brigade, whose soldiers wear the UN blue beret, is stationed in Nankou, northwest of Beijing, and has been visited by the foreign attaché corps assigned to China.[38] To maintain its multiple commitments to UN missions, the PLA must train and plan for the rotation of appropriate forces for extended periods of time. In late 2004, the General Logistics Department issued training material entitled, "Logistics Support for Peacekeeping Forces," based on UN guidance and the PLA's own experience.[39]

Table 8.1 Chinese participation in UN peacekeeping missions (February 2005)[40]

		Military observers	Military personnel	Civilian police
UN mission for the Referendum in Western Sahara	MINURSO	19		
UN organization mission in the Democratic Republic of the Congo	MONOC	10	220	
UN operation in Burundi	ONUB	3		
UN mission in Sierra Leone	UNAMSIL	3		
UN mission in Ethiopia and Eritrea	UNMEE	7		
UN mission in Liberia	UNMIL	5	568	24
UN operation in Côte d'Ivoire	UNOCI	3		
UN truce supervision organization	UNTSO	6		
UN stabilization in Haiti	MINUSTAH			133
UN mission in Kosovo	UNMIK			19
UN mission of support in East Timor	UNMISET			16

The PLA PKO force in the Congo is composed of an engineer company with about 175 personnel and a medical platoon of roughly 40 people.[41] In order to fulfill this mission, the PLA assigns its forces for an eight-month tour in the country.[42] Over time, and depending on the needs of the mission, the size and composition of Chinese contributions to individual peacekeeping operations may vary. In Liberia, the first PLA contingent was composed of an engineering company from the Shenyang Military Region, a medical team from the Nanjing Military Region, and a transportation team from the General Logistics Department, making it the largest Chinese PKO to date with over 550 personnel.[43] The engineering unit deployed to Liberia was a reserve water supply company that received three months of special training before departing in February 2004.[44] This development reflects greater integration of reserve units into the active PLA force than might have been expected only a few years earlier.

The Chinese deployment of Ministry of Public Security riot police to Haiti in 2004 caused considerable confusion outside of China. The initial batch of 125 personnel, composed of civilian policemen and women who received special peace-keeping training before their deployment, came from the four centrally administered cities of Beijing, Tianjin, Shanghai, and Chongqing.[45] Despite the large amount of information readily available both in English and Chinese, this force was mistakenly identified as part of the PAP in several foreign articles.[46] Photographs of the force revealed their blue uniforms, police rank insignia, and unit patches, showing that these anti-riot police were from the Ministry of Public Security system and not part of the PAP. Moreover, the leadership of the Ministry of Public Security, not the Central Military Commission, took the lead in publicizing the force. Perhaps some foreign confusion was due to the force's pre-deployment training, which was conducted at a PAP academy in Langfang, south of Beijing, established in 2002 to conduct PKO training for Chinese police peacekeepers.[47]

The Chinese media has paid a lot of attention both to the PLA's and to the civilian police's role in UN PKO missions. This positive image may be useful in appealing to Chinese civilians who want to see their military and police force engaged in socially beneficial functions and their country taking an active role as a responsible member of the international community. As such, these missions may be a positive factor in promoting overall civilian support to the armed forces and civilian police force.

Many PLA actions to improve its image and support the Chinese people are not unique to China; militaries in many countries routinely undertake similar activities. Nonetheless, there are numerous significant consequences for China and the PLA of these actions. First, the Chinese armed forces' relationship with the Chinese people has a direct influence on personnel recruitment and retention as well as the population's willingness to provide support to future PLA operations. Especially as the Chinese economy continues to grow, the rigor of service in the armed forces is not an attractive option to educated youth seeking to make money in the commercial sector. The PLA must find ways to appeal to and retain dedicated and educated personnel and supplement those forces in times of emergency with skilled citizens. Moreover, because of logistics restructuring over the past five years, the PLA now depends on local civilian personnel, material, and transportation assets to support any extended operation inside or outside of China. A PLA that is perceived as a drain on society, rather than a productive component of China's social structure, is not likely to receive the moral, manpower, or material support from the population it needs to modernize and accomplish its missions. Thus, the Chinese leadership has clear operational motivation to create and maintain good relations between the people and the army.

Civil–military relations, especially the manner by which Chinese security forces deal with peaceful demonstrations and public assemblies, also are important to China's international relations. Many outsiders continue to level moral condemnation and opprobrium toward the PLA for its role at Tiananmen. The PLA's relationships with the governments of many countries are still strained to varying degrees by sanctions imposed after the Tiananmen massacre.[48] Thus, foreign perceptions of the PLA have an impact both on its operational capabilities (primarily in the types of weapons and technology it may purchase from abroad) and the way the PLA interacts with professional militaries of other countries. Nevertheless, the PLA cannot be expected to initiate changes in its foreign relations contrary to policy prescribed by the country's civilian leadership. The subordinate position of the army to the Chinese Communist Party is of ultimate importance in defining its loyalties and priorities now and in the future.

9

CONCLUSIONS AND THE
GHOSTS OF TIANANMEN

The People's Liberation Army is in the third decade of a complex modernization process. The increase in speed and intensity of modernization seen since 1999 could not have been accomplished without the foundation established in the first 20 years of reform. Nevertheless, much remains to be done and, according to the PLA leadership, another 10–20 years are needed for it to reach "advanced world standards" in equipment, personnel, and training.[1] For example, the 2004 Defense White Paper laid out a decades-long goal for improving the quality of PLA personnel:

> In August 2003, the CMC began to implement its Strategic Project for Talented People. The Project proposes that *in one to two decades*, the PLA will possess a contingent of [commanders] capable of directing informationalized wars and of building informationalized armed forces, a contingent of staff officers proficient in planning armed forces building and military operations, a contingent of scientists capable of planning and organizing the innovative development of weaponry and equipment and the exploration of key technologies, a contingent of technical specialists with thorough knowledge of new- and high-tech weaponry performance, and a contingent of NCOs with expertise in using weapons and equipment at hand. The Project will be implemented in two stages. *By the end of 2010*, there will be a remarkable improvement in the quality of military personnel, and a big increase in the number of well-educated personnel in combat units. *The following decade* will witness a big leap in the training of military personnel.[2]
>
> (emphasis added)

Given the multifaceted nature of the modernization process underway, the low level from which the PLA began, and the relatively limited funding dedicated to the military from 1979 to 1999, this time-frame is not unreasonable. The Chinese leadership understands there is no quick, easy fix to acquiring military capabilities. An NCO corps is not built overnight, and providing large portions of the officer corps with the opportunity to pursue postgraduate education takes many years to achieve. PLA doctrine acknowledges that the force's new weapons and systems, including the much misunderstood *shashoujian* or "assassin's mace" weapons, must be employed into integrated, synchronized, and unified efforts incorporating all elements of combat power and support. Building upon classroom study and command post exercises, PLA units must repeatedly undergo realistic field training exercises to perfect the skills necessary to implement their new doctrine. Training over a period of years is necessary to consolidate and expand the basics practiced in the initial stages of doctrinal revision. Further progress is likely to be seen in future "integrated joint training" exercises and modifications to the PLA's training regimen as highlighted by new slogans and media emphasis.

The PLA's persistent *simultaneous* references to People's War, Local War under a variety of conditions, and the Revolution in Military Affairs with Chinese characteristics reveal continuity with past practices and traditions while transforming and modernizing the force for twenty-first century requirements. The official adoption of all three of these concepts in the 2004 Defense White Paper serves as a reminder that Chinese military modernization cannot be judged by foreign standards. China's unique circumstances and national strengths and weaknesses have resulted in a blend of old with new that has yielded great change, but has yet to be proved effective in battle. The Chinese Communist Party and government are committed to military modernization as part of the nation's strategic development plan. With more time and money, PLA capabilities will continue to improve – likely along the trajectory of recent years.

General trends after 1999

China's relations with its continental neighbors have improved greatly in the past decade and the likelihood of a land invasion of the Chinese mainland is extremely remote. A major amphibious assault against China's eastern or southern coasts is also improbable. China's size, population, and military improvements over the past decades greatly reduce the chance of political success for any ground-oriented military operation directed against the mainland, except for terrorist action and possibly minor border raids. However, the elevation of planning for the Taiwan contingency in the late 1990s presents Chinese military planners with requirements unlike those they face in defending China's land borders. The PLA must now be prepared to project and sustain force over 100 miles of sea and air while protecting its coastline from long-range attack. By definition, this assignment calls for the expansion of naval, air, and missile forces.

Because the speed and emphasis of PLA transformation shifted dramatically around the turn of the century, more change in the PLA has been visible since the year 1999 than in the previous two decades. The general trends, previously foreseen by much foreign analysis, are now recognized by authoritative Chinese sources in leadership speeches and official documents.[3] For example, the 2004 Defense White Paper confirmed several trends, which had been apparent in doctrinal writings and reports from the Chinese media, such as:

- The PLA will promote coordinated development of firepower, mobility and information capability, enhance the development of its operational strength *with priority given to* the Navy, Air Force and Second Artillery Force, and strengthen its comprehensive deterrence and warfighting capabilities.[4]
- In accordance with the principle of smaller but more efficient troops, the PLA Navy compresses the chain of command and reorganizes the combat forces in a more scientific way while giving prominence to the building of maritime combat forces, *especially amphibious combat forces* . . . the Air Force has *gradually shifted* from one of territorial air defense *to one of both offensive and defensive operations.*[5]

(emphasis added)

Specific details of these developments, however, are difficult for outsiders to verify. The White Paper also provided little definitive insight into ground force development except for general references to joint training, logistics reform, and the importance of political work.

As might be expected, the Chinese themselves do not provide official evaluations of the PLA's operational capabilities or specify the exact number and status of units. Based on the study of Chinese media reports (including photographs and video clips) and the few comments of foreign observers who have had the opportunity to see the PLA up close, it is reasonable to conclude that many of the PLA's new capabilities remain in the rudimentary stage and Chinese estimates of another 10–20 years of development are not unwarranted. If, however, at any point in this process the PLA is called to action by its political leaders, it will make the best use of progress in the force to that date and follow the orders of the party with the troops available. In any scenario, the PLA will rely heavily on the physical strength and stamina of its soldiers, sailors, airmen, and marines to make things work in spite of hardships. The PLA political system, in conjunction with the military commander system, will ensure that the force is motivated and committed to tasks assigned. Its logistics and armaments systems are working to sustain and maintain the force for extended periods. Many other factors, however, will also contribute to the outcome of any future Chinese use of force.

Given the likelihood of dominance of naval, air, and missile operations in the early phases of potential military campaigns, the ground force is striving to retain its relevance in future operations. While other services have received priority for development, the ground forces have emphasized developing forces that can get to and influence the battle in its early stages, such as Special Operations Forces, airborne and helicopter units, long-range artillery, and missile units. Especially in a campaign in the Taiwan Strait, large scale, ground force-dominated operations are likely to be a last resort following the execution of other options, including missile, air, and naval strikes or blockades. Airborne and ground force SOF and helicopter units may augment the initial operations of the other services, but the main effort is likely *not* to involve large ground units in the early stages of conflict. At the same time, ground force units will mobilize, move to emergency deployment locations, and assist in the air defense of the mainland. The scale of these movements may serve to distract prying eyes and electronic sensors from the activities other services may be executing. Nonetheless, peacetime training for the difficult amphibious contingency hones other military skills as well, and, perhaps more importantly, sends a message about China's commitment in the psychological battle of deterrence.

Conventional deterrence and action if deterrence fails

As seen in the portion of the 2004 White Paper excerpted above, Chinese forces have both a deterrence and warfighting role. While "preparing for military struggle," PLA ground force modernization also contributes to China's conventional deterrence posture. In order for deterrence to be credible, Chinese writings discuss three tasks that must be accomplished:

1 China must have a force capable of conducting a variety of combat missions.
2 China must display the intention and determination to employ that force if necessary.
3 The potential enemy must perceive China's force as capable and understand Beijing's willingness to use it.

Conventional deterrence thus involves not only military dimensions but also political, economic, and diplomatic components.[6] Political signals may be sent through (1) public or private diplomacy at international organizations, such as the United Nations, and/or directly to other governments or persons, (2) the use of the Chinese and foreign media in official statements or "opinion pieces" written by influential persons, (3) non-military actions, such as restrictions on travel or trade, or (4) by the use of military demonstrations, exercises, deployments, or tests, which do not involve the use of deadly force. The PLA's propaganda system is likely to be involved in the transmission of messages through capabilities developed in "three wars" training.

These signals will be crafted to portray China as the aggrieved party in any dispute and undermine the opponents' justification for whatever has precipitated the emergency. China is unlikely ever to admit that its own actions or policies could lead to a crisis and therefore will always portray itself as being forced to act to protect its sovereignty from the aggressions of others. Any measures China may take will be framed as "self-defensive" in nature and made reluctantly in response to the actions of others. Based on their calculations of comprehensive relative strengths and demonstrated capabilities, Chinese leaders would prefer to have a high degree of confidence that the actions they take will result in a successful political conclusion to a crisis.

If deterrence fails, actual combat measures may be needed to resolve the political situation. The Chinese government may decide to act preemptively before an enemy strikes, but will represent its action as a "counterattack" to foil a threat to China's sovereignty or national interests. Official Chinese statements attest to the PLA's commitment to defending China's sovereignty. If the situation calls for the use of force after other measures have failed, even something as important as the 2008 Olympics would not be an impediment to ordering the PLA to protect China's vital interests.

The PLA's military performance, however, will be a function of many variables that change with each scenario, not all of which are under China's or the PLA's control. Most important are the political objectives to be attained through the use of military force (as defined by the Chinese political leadership) and who the PLA's enemy is, especially his will to fight. Beyond Beijing's direct control, the international political/security situation at the time and events outside of China may affect both the PLA's and its adversaries' courses of action. The PLA is likely to have some influence over where the campaign is waged by decisions about the location of the main and supporting efforts, though political imperatives may dictate expansion or contraction of the area of operations. Enemy actions will also frame the size of the battlefield and influence the weapons and tactics employed. And while the PLA leadership may have input into the timing of military action, the season and weather will impact operations in unpredictable ways.[7] Each of these factors must be considered in the assessment of the possibility of success for any particular campaign. Adding to these uncertainties is the fact that no PLA commander or staff officer has personal experience directing operations of the complexity and scale envisioned by current Chinese doctrine against a foreign foe.

Overall improvements in PLA capabilities to date have demonstrably contributed to the PLA's role in deterrence as seen in the notoriety given to extended amphibious exercises since 2001. Moreover, Chinese strategic and military planners now have an increased number of options available to them should deterrence fail and the use of force be necessary. Although operational improvements are apparent, definitive conclusions as to exactly what and how widespread these improved capabilities are cannot be made solely through the examination of Chinese statements and media reporting. In other words, based only on information publicly available, judgments such as the PLA can conduct a division-sized airborne operation or insert 1,000 SOF troops behind enemy lines successfully *cannot* be made with any degree of certainty. Though elements of some 20 divisions and brigades likely have conducted amphibious training to some degree since 2001, this *does not* mean the PLA has 20 divisions and brigades fully trained, equipped, and capable of conducting a coordinated, large-scale sea-crossing and landing operation. On the other hand, the Central Military Commission probably does have a reasonable estimate of the status and readiness of all the PLA's forces. It also understands that capabilities are not static and must be evaluated objectively on a regular basis.

Numbers can be deceiving

The size of the army's main combat force, 18 corps-sized group armies, some 40 divisions and about 43 maneuver brigades, supported by another 40 artillery, AAA, and air defense divisions and brigades, sounds formidable in its absolute numbers. But these units are generally smaller and *do not* equate in firepower and capabilities to similarly named units in western militaries. The Chinese tacitly acknowledge this disparity by the fact that senior colonels, who command divisions and brigades, are not considered general officers, whereas divisions and many brigades in western forces are commanded by generals or brigadiers. A group army with an all-brigade structure likely does not equate in firepower to a western division, especially a US Army or Marine division, both of which have much greater organic helicopter support than is found in the PLA's two most powerful group armies. Accordingly, the mere number of ground force units available to Chinese military planners is not a good indicator of the PLA's offensive capacity.

Nevertheless, much discussion of the PLA ground forces inevitably falls back on the size of the Chinese army and often implies, given an unlimited amount of time, that sheer numbers will prevail. For example, as late as 2003 the US Department of Defense's report on China's military power stated: "China's primary ground force advantage is its overwhelming size, provided these forces could be delivered to the battleground."[8] The final caveat, about being delivered to the battleground, however, is an important factor in the analysis of Chinese army capabilities well into the future.

Heavy armored and mechanized infantry units now comprise over 40 percent of ground force maneuver units (approximately 36 of some 83 maneuver divisions and brigades). Over the course of the two personnel reductions implemented since 1997, the size of the PLA armored force (tank divisions and brigades) decreased from about 12 tank divisions and 13 brigades in 1997 to roughly 10 armored divisions and 11 brigades in 2004, with many of the remaining units receiving new equipment.[9] Over the same period, the number of old-style infantry units was cut considerably, while the size of the mechanized infantry force increased significantly, including the creation of two *amphibious* mechanized divisions. Prior to 1997 approximately five mechanized divisions were assigned to group armies in the Beijing and Shenyang Military Regions and no mechanized infantry brigades existed.[10] In less than ten years the number of mechanized divisions had nearly doubled and at least five new mechanized infantry brigades were added to the force, all accomplished by transforming motorized infantry divisions. Mechanized infantry units are now found in all Military Regions except for Chengdu, where mountains and difficult terrain reduce their effectiveness. Increased numbers of mechanized infantry units improve capabilities in China's western and northern deserts and plains, but less so in the mountains and jungles to the south or on China's seacoast, unless adequately supported by transportation assets.

The mechanization of the infantry force increases the army's firepower and battlefield mobility. Moreover, new tanks, APCs, and self-propelled artillery are symbolic of an advanced military and important to the PLA's self-image. But increased mechanization complicates the problem of transporting a heavy force to the fight. While mechanized forces can move by rail or road throughout the mainland and across land borders, projecting the power of the mechanized units beyond China's shores remains problematic.

The ground force's heavy units (armored and mechanized infantry) are dependent on the joint capabilities of the PLA Navy and Air Force, augmented by civilian assets, to get to the most likely battlefields beyond China's coastline – a prime example of the PLA's new joint doctrine. Chinese ground forces also rely to a great extent on PLA Navy and Air Force air defense capabilities to protect them from long-range strikes while assembling on land, and even more so during the vulnerable period of transit to enemy territory. Mechanized units, even the two amphibious mechanized divisions, must use specialized amphibious lift capabilities if they are to be landed in a hostile environment. (The PLA's amphibious tanks, APCs, and artillery can "swim" the last few kilometers to shore, but they cannot cross long distances of open water such as the Taiwan Strait.) Though the size of the amphibious fleet has expanded to some extent, the PLA Navy's amphibious transport force and the army's three ship transport units do not have enough amphibious vessels to simultaneously transport the two amphibious mechanized divisions and the two PLA Navy marine brigades, amounting in total to some 3,000 vehicles. Techniques to increase sea transport capabilities include rapid turn-around of the existing fleet and the use of large civilian vessels if port or dock facilities have been secured, allowing for the administrative offloading of heavy equipment.

Mechanized forces also require much greater transport air-lift capacity than lighter infantry forces. Given the current status of the PLA's air transport capabilities, mechanized infantry troops can be transported by air without much of their heavy equipment, but they lose many of the intrinsic benefits of their organization and organic armament. Even road movement of heavy forces complicates logistics support: when possible it is preferable to load tanks and APCs on heavy transport trailers to save wear and tear on the tracked vehicles themselves and the roads they travel on. But, unless adequately protected by air defense assets, such operations are particularly susceptible to air strikes both on the road and while loading and offloading heavy equipment.

The PLA has practiced small-scale administrative movements of personnel and equipment over long distances into non-hostile environments with its deployment of UN PKO forces to Africa. Given its strengths in planning, the PLA would likely be able to organize the movement of much larger formations to distant locations using a variety of military and civilian assets provided there is no enemy opposition en route or at the point of disembarkation. Forced insertion of PLA ground forces by air or sea over long distances into a hostile situation, however, would depend on the unproven, but growing, long-range fire support capabilities of naval, air, and missile forces. While exact capabilities are open to speculation, the Chinese media provides hints at improving capabilities and enduring shortfalls.

Assessing training

Careful analysis of Chinese media reports of PLA exercises often can provide insight into the *quantity* and *content* of training activity, but based only on these sources evaluation of the *quality* of that training is tenuous. The media may be used to obscure genuine developments, misdirect attention, or exaggerate realities; in other cases, it can be revealing of actual conditions. In some instances, the intention of publishing certain stories and photographs is to illustrate the distribution of new weapons and equipment to the force. Similarly, many other photos document the presence of much older equipment remaining in the force. Television video segments of some training exercises often provide useful insights; the mud, sweat, and ripped uniforms associated with realistic training are more likely to be seen in video clips than in staged still photos. Other television segments are mere firepower displays aimed at impressing audiences with loud noises and explosions. Analysts of the PLA must use caution and exercise judgment in reviewing the various sources of material becoming increasingly available to the public.[11]

Many photographs are obviously staged for visual impact rather than the realistic portrayal of conditions or capabilities. For example, merely looking at photographs in the *PLA Daily* or the glossy *PLA Pictorial* (*Jiefangjun Huabao*) one would conclude Chinese soldiers always have every button of their uniforms buttoned and their headgear secured, whether in the field or in a command shelter using computers. Other dubious photos show commanders in sandbagged, forward command posts with computers, while tanks, infantry with flamethrowers, artillery, and helicopters pass by in assault on enemy positions. Unfortunately, this type of stagecraft is the propaganda system's idea of how to demonstrate the PLA's understanding of the need for combined arms and joint operations and not a reflection of actual training conditions.

Many recent photographs of small-unit training depict soldiers and equipment bunched together in groups that would be very vulnerable to incoming fire. Some of these photos may be intended to portray administrative situations, which in theory would not be subject to enemy interdiction. Still, a number of such pictures clearly illustrate tactical conditions or exercises, and actually reveal poor dispersion discipline. Perhaps the most egregious examples are found in photos of artillery or air defense units conducting live fire exercises. Nearly every image shows guns (or multiple rocket launchers) arrayed in straight lines with only a few meters separating them from one another. Rarely is artillery dug in or deployed in staggered formations to provide protection from enemy fire. Similar dispersal patterns are frequently seen in photos of dismounted infantry and APCs assaulting enemy positions. Close formations may be staged for artistic impact, but the prevalence of this type of spacing could be a sign of "the way you train is the way you fight." Such photos also suggest training at a basic level focused on individual and crew skills and small-unit tactics, not yet integrated into larger unit scenarios.

Many video clips of joint exercises show PLA Air Force fighters flying in formation near ground force activities, implying that they are supporting operations on the ground. Most reporting of fighter and helicopter support to the ground force, however, appears to describe attacks on pre-planned targets, in which the aircraft are not under the control of forward observers or air controllers in ground force units. Missions as such would be termed "battlefield air interdiction" and have an important place in joint operations. On the other hand, "close air support" or CAS, which is conducted in close proximity to friendly forces and in coordination with the fire and movement of ground forces, still does not appear to be routinely practiced by the PLA. This situation may change in the future as target designators and compatible radios are issued to ground and air forces. Once properly equipped, units will require time to refine procedures for controlling aircraft attacking enemy positions near friendly forces and gain confidence in their ability to safely perform advanced tactical techniques.

The shortcoming in CAS capabilities hints at another possible problem in PLA training. The PLA has established a number of "Blue" force units which are organized as potential enemies and execute foreign tactics and operational techniques. Though it is feasible to *simulate* many foreign capabilities, it is much less likely these "Blue" units can actually implement many tactics of foreign forces given the PLA's own shortfalls in many capabilities common to foreign armies, such a close air support, large air mobile operations, and long-range intelligence, surveillance, and targeting capabilities. Many articles describe the use of balloons or model airplanes to simulate enemy land attack cruise missiles or stealth aircraft for air defense target practice. Though these artificialities may encourage PLA commanders to consider this type of threat in their operational planning, such measures are extremely unlikely to represent realistically the capabilities of high technology weapons on the battlefield today. Some commanders have commented on the lack of realism in such training and the potential that soldiers may be deceived or become overconfident by successes from such "idealism" in training.[12]

In any case, accurately recreating battlefield conditions in a training environment is a challenge to all armies. The PLA obviously has demonstrated its commitment to increasing realism in training by the construction of many combined arms training areas throughout the country and increased training opportunities for its forces. Future improvements will require additional funding and sustained dedication to the complex task of preparing for modern warfare.

Future trends

The PLA ground force is likely to continue adjusting its organizational structure beyond the end of the 200,000-man reduction initiated in 2003. Additional manpower cuts may result in the elimination of units that have not been upgraded with new equipment in recent years. Other units will likely be restructured into smaller formations. For example, more divisions may transform an existing infantry regiment to an armored regiment, resulting in only three maneuver regiments under division control. These smaller divisions would likely have a total of about nine infantry and armored battalions (compared to 12 battalions in a fully manned and equipped old-style division). Other divisions may be downsized to brigades, with no intermediate regimental headquarters, and approximately five maneuver battalions. Despite the formation of brigades, many divisions continue to be upgraded to increase their firepower and mobility. Though their total numbers may continue to decrease, it appears the division will remain an important organizational level in the future PLA force structure.

Actual PLA ground force capabilities would probably be increased by the reduction of another 200,000 to 300,000 personnel billets through force structure cuts, unit reorganization, logistics reform (including the out-sourcing of many tasks), and headquarters and educational infrastructure streamlining. Increased mechanization of the force will probably allow for less painful manpower reductions than those named above due to efficiencies gained through high technology and simple labor-saving machinery, such as fork-lifts and cranes. These billets could be applied to other services if necessary or removed completely from the PLA's roster. The smaller force would require less equipment for modernization, and *if* the army's budget was not decreased by an amount proportional to the personnel cuts additional funds could be applied to the costs of training, ammunition, maintenance, and spare parts needed for its higher operations tempo. Given the tradition of ground force dominance of the PLA, and lacking a firm commitment not to cut the army's budget, however, institutional opposition to more cuts could be expected.

In the first decades of modernization it was logical to provide only a portion of the large force priority in new equipment and training opportunities. This small segment of the force was assigned the responsibility for early deployment and designated as the "rapid reaction" force. Units with lower priorities were given more time to mobilize and prepare for deployment to reinforce the early response units. As the PLA ground force decreases in size and training intensity is increased, most, if not all, units are required to achieve rapid mobilization and deployment capabilities. Instead of relying on only a handful of permanently designated "rapid reaction units," Military Regions and group armies now are likely to rotate alert status on a periodic basis among all the units under their commands. In this way a portion of the force would be ready for rapid deployment to support real-world situations while other parts of the force can be involved in out-of-garrison training, repair and recovery from training, or other missions. Such a development would reflect confidence by the PLA leadership in a higher level of the combat capabilities for a larger proportion of the force. Specific capabilities of units would vary over time and depend on training accomplished, equipment availability, support capacity, and personnel status. The total number of fully trained and equipped units currently in the ground forces likely amounts to a significantly larger absolute number of units than a decade before.

But the PLA is still limited in how much force it can project over water to defend its claims to sovereignty. Increased PLA ground force expeditionary capabilities require much greater PLA Navy and Air Force lift capacity. Additional purchases of large foreign transport aircraft or sustained domestic building programs within the Chinese defense aviation and shipbuilding industries would indicate a major step toward the development of long-range force projection capabilities. Concomitantly, the PLA Navy and Air Force would also have to build capabilities to protect and sustain these assets in transit and after they reached their destination. Someday (if it has not happened already) there may be an interesting debate among the PLA's increasingly joint senior leadership over whether funds saved by cuts in the ground force should be applied to acquiring more transportation assets in the PLA Navy and Air Force.

Given the relative proximity of Taiwan to the mainland, the PLA ground force could boost its own self-deployment capability for this scenario by increasing the size of its helicopter force and concentrating that growth in the Nanjing and Guangzhou Military Regions. Since the establishment of the Army Aviation Bureau in the mid-1980s, the growth of the helicopter force has been modest to the point that only about 400 aircraft are in service for the entire army. Emphasis in recent years has been on expanding the capabilities of the force to include attack and other missions over and above traditional transport roles. With this expansion in missions, the helicopter force *may* be on the verge of a significant expansion in size. More aircraft would permit more ground force units to increase proficiency in airmobile operations conducted at battalion and larger size. If enough helicopters became available, formation of a ground force unit of brigade or division size dedicated primarily to airmobile operations over a period of about five years would not be surprising.[13]

The ghosts of Tiananmen

As the PLA ground forces get smaller in size, more mechanized, and better trained in joint operations, they become less suitable and less available to internal security roles. For instance, units from the 42nd Group Army engaged in extended landing exercises with new amphibious tanks, APCs, and self-propelled artillery on Dongshan island are not readily redeployed to put down riots in Guangzhou. Nevertheless, the Chinese Communist Party continues to regard the PLA as its last line of defense against domestic turmoil. But other government decisions have strengthened the Ministry of Public Security police and the People's Armed Police forces' ability to respond to and handle the riots, demonstrations, and protests that result from economic disparities, unemployment, government malfeasance, official corruption, and limited political reform. Though there has been no official apology or expression of regret for the events of June 1989, Chinese political and military leaders do not want internal conditions in any part of the country to deteriorate to the point that another massive violent suppression of dissent or demonstrations by the PLA is necessary.

The debate in the United States and Europe in 2004 and 2005 over lifting the arms embargo on China imposed after Tiananmen illustrates that many foreigners have not forgotten nor forgiven the PLA for its actions in June 1989.[14] Within China, and indeed within the PLA itself, similar arguments are undoubtedly held *sotto voce*.[15] Though some younger Chinese, who are more concerned with improving their lifestyle, may not feel as deeply about Tiananmen as their parents and grandparents, a significant portion of the population still is concerned about "setting the record straight."[16] Nonetheless, within the CCP itself no compromise is permitted to allow for the reevaluation of the "Tiananmen verdict." Therefore, as a loyal servant of the party, the PLA alone cannot disassociate itself from the stigma attached to the events of 1989.

A rare insight into the inner struggle within the party and the PLA was provided by the experience of SARS whistle-blower Dr Jiang Yanyong (see Chapter 8, p. 173) in early 2004. In a letter to the Chinese leadership in February, Dr Jiang called for a reassessment of the Tiananmen massacre, stating that former president and military leader Yang Shangkun had told him that "4 June was the worst mistake the party had made in its history and he believed it would be rectified, though he was not able to correct it anymore."[17] A few months later, Dr Jiang was detained and placed into military custody for violating "military discipline." Based on orders issued at the highest party and government level, the army was instructed to "help and educate" the doctor.[18] After about six weeks of bad publicity and international pressure, Jiang was released in July and not charged with any crime.[19]

The treatment of Dr Jiang foreshadowed the party's appraisal of Zhao Ziyang, general secretary of the CCP removed from office for supporting the student demonstrations in the spring of 1989. After his death on 17 January 2005, the party officially concluded that Zhao had "committed serious mistakes in the political turmoil that occurred in the spring and summer of 1989."[20] This assessment and his tightly controlled funeral service further indicate little likelihood of a reevaluation of the Tiananmen verdict while officials responsible for decisions at the time are still alive.

Nevertheless, *if* the Chinese Communist Party can reevaluate that black period, the PLA certainly will quickly follow. A reassessment of Tiananmen, along the lines of the 70/30 assessment of Mao after his death, would elevate the status of the PLA in the eyes of many of the Chinese people more than all the new equipment they may be issued or any amount of blood soldiers may donate to local hospitals. Until the stain on the Chinese army's reputation is addressed openly, the PLA will continue to be haunted both inside and outside of China by the ghosts of Tiananmen.

Final vignettes

Shortly after the bloodshed in Beijing, many soldiers involved in the military action were awarded silver wristwatches for their participation. At the top of the watch's yellow face was a red outline of the Tiananmen rostrum; on the bottom, a profile of a PLA soldier wearing a green helmet. Under the soldier were the figures "89.6" (for the date June 1989) and the characters "In Commemoration of Quelling the Rebellion." Inscribed on the back were the characters "Presented by the Beijing Committee of the Chinese Communist Party and the People's Government of Beijing." In the following years, these watches were often found in flea markets in Beijing, broken, their hands no longer working, discarded by the soldiers to whom they had been presented.[21]

One of the few PLA officers who ever spoke to me about June 1989 interpreted the image of the one man in the white shirt standing in front of the column of tanks differently from most of the rest of the world. The officer said this photo actually demonstrated the discipline of the Chinese soldiers. "It would have been easy for the tank commander to run over the demonstrator, but he didn't and by his restraint he let that one man stop the entire column." The man was pulled away from the column of tanks; his fate is unknown.

On a train from Baotou, Inner Mongolia to Beijing, a Chinese businessman told me: "Many foreigners only see how far China is behind the west, and how we can never catch up. On the other hand, we Chinese see how far we have come [since 1979]. In order to understand what is happening in China, you must be able to look through both of these lenses at the same time."

The Chinese businessman's admonition is a reminder against oversimplification of a complex topic. In absolute terms ("how far we have come"), based on 20 years of slowly building momentum, China's military modernization program has resulted in dramatic improvements in capabilities over the past six years. But in relative terms ("how far China is behind"), are improvements in the PLA's capabilities sufficient to give the Chinese leadership confidence it will prevail on a future battlefield? Many factors must be considered to answer that question or any balance of military power equation. Professional planners in the PLA undertake such analysis on a routine, recurring basis. This book seeks merely to serve as a starting point for future study and further research on developments yet to be identified.

NOTES

1 INTRODUCTION

1 For comprehensive studies of the big issues facing the PLA as it entered the twenty-first century, see David Shambaugh, *Modernizing China's Military*, Los Angeles: University of California Press, 2002, Andrew J. Nathan and Robert S. Ross, *The Great Wall and The Empty Fortress: China's Search for Security*, New York: W.W. Norton & Company, 1997. For the PLA Navy, see Bernard D. Cole, *The Great Wall at Sea: China's Navy Enters the Twenty-First Century*, Annapolis: United States Naval Institute, 2001. For the PLA Air Force, see any of numerous essays and articles by Kenneth W. Allen, including his groundbreaking work co-authored with Jonathan Pollack and Glenn Krumel, *China's Air Force Enters the 21st Century*, Santa Monica: RAND, 1995. For strategic missile forces, see Mark A. Stokes, *China's Strategic Modernization: Implications for U.S. National Security*, Carlisle: Strategic Studies Institute, 1999; Bates Gill and James Mulvenon, "The Chinese Strategic Rocket Forces: Transition to Credible Deterrence," Paper presented to the National Intelligence Council Conference, 5 November 1999; or Bates Gill, James Mulvenon, and Mark Stokes, "The Chinese Second Artillery Corps: Transition to Credible Deterrence," in James Mulvenon and Andrew N.D. Yang (eds), *The People's Liberation Army as Organization Reference Volume v1.0*, Santa Monica; RAND, 2002. For China's strategic culture, see Alastair Iain Johnston, *Cultural Realism: Strategic Culture and Grand Strategy in Chinese History*, Princeton: Princeton University Press, 1995; Michael D. Swaine, *The Role of the Chinese Military in National Security Policymaking*, Santa Monica: RAND, 1998; and Andrew Scobell, *China and Strategic Culture*, Carlisle: Strategic Studies Institute, 2002. To examine civil–military relations, see any of the works of Ellis Joffe, especially *The Chinese Army After Mao*, Cambridge, Mass.: Harvard University Press, 1987. For doctrine and strategy, see Michael Pillsbury (ed.), *Chinese Views of Future Warfare*, Washington, D.C.: National Defense University Press, 1997; Michael Pillsbury, *CHINA Debates the Future Security Environment*, Washington, D.C.: National Defense University Press, 2000; Bates Gill, "China and the Revolution in Military Affairs: Assessing Economic and Socio-Cultural Factors," and Lonnie Henley, "China's Capacity for Achieving a Revolution in Military Affairs," in *China and the Revolution in Military Affairs*, Carlisle: Strategic Studies Institute, 1996. David M. Finkelstein, Paul H.B. Godwin, and Harlan Jencks also have written numerous articles on doctrine and strategy, many of which are found in the edited volumes listed in the bibliography. James Mulvenon is the acknowledged guru on Chinese information warfare; see also Timothy Thomas, "Like Adding Wings to the Tiger: Chinese Information War Theory and Practice," Foreign Military Studies Office, Fort Leavenworth, at http://www.iwar.org.uk/iwar/resources/china/iw/chinaiw.htm (accessed 2 April 2005). For detailed examinations of the PLA's business empire, see Tai Ming Cheung, *China's Entrepreneurial Army*,

Oxford: Oxford University Press, 2001; James C. Mulvenon, *Soldiers of Fortune: The Rise and Fall of the Chinese Military-Business Complex: 1978–1998*, Armonk: M.E. Sharp, 2000.

2 Students of the PLA are well advised to read and be familiar with information in all of the Defense White Papers. These documents are official statements of the Chinese government, reflecting current policy, and compiling many recent statistics. Links to all China's White Papers can be found at http://www.china.org.cn/e-white/index.htm (accessed 3 April 2005). While they are good summary documents, many more details can be derived from other official sources such as the Chinese-language *Jiefangjun Bao* (*Liberation Army Daily*), the English-language *PLA Daily, People's Daily*, and *Xinhua* (New China News Agency). All four of these sources are available online on the Internet. *PLA Daily* online carries its own translations of articles and editorials that appear in the Chinese-language *Jiefangjun Bao*; however, many of the *PLA Daily* online articles are shorter and do not contain as much detail as in the original Chinese version.

3 The author uses "modernization" and "transformation" with regard to the PLA almost interchangeably because as the PLA modernizes it is simultaneously transforming itself into an organization quite different from its previous structure. For militaries that are already modernized, like the United States military, modernization has more of an implication of upgrading and improving already advanced weapons and equipment, while transformation refers more to major changes in force structure and the way forces are employed, aided to a large degree by advanced electronics and other high technologies.

4 Detailed discussions of national-level headquarters are found in Shambaugh, *Modernizing China's Military* and Mulvenon and Yang, *The People's Liberation Army as Organization Reference Volume v1.0*.

5 Zhou Enlai, Deng Xiaoping, and Hua Guofeng were associated with the concept of the "Four Modernizations" as far back as 1975. (At the time military modernization was listed third, before science and technology.) The concept was revived in February 1978 by Hua, but not formally adopted until December at the 11th Plenum. See Jonathan D. Spence, *The Search for Modern China*, New York: W.W. Norton & Company, 1990, pp. 644–45, 654–57.

6 For review of Chinese military operations since 1949, see Gerald Segal, *Defending China*, Oxford: Oxford University Press, 1985; Mark A. Ryan, David M. Finkelstein, and Michael A. McDevitt (eds), *Chinese Warfighting: The PLA Experience Since 1949*, Armonk: M.E. Sharpe, 2003.

7 Nathan and Ross, *The Great Wall and The Empty Fortress*, p. 144.

8 For detailed analysis of the US–China–Taiwan triangle during the 1990s, see Robert L. Suettinger, *Beyond Tiananmen: The Politics of U.S.–China Relations 1989–2000*, Washington, D.C.: Brookings Institution Press, 2003. For a comprehensive account of US–China–Taiwan relations since 1979, see Alan D. Romberg, *Rein In at the Brink of the Precipice: American Policy Toward Taiwan and U.S.–PRC Relations*, Washington, D.C.: Henry L. Stimson Center, 2003.

9 This last element of reform is perhaps demonstrated best by the government first allowing and encouraging the PLA to enter into commercial activities in the 1980s in order to earn money to help support itself, and then in 1998 ordering the PLA to divest itself of commercial ventures because of problems of graft, corruption, and abuse that inevitably resulted.

10 Mao Zedong, "Problems of War and Strategy," 6 November 1938, available at the "Mao Tse-tung Internet Library" at http://www.marxists.org/reference/archive/mao/selected-works/volume-2/mswv2_12.htm (accessed 2 April 2005).

11 The "Three Represents" are defined as "the Party must always represent the requirements of the development of China's advanced productive forces, the orientation of the development of China's advanced culture, and the fundamental interests of the

overwhelming majority of the people in China." From Jiang Zemin's "Speech at the Rally in Celebration of the 80th Anniversary of the Founding of the Communist Party of China," 1 July 2001.

12 "RMRB Commentator on Promoting Military–Civilian Unity," in Foreign Broadcast Information System (FBIS) Beijing, *Renmin Ribao* (Internet version-WWW), in Chinese, 10 January 2004, p. 6.

13 *China Defense White Paper*, "National Defense Policy," 16 October 2000.

14 "Jiang Zemin's Book on Technology, Army Building Viewed," in FBIS Guangzhou, *Yangcheng Wanbao* (Internet version-WWW), in Chinese, 13 February 2001.

15 *China's National Defense in 2004*, "Foreword," December 2004.

16 "PLA Daily editorial: faithfully implement the army's historical mission in the new period of the new century," *PLA Daily* online, 16 March 2005; "Chinese military urged to perform 'historical mission,'" *Xinhua* online, 13 March 2005.

17 "NPC proposes $30 bln military spending for 2005," *Xinhua* online, 4 March 2005. See Shambaugh, *Modernizing China's Military*, p. 189, for 1994 and 1999 numbers.

18 *China's National Defense in 2002*, "National Defense Building," December 2002.

19 See Shambaugh, *Modernizing China's Military*, Chapter 5, pp. 184–224, and Richard Bitzinger, "Chinese Defence Spending and Military Modernization," in the Royal United Services Institute, *Chinese Military Update*, Vol. 2, No. 1, June 2004, pp. 3–5, for in-depth examinations of the defense budget issue.

20 According to "Chinese military urged to perform 'historical mission,'" Hu also "underlined the necessity to well coordinate and balance the country's economic development and national defense building, urging the military to seek a new path of modernization with 'low cost yet high efficiency.'"

21 Yanan Ju, *Understanding China: Center Stage of the Fourth Power*, Albany: State University of New York Press, 1996, p. 47.

22 William Whitson and Chen-hsia Huang, *The Chinese High Command: A History of Communist Military Politics, 1927–71*, New York; Praeger Publishers, 1973. Whitson's study was brought into the 1990s by Michael Swaine, *The Military & Political Succession in China*, Santa Monica: RAND, 1992.

23 *China's National Defense in 2004*, "National Defense Policy," December 2004.

24 David M. Finkelstein, "China's National Military Strategy," in James C. Mulvenon and Richard H. Yang (eds), *The People's Liberation Army in the Information Age*, Santa Monica: RAND, 1999, pp. 135–38.

25 The concept of "Information Technology application" is often awkwardly translated as "informationization" or "informationalization," a direct translation of the Chinese term *xinxihua*.

26 Significantly, on 1 January 2004 the *Jiefangjun Bao* published an editorial on "advancing the RMA with Chinese characteristics" as a strategic move to accelerate the modernization of China's armed forces.

27 Also in late 2004, after more than a decade of studying the RMA, the PLA Press published a 12-volume set on *New World Revolution in Military Affairs*, described as "China's first great work that has systematically elaborated the new world revolution in military affairs" with the intent of "accelerating the military changes with Chinese characteristics." See "New World Revolution in Military Affairs series published," *PLA Daily* online, 23 December 2004.

28 For a comprehensive discussion of building the PLA to meet future challenges, see "PRC: Military Journal on 'Comprehensive Integration' and RMA With Chinese Characteristics," in FBIS Beijing, *Zhongguo Junshi Kexue*, in Chinese, 20 April 2004, pp. 96–100.

29 "Jiang Zemin's Book on Technology, Army Building Viewed," in FBIS Guangzhou, *Yangcheng Wanbao* (Internet version-WWW), in Chinese, 13 February 2001.

30 The 1999 US Department of Defense Report to Congress on "The Security Situation in

the Taiwan Strait" mentioned ground force morale as "poor." Since that time there has been no mention of morale problems in this series of reports.

2 WHAT IS THE PLA?

1 The US State Department uses this term in its annual report on Human Rights in China. Also included in this definition of the Chinese "security apparatus" are "the state judicial, procuratorial, and penal systems."

2 In US terminology, "paramilitary forces" are defined as "forces or groups distinct from the regular armed forces of any country, but resembling them in organization, equipment, training, or mission." See Joint Publication 1-02, *Department of Defense Dictionary of Military and Associated Terms*, at http://www.dtic.mil/doctrine/jel/new_pubs/jp1_02.pdf (accessed 5 April 2005).

3 The responsibilities of the Ministry of Public Security, taken from the webpage "The Organizational Structure of the State Council," found at http://www.china.org.cn/english/kuaixun/64784.htm (accessed 5 April 2005).

4 "33,761 unqualified policemen dismissed in clean-up campaign," *Xinhua* online, 7 January 2004.

5 "China to enhance anti-riot police force," *Xinhua* online, 27 January 2001.

6 The responsibilities of the Ministry of State Security are taken from the webpage "The Organizational Structure of the State Council," found at http://www.china.org.cn/english/kuaixun/64784.htm (accessed 5 April 2005).

7 The premier is appointed by the PRC president and approved by the National People's Congress.

8 According to *China's National Defense in 2002*, "The Armed Forces," "The General Staff Headquarters administers the building of the militia under the leadership of the State Council and the CMC." Furthermore, management of the militia's role in maintaining the public order must "be guided by the policies and principles of the party Central Committee, the State Council and the Central Military Commission"; see "CPC, PLA Issue Circular on Improving Militia's Role in Maintaining Public Order," in FBIS Beijing, *Jiefangjun Bao* (Internet version-WWW), in Chinese, 16 December 2003, p. 1. The close scrutiny local governments give to all reserve forces is represented by comments of Zhang Zhongwei, Sichuan deputy party secretary, "No government, at whatever level it may be, is allowed to regard the work of militia and reserve forces as a matter only within the duties of military organs." See "PRC Sichuan Holds Meeting on Party's Control Over Armed Forces," in FBIS Chengdu, *Sichuan Ribao* (Internet version-WWW), in Chinese, 20 December 2000.

9 "Law of the People's Republic of China on National Defense, adopted at the fifth Session of the Eighth National People's Congress [NPC] on 14 March 1997," Beijing *Xinhua* Domestic Service, in FBIS-CHI-97-055.

10 A similar table is found in Dennis J. Blasko, "People's War in the 21st Century: The Militia and the Reserves," in David Finkelstein and Kristen Gunness (eds), *Swimming in a New Sea: Civil–Military Issues in Today's China*, Armonk: M.E. Sharpe, forthcoming.

11 *China's National Defense in 2004*, "Revolution in Military Affairs with Chinese Characteristics," and International Institute for Strategic Studies (IISS), *The Military Balance, 2004–2005*, London: Oxford University Press, 2004, p. 170.

12 IISS, *The Military Balance, 2004–2005*, pp. 170–72.

13 *China's National Defense*, "Reducing Military Personnel," July 1998.

14 *China's National Defense in 2002*, "The Armed Forces," outlines the types of units found in each arm of the ground forces. Chinese sources do not include logistics and armament units as separate branches. They are included in this listing because of their increasing importance to the PLA.

15 Kenneth Allen, "Introduction to the PLA's Administrative and Operational Structure," in James Mulvenon and Andrew N. D. Yang (eds), *The People's Liberation Army as Organization Reference Volume v1.0*, Santa Monica: RAND, 2002, p. 6.

16 *China's National Defense*, "Reducing Military Personnel," July 1998.

17 US Department of Defense, "Annual Report on the Military Power of the People's Republic of China," 12 July 2002, p. 23, and Dennis J. Blasko, "PLA Ground Forces: Moving Toward a Smaller, More Rapidly Deployable, Modern Combined Arms Force," in Mulvenon and Yang (eds), *The People's Liberation Army as Organization Reference Volume v1.0*, pp. 319–20.

18 This section is based upon Dennis J. Blasko, "People's War in the 21st Century: The Militia and the Reserves."

19 "*Jiefangjun Bao* 'Roundup' on Reserve Forces Building Under Jiang Zemin," in FBIS Beijing, *Jiefangjun Bao* (Internet version-WWW), in Chinese, 20 October 2002, p. 1.

20 *China's National Defense in 2004*, "The Military Service System."

21 IISS, *The Military Balance, 2004–2005*, p. 173.

22 The PAP Beijing *zongdui* has an organizational level one step higher than division. The PAP uses different terminology than the PLA for its organizational structure: *zongdui* for division (*shi*) in the PLA; *zhidui* for regiment (*tuan*), *dadui* for battalion (*ying*), and *zhongdui* for company (*lian*).

23 IISS, *The Military Balance, 2004–2005*, p. 173. See also Tai Ming Cheung, "The People's Armed Police: First Line of Defense," in *The China Quarterly*, Special Issue: *China's Military in Transition*, June 1996.

24 By definition, PLA and PAP *conscripts* are ordered into service by the Chinese government. Preferably, civilians inducted enter the service willingly, though many stories can be found about young men attempting to avoid service for a variety of reasons. An unknown number of conscripts probably volunteer to enter the PLA or PAP based on various personal motivations, such as patriotism, economic opportunity, the thrill or challenge of military life, etc. The *CIA Factbook* estimates over 12 million males reach military service age annually; see http://www.odci.gov/cia/publications/factbook/geos/ch.html (accessed 3 April 2005). Based on percentages estimated in Chapter 3, the PLA and PAP may need to induct a total of approximately 500,000 young men annually to meet their requirements for new soldiers.

25 *China's National Defense in 2002*, "The Armed Forces." All quotes in this section are from that source.

26 *China's National Defense in 2004*, "National Defense Mobilization and Reserve Force Building," states: "primary militia members aged 18–22 receive 30–40 days of military training." It does not specify why only militia personnel within that age range receive this amount of training.

27 "HK Daily on PLA Circular Requiring Overseas-Funded Firms to Build Militia," in FBIS Hong Kong, *Ching Chi Jih Pao*, in Chinese, 30 September 2002, p. A17.

28 *China's National Defense in 2004*, "National Defense Mobilization and Reserve Force Building."

29 "CPC, PLA Issue Circular on Improving Militia's Role in Maintaining Public Order," in FBIS Beijing, *Jiefangjun Bao* (Internet version-WWW), in Chinese, 16 December 2003, p. 1.

30 "*Jiefangjun Bao* 'Roundup' on Reserve Forces Building Under Jiang Zemin," in FBIS Beijing, *Jiefangjun Bao* (Internet version-WWW), in Chinese, 20 October 2002, p. 1.

31 For more detailed discussions of the PLA national command structure and the four general headquarters departments, see David Shambaugh, *Modernizing China's Military*, Los Angeles: University of California Press, 2002, Ch. 4, and Mulvenon and Yang (eds), *The People's Liberation Army as Organization Reference Volume v1.0*, Chs 2–7. Details for this section are derived primarily from the *Year 2000 Chinese Defense White Paper*,

the Qianlong website "China Overview" webpage at http://mil.qianlong.com/5051/2003-7-30/145@240625.htm (accessed 5 April 2005), and the *Directory of PRC Military Personalities, October 2003.*

32 Membership in the State CMC is announced and adjusted during the annual meetings of the National People's Congress in March, while Party CMC membership is adjusted in the fall. When Jiang Zemin stepped down from the Party CMC chairman position in September 2004, he retained the State CMC chairman position until the following year's meeting of the National People's Congress in March.

33 "'Full Text' of Revised Routine Service Regulations for PLA," in FBIS Beijing, *Jiefangjun Bao* (Internet version-WWW), in Chinese, 1 Apr 2002, pp. 4–8, Article 74.

34 For discussion of protocol order, rank structure, duty positions, and many other aspects of PLA organization, see Kenneth Allen, "Introduction to the PLA's Administrative and Operational Structure," in Mulvenon and Yang (eds), *The People's Liberation Army as Organization Reference Volume v1.0*, pp. 28–44.

35 GLD logistics bases include the Qinghai-Tibet Army Depot Department, Wuhan Rear Base, Nenjiang Base, and Chen Hu Base in Hubei.

36 "Steady agriculture and sideline production in the army stressed by GLD," *PLA Daily* online, 17 June 2004. PLA regulations call for "Units with the necessary conditions shall gradually strive for self-sufficiency or basic self-sufficiency in meat and vegetable. Proceeds from production shall mainly be spent on the improvement of food and the subsidizing of livelihood needs. Income of grass-roots units from production belongs to grass-roots units." See Articles 251 and 252 in "'Full Text' of Revised Routine Service Regulations for PLA," in FBIS Beijing, *Jiefangjun Bao* (Internet version-WWW), in Chinese, 1 April 2002, pp. 4–8.

37 Kristen Gunness, *Swimming in a New Sea: Civil–Military Issues in Today's China*, Alexandria: The CNA Corporation, May 2004, p. 28. An update to the number of factories controlled by the GLD was made in the article "Remarkable progress made in PLA logistics socialization," *PLA Daily* online, 10 April 2005, which somewhat unclearly stated, "All quartermaster factories have been handed over to civil organizations, and 45% military supplies and clothing and accoutrements are ordered from society through open tender." If *all* quartermaster factories are now run by civilian organizations, why is only 45 percent of "clothing and accoutrements" bought on the open market? What factories make the other 55 percent? This report is a good example of imprecision in PLA media reporting and statistics "with Chinese characteristics."

38 Lonnie Henley, "PLA Logistics and Doctrine Reform, 1999–2009," in Susan M. Puska (ed.), *People's Liberation Army After Next*, Carlisle: Strategic Studies Institute, 2000, pp. 55–77; Dennis J. Blasko, "Chinese Military Logistics: The GLD System," The Jamestown Foundation, *China Brief*, Volume 4, Issue 19, 30 September 2004.

39 The protocol order for the Military Regions was established by the sequence each region came under control of communist forces in the civil war. This listing *does not* represent priorities in missions or funding currently assigned to the regions.

40 The Hong Kong and Macao Garrisons are located in the Guangzhou MR, but they are subordinate to the CMC. See *China's National Defense*, "National Defense Construction," July 1998; *Year 2000 Chinese Defense White Paper*, "National Defense Construction."

41 Chinese terminology for duty positions used throughout is derived from *Xiandai Jundui Zhihui (Command of Modern Armies)*, Beijing: National Defense University Press, 1993, Appendix 5, pp. 518–22, and *A New English–Chinese Chinese–English Dictionary of Military Terms*, Beijing: Defense Industries Press, 1999.

42 *China's National Defense*, "National Defense Construction," July 1998.

43 *White Paper on China's National Defense in 2002.*

44 *Year 2000 Chinese Defense White Paper*, "National Defense Construction."

45 Details of the NDMC functions are found in *China's National Defense in 2002*, "National Defense Building."

46 Except where noted, information in this section is derived primarily from "'Full Text' of Revised Routine Service Regulations for PLA," Articles 26 through 56.

47 The change from mess officers to mess NCOs is mentioned in the article "Food allowances for soldiers raised," *PLA Daily* online 19 April 2004.

48 Mortars are manned by infantry or armored troops and are not considered artillery weapons.

49 "'Full Text' of Revised Routine Service Regulations for PLA," Article 138.

50 The priority given to divisions for new equipment and the shift to brigades was synthesized by the author from a review of Chinese military newspaper articles from 1998 on.

51 This table updates information found in Dennis J. Blasko, "PLA Ground Forces: Moving Toward a Smaller, More Rapidly Deployable, Modern Combined Arms Force," p. 319.

52 The general organization structure of group armies is synthesized from Tables 4.1–4.7.

53 The number of workers in the Chinese defense industry is derived from information available on their websites and promotional literature.

3 WHO IS THE PLA?

1 "New Uniforms for the People's Army," 1 December 2004, at http://service.china. org.cn/link/wcm/Show_Text?info_id=113688&p_qry=pla (accessed 5 April 2005). Pictures of PLA uniforms, ranks, and insignia can be found at the English-language *PLA Daily* website at http://english.pladaily.com.cn/special/uniforms/index.htm (accessed 5 April 2005), http://english.pladaily.com.cn/special/cpla/3/index.htm (accessed 5 April 2005), and http://english.pladaily.com.cn/special/cpla/2/index.htm (accessed 5 April 2005).

2 These insignia differentiate the PLA from the PAP who wear different collar and cap insignia in addition to a different (more metallic) shade of green uniform. Other uniform differences which distinguish the PAP from PLA include a different color scheme (red for enlisted troops) for shoulder epaulets, yellow and red stripes at the bottom of jacket sleeves, predominately yellow stripes (piping) down the side of trouser legs, and very thin yellow and red stripes on service caps along with a gold band over the hat brim. In 2005, the PAP also began wearing distinctive shoulder patches and chest badges to identify specific units, localities, and unit functions. Although the difference between PLA and PAP uniforms is striking once seen side by side, many media sources, both outside and inside China, confuse the two forces and misidentification of PAP for PLA and vice versa is common.

3 "Decision of State Council, Central Military Commission on Amending Conscription Work Regulations," in FBIS Beijing, *Xinhua* Domestic Service, in Chinese, 0604 GMT, 9 September 2001.

4 *China's National Defense in 2004*, "The Military Service System."

5 Information for this section is derived from numerous articles in *PLA Daily* online during the winter of 2003–04, each of which provides a small glimpse into the conscription and basic training process.

6 According to *China's National Defense in 2004*, "The Military Service System," "Enlistment in peacetime usually takes place once a year." This statement leaves room for additional conscription orders to be levied in time of emergency.

7 "'Full Text' of Revised Routine Service Regulations for PLA," in FBIS Beijing, *Jiefangjun Bao* (Internet version-WWW), in Chinese, 1 April 2002 pp. 4–8.

8 "PLA Takes Measures To Broaden Ranks of NCOs," in FBIS Beijing, *Xinhua* Domestic Service, in Chinese, at 0815 GMT, 14 October 2004.

9   *Qianwei Bao* (Jinan Military Region newspaper), 4 January 2002.

10 Unless otherwise noted, information for this section is derived from "PLA Regulations for Managing Noncommissioned Officers," in FBIS Beijing, *Jiefangjun Bao* (Internet version-WWW), in Chinese, 23 May 2001, p. 2 and "New Revised Military Service Regulations," in FBIS Beijing, *Xinhua* Domestic Service, in Chinese, 0918 GMT, 11 July 1999.

11 "NCO training and recruitment to commence soon," *PLA Daily* online, 23 December 2004, and *Jiefangjun Bao* online, in Chinese, 23 December 2004.

12 "New Revised Military Service Regulations," in FBIS Beijing, *Xinhua* Domestic Service, in Chinese, 0918 GMT, 11 July 1999, Article 9.

13 "PLA Regulations for Managing Noncommissioned Officers," Articles 9–13.

14 For an example, see "NCOs invited to teach in air force institute," in *PLA Daily* online, 21 April 2004.

15 "NCO training and recruitment to commence soon," *PLA Daily* online, 23 December 2004.

16 *Jiefangjun Bao* online, in Chinese, 23 April 2003.

17 "China enrolls record number of sergeants to beef up high-tech capability," *People's Daily* online, 18 July 2005.

18 *China's National Defense in 2004*, "The Military Service System," provides an outline of the system of ranks and classifications for officers, NCOs, and conscripts described in this chapter. The terminology for officer categories, military ranks, grades, and duty or post positions varies widely according to sources, both in Chinese and English. Despite these variations in translation, the meaning of each term can usually be understood in context.

19 See James C. Mulvenon, *Professionalization of the Senior Chinese Officer Corps: Trends and Implications*, Santa Monica: RAND, 1997. The Qianlong website "China Overview" webpage at http://mil.qianlong.com/5051/2003-7-30/145@240625.htm (accessed 1 June 2004) identifies the duty categories and ranks for PLA officers. See also Kenneth W. Allen and John F. Corbett, Jr., "Predicting PLA Leader Promotions," in Andrew Scobell and Larry Wortzel (eds), *Civil–Military Change in China: Elites, Institutes, and Ideas After the 16th Party Congress*, Carlisle: Strategic Studies Institute, 2004, pp. 257–77; Kenneth Allen, "Introduction to the PLA's Administrative and Operational Structure," in James Mulvenon and Andrew N. D. Yang, (eds), *The People's Liberation Army as Organization Reference Volume v1.0*, Santa Monica: RAND, 2002, pp. 28–35.

20 The background color for officer epaulets is gold for dress, spring/autumn, and winter uniforms with thin red stripes. These are also known as "hard" epaulets because of their stiff backboard; all hard officer epaulets also have thin red stripes along the outside edges. Epaulets for summer and camouflage/fatigue uniforms are known as "soft epaulets" and have a dark green-black background and no gold stripes along the edges.

21 A similar table can be found in Kenneth Allen, "Introduction to the PLA's Administrative and Operational Structure," pp. 32–33. The same information is found at the Qianlong website "China Overview" webpage at http://mil.qianlong.com/5051/2003-7-30/145@240625.htm (accessed 5 April 2005). Information from *China's National Defense in 2004* was also used to update these sources.

22 Correspondence with PLA officer, 24 May 2004.

23 For discussion of "mountain-topism," see Harlan W. Jencks, *From Muskets to Missiles: Politics and Professionalism in the Chinese Army, 1945–1981*, Boulder: Westview Press, 1982, pp. 71, 176, 229–30, 243.

24 Qianlong website "China Overview" webpage at http://mil.qianlong.com/5051/2003-7-30/145@240625.htm (accessed 5 April 2005).

25 Kenneth Allen, "Introduction to the PLA's Administrative and Operational Structure," p. 35.

26 "Military officers score scientific achievements in Tibet," *Xinhuanet* online, 16 April 2004.

27 "PLA Department, Tianjin University Sign Agreement on Training Military Cadres," in FBIS Beijing *Zhongguo Xinwen She*, in Chinese, 0910 GMT, 31 May 2002.

28 "Tsinghua University holds commencement for national defense students of 2005," *PLA Daily* online, 13 July 2005.

29 "Chinese institutions of higher learning to enroll 12,000 national defense-oriented students," *PLA Daily* online, 25 April 2005 and "More university students trained for military service," *Xinhuanet* online, 7 May 2004.

30 "1000 national defense graduates entered the PLA talents matrix," *PLA Daily* online, 4 July 2003, and "First batch of national defense students graduate from Tsinghua University," *PLA Daily* online, 14 July 2004.

31 "Military academies to recruit 20,000 high school graduates in 2004," *PLA Daily* online, 27 April 2004.

32 "Military colleges to enroll some 20,000 fresh senior secondary school graduates," *PLA Daily* online, 25 April 2005.

33 "Four military colleges and universities turned over to local governments," *PLA Daily* online, 25 August 2004.

34 The list of PLA academies and their subordination is derived primarily from *Directory of PRC Military Personalities, October 2003*, pp. 233–46. A somewhat outdated list of many PLA schools, with links to descriptions of each school, is found on the Chinese language *Jiefangjun Bao* website at http://www.pladaily.com.cn/item/jxzs/tmp/bkzn/bt.htm (accessed 5 April 2005) and was also used in the compilation of Table 3.3. Table 3.3 does not include institutions that educate officers for the PLAN, PLAAF, or Second Artillery.

35 "Guangzhou Military Region Integrated Training Base Established, Guilin Army Academy Mission Accomplished," *Xinhuanet* online, 4 February 2005.

36 "Forging talents within the limit," *PLA Daily* online, 25 June 2003. An unconfirmed report suggests the Physical Culture (Sports) Academy at Guangzhou has been turned over to local civilian control.

37 "High-caliber talent program runs smoothly," *PLA Daily* online, 29 September 2003.

38 *China's National Defense in 2004*, "Revolution in Military Affairs with Chinese Characteristics."

39 *China's National Defense in 2004*, "Revolution in Military Affairs with Chinese Characteristics."

40 "A foreign officer's Chinese-style wedding," *PLA Daily* online, 18 March 2005.

41 "China Establishes First Air Defense Command Academy," in FBIS Beijing, *Xinhua*, in English, 1356 GMT, 14 June 2004.

42 *Hebei Daily*, 26 July 2004, and "PRC-Owned HK Daily: CMC Decree Renames, Upgrades PLA Missile Academy," in FBIS Hong Kong, *Hsiang Kang Shang Pao*, in Chinese, 27 July 2004, p. A3.

43 *China's National Defense in 2004*, "Revolution in Military Affairs with Chinese Characteristics."

44 "NDU intensifies training of commanding professionals," *PLA Daily* online, 12 April 2005.

45 "'Historic leap' for foreign military trainees," *PLA Daily* online, 9 August 2004.

46 "Senior commanders to teach in university," *PLA Daily* online, 2 September 2003.

47 "NUDT establishes student resource bases in 100 prestigious middle schools," *PLA Daily* online, 2 June 2004, and "NUDT celebrates its 50th anniversary," *PLA Daily* online, 2 September 2003.

48 "NUDT celebrates its 50th anniversary," *PLA Daily* online, 2 September 2003.

49 "12 new subjects on curriculum at UNDST," *PLA Daily* online, 3 June 2003.

50 "NUDT explores new ways of training competent commanding personnel," *PLA Daily* online, 24 June 2004.

51 "Army to enroll nonmilitary personnel on contract basis," *PLA Daily* online, 5 July 2005.
52 Qianlong website "China Overview" webpage at http://mil.qianlong.com/5051/2003-7-30/145@240625.htm (accessed 5 April 2005).
53 Conversation with PLA civilian, September 1996.

4 WHERE IS THE PLA?

1 *China's National Defense*, "National Defense Policy," July 1998, and *China's National Defense in 2000*, "National Defense Policy."
2 *China's National Defense in 2002*, "National Defense Policy."
3 *China's National Defense in 2002*, "The Armed Forces."
4 *China's National Defense in 2004*, "National Defense Policy."
5 *China's National Defense in 2004*, "National Defense Policy."
6 Kenneth Allen, "Introduction to the PLA's Administrative and Operational Structure," in James Mulvenon and Andrew N. D. Yang (eds), The People's Liberation Army as Organization Reference Volume v1.0, Santa Monica: RAND, 2002, p. 12.
7 "Chairman Jiang signs order to honor advanced units and individuals," *PLA Daily* online, 18 June 2004.
8 "PLA starts to renew number plates for military vehicles," *PLA Daily* online, 1 December 2004.
9 Locations for the 15th Airborne Army are found in the *Directory of PRC Military Personalities*, October 2003, p. 64. For identification of transport regiments and airfields supporting the 15th Airborne, see the webpage "Aviation of the People's Liberation Army," at http://www.china-military.org/units/guangzhou/13div.htm (accessed 6 April 2005).
10 The numbers of the various types of units cited in this paragraph, except for local forces, are based on a summary of the listings in Tables 4.1–4.7.
11 The International Institute for Strategic Studies, *The Military Balance, 2004–2005*, London: Oxford University Press, 2004, p. 170, lists 12 infantry divisions, one mountain brigade, four infantry brigades, and 87 regiments/battalions as "Local Forces (Garrison, Border, Coastal)."
12 *China's National Defense in 2002*, "National Defense Building."
13 "China's terrestrial frontier defense infrastructure takes shape," in *People's Daily* online, 5 August 2004.
14 "Renmin Wang Refutes Western Reports on PLA Buildup on DPRK Border," in FBIS Beijing, *Renmin Wang* (Internet version-WWW), in Chinese, 22 September 2003.
15 *China's National Defense*, "National Defense Construction," July 1998, and *Year 2000 Chinese Defense White Paper*, "National Defense Construction."
16 For details of the 1997–2000 restructuring, see Dennis J. Blasko, "PLA Ground Forces: Moving Toward a Smaller, More Rapidly Deployable, Modern Combined Arms Force," in Mulvenon and Yang (eds), *The People's Liberation Army as Organization Reference Volume v1.0*, pp. 326–36.
17 *Directory of PRC Military Personalities, October 2004*, p. v.
18 In order to compile this listing, the author has used the *Directory of PRC Military Personalities, October 2004* (and previous annual editions of this work) as a baseline and updated it with information derived by Ellis Melvin and his study of the Chinese media. US government personnel who have made official visits to PLA units have provided additional information, along with additional reporting from the Chinese press. Details of the organization of logistics subdepartments were derived from three Chinese Internet postings provided by Ellis Melvin in 2003, 2004, and 2005. These postings provide the most detailed look at this otherwise unstudied element of the force. The accuracy of the data on logistics subdepartments has not been verified by other sources, but is provided as a "best-guess" estimate.

19 An all-brigade structure makes this group army – technically a corps-size formation – closer to a division in size, as found in other armies, rather than a true corps composed of multiple full divisions and support elements.

20 "Zhangjiakou Army Reserve Antiaircraft Artillery Brigade Formed 27 Apr," in FBIS Shijiazhuang, *Hobei Ribao* (Internet version-WWW), in Chinese, 28 April 2005, and "Qinhuangdao Army Reserve Artillery Brigade Formed 28 Apr," in FBIS Shijiazhuang, *Hobei Ribao* (Internet version-WWW), in Chinese, 29 April 2005.

21 *Xinhuanet* online, in Chinese, 28 May 2004, republishing an article from *Jiefangjun Bao*.

22 "Hubei's Yichang Army Reserve AAA Brigade Activated 29 Apr," in FBIS Wuhan, *Hubei Ribao* (Internet version-WWW), in Chinese, 1 May 2005.

23 Numbers of reserve units in 1998 derived from *Directory of PRC Military Personalities, June 1998*.

24 *Directory of PRC Military Personalities, October 2004*, pp. 89–94.

25 *China's National Defense in 2004*, "National Defense Mobilization and Reserve Force Building."

26 "PRC: Investigative Report on Tianjin Enterprise's Militia Organization," in FBIS Beijing, *Zhongguo Minbing*, in Chinese, 10 January 2004, pp. 18–19.

27 "PRC: Remarkable Achievements in Construction of People's Air Defense Facilities," in FBIS Beijing, *Xinhua* Domestic Service, in Chinese, 0732 GMT 26 September 2003.

28 Diagram in *Houqin Jijuan Changyong Wenshu Xiezuo Shili* (*Examples of Writing Common Documents for Logistic Organs*), Yellow River Publishing House, 2001, p. 279.

29 Information Office of the State Council of the People's Republic of China, "History and Development of Xinjiang," May 2003, http://www.china.org.cn/e-white/20030526/9.htm (accessed 6 April 2005). Numbers for the total size of the Corps are from this source.

30 See Charles Hutzler, "From corps to corp., Chinese paramilitary seeks money to grow," 19 December 1998, at http://www.uyghuramerican.org/mediareports/1998/apdec1998.html (accessed 8 June 2004). The 100,000 figure is repeated as the number of militia in the Corps in Matt Forney, "One Nation-Divided Since Sept. 11, Beijing has been cracking down in Xinjiang," *Time* Magazine, 25 March 2002 at http://www.time.com/time/asia/magazine/article/0,13673,501020325-218371,00.html (accessed 6 April 2005).

31 White Paper, "History and Development of Xinjiang."

5 HOW WILL THE PLA FIGHT?

1 Xiaobing Li, "PLA Attacks and Amphibious Operations During the Taiwan Strait Crises of 1954–55 and 1958," in Mark A. Ryan, David M. Finkelstein, and Michael A. McDevitt (eds), *Chinese Warfighting: The PLA Experience Since 1949*, Armonk: M.E. Sharpe, 2003, pp. 154–56.

2 See Paul H.B. Godwin, *China's Defense Modernization: Aspirations and Capabilities*, Alexandria: The CNA Corporation, 2001; Paul H.B. Godwin, "Assessing the Evolving Doctrine and Strategy of Chinese People's Liberation Army: Developing a Framework for Analysis," discussion paper prepared for "Chinese Military Studies: a Conference on the State of the Field," sponsored by the National Defense University, Institute for National Strategic Studies, 26–27 October 2000, Fort L.J. McNair, Washington, D.C., 20319, found at http://www.ndu.edu/inss/China_Center/CMA_Conf_Oct00/paper 12.htm (accessed 7 April 2005); and Bates Gill and James Mulvenon, "The Chinese Strategic Rocket Forces: Transition to Credible Deterrence," paper presented to the National Intelligence Council: Conference, 5 November 1999.

3 The author simplistically considers "doctrine" to be a statement of how a military fights. The PLA has no single word for "doctrine," and what is considered its warfighting doctrine is found in a variety of regulations and official documents, including teaching material used in its military education institutes. These various publications provide guidelines and directives on how its various forces will be employed.

4 Sun Haichen (ed.), *The Wiles of War: 36 Military Strategies from Ancient China*, Beijing: Foreign Languages Press, 1993, p. 328. In December 1994, a PLA NDU professor of Marxism pointed out to me that this last stratagem, "Running Away as the Best Choice," had particular relevance to the PLA at the time.

5 Sun Tzu, *The Art of War*, translated by Samuel B. Griffith, London: Oxford University Press, 1963, p. 63, Ch. I, Verse 1. All quotations are from this translation and will be identified in the text by chapter and verse, for example, I.1.

6 "On Protracted War" (May 1938), from *The Quotations of Mao Tse tung*, found at http://www.marxists.org/reference/archive/mao/works/red-book/ch08.htm (accessed 7 April 2005).

7 "Problems of Strategy in China's Revolutionary War," (December 1936) found at http://www.marxists.org/reference/archive/mao/works/1936/12.htm#s5-1 (accessed 7 April 2005). The term "military strategy" to describe the "Active Defense" is found in the *Year 2000 China Defense White Paper*, "National Defense Policy."

8 "The Present Situation and Our Tasks," (25 December 1947), *Selected Military Writings*, 2nd edn, pp. 349–50, found at http://www.marxists.org/reference/archive/mao/works/red-book/ch08.htm (accessed 7 April 2005).

9 See Lonnie Henley, "PLA Logistics and Doctrine Reform, 1999–2009," in Susan M. Puska (ed.), *People's Liberation Army After Next*, Carlisle: Strategic Studies Institute, 2000, p. 55, and US Department of Defense, "Annual Report on the Military Power of the People's Republic of China," 12 July 2002, p. 13, for reference to the initial issue of new warfighting regulations. The new regulations are actually a set of regulations covering all elements of PLA operations. New regulations continue to be issued. While there are many news reports of new regulations being promulgated and books published to explain them, the entire body of regulations is not available to foreign observers.

10 Wang Houqing and Zhang Xingye (eds), *On Military Campaigns*, translated by Language Doctors, Inc, Beijing: National Defense University Press, May 2000.

11 *On Military Campaigns*, Ch. I, Sect. 2.

12 Excerpted from *On Military Campaigns*, Ch. III, Sect. 2. The author has made a few grammatical and word changes for clarity and readability. This chapter's discussion of *On Military Campaigns* has been guided and influenced by numerous discussions with Dr David Finkelstein of the Center for Naval Analyses.

13 The PLA considers a campaign against Taiwan to be a domestic use of force with the likely intervention of a foreign force.

14 The term "*baozhang*" is sometimes translated as "guarantee" or "safeguard"; however, in most military cases, the preferred rendering should be "support."

15 *On Military Campaigns*, Ch. II, Sect. 2.H.

16 Information for this section is derived from *On Military Campaigns*, Ch. VI, Sect. 1.

17 *On Military Campaigns*, Ch. VI, Sect. 1.

18 Joint Publication 1-02, *Department of Defense Dictionary of Military and Associated Terms*, 12 April 2001, found at http://www.dtic.mil/doctrine/jel/new_pubs/jp1_02.pdf (accessed 4 April 2005).

19 Information for this section is derived from *On Military Campaigns*, Ch. VI, Sect. 2.

20 See *Department of Defense Dictionary of Military and Associated Terms* for definition of "air interdiction" and "close air support," found at http://www.dtic.mil/doctrine/jel/new_pubs/jp1_02.pdf (accessed 31 March 2005). Kenneth W. Allen, Jonathan Pollack, and Glenn Krumel, *China's Air Force Enters the 21st Century*, Santa Monica: RAND,

1995, p. 118, noted that "the PLAAF had backed away almost completely from the idea of close air support by 1990." So far, there is little evidence to support changing that conclusion.

21 Information for this section is derived from *On Military Campaigns*, Ch. VI, Sect. 3.
22 Information for this section is derived from *On Military Campaigns*, Ch. VI, Sect. 4.
23 *On Military Campaigns*, Ch. VI, Sect. 4.
24 Information for this section is derived from *On Military Campaigns*, Ch. XI, Sect. 1.
25 *On Military Campaigns*, Ch. XX.
26 *On Military Campaigns*, Ch. XIV, Sect. 3.
27 *On Military Campaigns*, Ch. XIV, Sect. 1.
28 Information for this section is derived from *On Military Campaigns*, Ch. XIV, Sect. 1 and 3.
29 Information for this section is derived from *On Military Campaigns*, Ch. XVII, and Xu Guoxin (ed.), *Zhanqu Zhanyi Houqin Baozhang (Theater Campaign Logistics Support)*, Beijing: National Defense University Press, June 1997.
30 Information for this section is derived from *On Military Campaigns*, Chapter XIX.
31 Information for this section is derived from *On Military Campaigns*, Chapter XX.
32 Zhang Xingye (ed.) *Zhanyi Lilun Xuexi Zhinan* (*Guide to the Study of Operational Theory*), Beijing; National Defense University Press, 2001, pp. 243–4.
33 Operational planning factors found at *Zhanyi Lilun Xuexi Zhinan*, pp. 246–47.
34 Information for this section is derived from *On Military Campaigns*, Ch. XXI.
35 Information for this section is derived from *On Military Campaigns*, Chs VIII and IX.
36 *Jiefangjun Bao*, 14 September 2001.
37 *Renmin Qianxian* (Nanjing Military Region newspaper), 19 October 2001.
38 *Renmin Qianxian* (Nanjing Military Region newspaper), 17 November 2002.
39 *On Military Campaigns*, Ch. I, Sect. 3.

6 WHAT EQUIPMENT DOES THE PLA USE?

1 Funding for equipment procurement is derived from the four Chinese Defense White Papers of 1998, 2000, 2002, and 2004.
2 See Richard A. Bitzinger, "Chinese Defence Spending and Military Modernization," in Royal United Services Institute, *Chinese Military Update*, Vol. 2, No. 1, June 2004, pp. 3–5.
3 The Stockholm International Peace Research Institute (SIPRI) database, dated 10 June 2005, accounts for $18.216 billion of *all foreign arms deliveries* to China from 1989 to 2004, with the majority of deliveries occurring during and after 1999; Russia (and the former Soviet Union) accounted for $16.767 billion of that total. See http://web.sipri. org/contents/armstrad/TIV_ind_imp_CHI_89-04.pdf (accessed 16 June 2005). SIPRI updates its information annually as new information becomes available, which sometime results in changing data from previous years.
4 An outstanding source of technical data for military equipment of all sorts is the series of Jane's *All the World's* publications; unfortunately, Jane's publications are not always readily accessible or available to general readers. Several sources available on the Internet provide photographs and technical data for Chinese ground force equipment. These sources vary in accuracy, completeness, and timeliness and include Chinese Defence Today at http://www.sinodefence.com/army/default.asp (a particularly well-organized and easy to use site, accessed 8 April 2005); GlobalSecurity.org at http:// www.globalsecurity.org/military/world/china/pla-inventory.htm (accessed 8 April 2005); the Federation of American Scientists at http://www.fas.org/man/dod-101/ sys/land/row/index.html (assessed 8 April 2005); and the Qianlong website at http://mil.qianlong.com/ (accessed 8 April 2005). *Zhongguo Changgui Wuqi Huici*

(*Chinese Conventional Weapons Assembled*), Beijing: Weapons Industry Press, 1991, and *Directory of Chinese Military Equipment 1987–88*, Hong Kong: Conmilit Press, 1987, were also used for older nomenclature and descriptions.

5 See Richard F. Grimmett, "Conventional Arms Transfers to Developing Nations, 1996–2003," Congressional Research Service Report to Congress (CRS), 26 August 2004. In the period from 1996 to 2003, as a *supplier* of arms, China was ranked fifth (behind the US, Russia, France, and the UK) in arms *agreements*, valued at $8.188 billion (page CRS-43). Actual arms *deliveries* made by China over this period was even less, at $5.3 billion (page CRS-59). After arms agreements are made, it may take many years for actual delivery of all equipment to take place. Like SIPRI, CRS updates and adjusts its data annually.

6 A number of Chinese news reports, magazines, and videos were issued to commemorate the parade. These include "On Vehicle Formations in Military Parade," in FBIS Beijing, *Zhongguo Xinwen She*, in Chinese, 1 October 1999; *Keji Zhoukan Zhongguo Dayuebing Jishi* (*Science and Technology Weekly China Grand Military Parade*), Beijing: Science and Technology Weekly Press, no date; *Zhongguo Zuixin Wuqi Zhuangbei* (*China's Newest Weapons and Equipment*), Beijing: Haihu Press, November 1999; and the DVD "China's 50th National Day Parade," Hong Kong: Mei Ah Disc Co. Ltd, n.d. The descriptions of the parade found in this chapter build upon and update information from Dennis J. Blasko, "PLA Ground Forces: Moving Toward a Smaller, More Rapidly Deployable, Modern Combined Arms Force," in James Mulvenon and Andrew N.D. Yang (eds), *The People's Liberation Army as Organization Reference Volume v1.0*, Santa Monica: RAND, 2002, pp. 336–44.

7 International Institute for Strategic Studies, *The Military Balance, 2004–2005*, London: Oxford University Press, 2004, p. 170.

8 Descriptions and details for much of the equipment identified in this chapter are based upon information found on the Chinese Defence Today website.

9 US Department of Defense, "Annual Report on the Military Power of the People's Republic of China," May 2004, p. 38. The DOD report from two years earlier (2002) estimated total production of 1,800 Type 96 tanks. No reason for the discrepancy was given when the number was downsized to 1,500 in 2003.

10 Christopher F. Foss, "China fields enhanced Type 98 main battle tank," *Jane's Defence Weekly*, 18 August 2004.

11 *The Military Balance, 2004–2005*, p. 170.

12 Chinese Defence Today website, Airborne Combat Vehicle webpage at http://www.sinodefence.com/army/armour/airborne.asp (accessed 8 April 2005).

13 Chinese Defence Today website, Type 92/90 Wheeled Armored Fighting Vehicle webpage at http://www.sinodefence.com/army/armour/wz551.asp (accessed 8 April 2005).

14 *The Military Balance, 2004–2005*, p. 170.

15 Details of the 152-mm and 155-mm guns are derived from the Chinese Defence Today website at http://www.sinodefence.com/army/artillery/tubeartillery/towed_152a.asp and http://www.sinodefence.com/army/artillery/tubeartillery/towed_155.asp (accessed 8 April 2005).

16 "On Vehicle Formations in Military Parade," in FBIS Beijing, *Zhongguo Xinwen She*, in Chinese, 1 October 1999.

17 Walter L. Williams and Michael D. Holthus, "Krasnopol: A Laser-Guided Projectile," *Field Artillery*, September–October 2002, p. 30–33 at http://sill-www.army.mil/FAMAG/Go_to_War_Primer/kransnopol.pdf (accessed 8 April 2005).

18 *The Military Balance, 2004–2005*, p. 170.

19 Christopher Foss, "China gets Smerch MRS technology," *Jane's Defence Weekly*, 29 March 2000, and Chinese Defence Today website, A-100 webpage at http://www.sinodefence.com/army/artillery/mlrs/a100.asp (accessed 8 April 2005).

20 Chinese Defence Today website, WS-1B webpage at http://www.sinodefence.com/army/artillery/mlrs/ws1b.asp (accessed 8 April 2005).
21 "PRC Magazine Compares B611 to Russian 'Tochka,' Sees Possibility of Ship-Launch," in FBIS Zhengzhou, *Jiandai Wuqi*, in Chinese, 1 December 2004, pp. 34–37, and China National Space Administration webpage, 2 November 2004, at http://www.cnsa.gov.cn/english/news_release/show.asp?id=112 (accessed 8 April 2005).
22 Unit identifications from "On Vehicle Formations in Military Parade," in FBIS Beijing, *Zhongguo Xinwen She*, in Chinese, 1 October 1999.
23 *The Military Balance, 2004–2005*, p. 170.
24 Chinese Defence Today website, HJ-9 webpage at http://www.sinodefence.com/army/artillery/antitank/hj9.asp (accessed 8 April 2005).
25 Unit identifications from "On Vehicle Formations in Military Parade," in FBIS Beijing, *Zhongguo Xinwen She*, in Chinese, 1 October 1999.
26 *The Military Balance, 2004–2005*, p. 170.
27 Chinese Defence Today website, Type 90 Twin 35-mm Anti-aircraft Artillery webpage at http://www.sinodefence.com/army/artillery/aaa/35.asp (accessed 8 April 2005).
28 "Article Features Anti-Aircraft Wheeled Vehicle CQW-2," in FBIS Beijing, *Bingqi Zhishi*, in Chinese, 5 May 2004.
29 *The Military Balance, 2004–2005*, p. 170, and Luke Colton, "Airborne Iron Fist," *Flight International*, 4–10 November, 2003, p. 43. Colton is a leading figure in the study of the PLA helicopter force. Over the years, *The Military Balance* numbers have changed to better reflect Colton's estimates.
30 "New gunship successful in first flight in E. China province," *People's Daily* online, 30 December 2004.
31 "PRC Magazine Publishes Roundup on UAVs at Zhuhai Air Show – PHOTOS," in FBIS Beijing *Junshi Shijie Huakan*, in Chinese, 1 January 2003 pp. 12–13; "PRC S&T: Changhong, China's High-Altitude, High-Speed UAV," in FBIS Beijing, *Guoji Hangkong*, in Chinese, 1 September 2003, pp. 50–51; and Roxana Tiron, "China Is Pursuing Unmanned Tactical Aircraft," in *National Defense*, May 2004 at http://www.nationaldefensemagazine.org/article.cfm?Id=1425 (accessed 17 August 2004).
32 Gavin Rabinowitz, "Israeli Official: U.S. demands Israel confiscate Chinese-owned drones," Associated Press (AP), 22 December 2004; Peter Enav, "China Official Slams U.S. on Weapons Deal," AP, 30 December 2004; Sinodefence.com, "*Harpy* Ground Attack Unmanned Aerial Vehicle," at http://www.sinodefence.com/airforce/uav/harpy.asp (accessed 8 April 2005).
33 "PRC S&T: China's Mini-UAVs – Soldiers' Flying Eyes," in FBIS Beijing, *Junshi Shijie Huakan*, in Chinese, 1 July 2003, pp. 26–27, and Roxana Tiron, "China Is Pursuing Unmanned Tactical Aircraft."
34 "PLA Reconnaissance Battalion Conducts Military Exercises," in FBIS Beijing, *Jiefangjun Bao* (Internet version-WWW), in Chinese, 10 May 2000, p. 2; *Renmin Jundui* (Lanzhou Military Region newspaper), 8 May 2001. The reconnaissance battalion was reported to have a subordinate "Instrument (apparatus) Reconnaissance Company," which operated the UAVs and battlefield ground surveillance radars, and an "Armed Reconnaissance Company," which also performed infiltration and "sabotage" operations behind enemy lines.
35 "PRC Unmanned Aerial Vehicles Described," in FBIS Beijing, *Bingqi Zhishi* in Chinese, 4 June 2000, pp. 14–16; "PRC Magazine Publishes Roundup on UAVs at Zhuhai Air Show – PHOTOS"; Roxana Tiron, "China Is Pursuing Unmanned Tactical Aircraft." Technical details for China's UAVs can be found on a number of Internet websites.
36 The Type 87 5.8-mm assault rifle and machine-gun were developed before the Type 95 series, but were not distributed in large numbers to the PLA. Technology from the unsuccessful Type 87 was used to develop the Type 95. See Chinese Defence Today

website, Type 87 5.8-mm assault rifle webpage, at http://www.sinodefence.com/army/individual/rifle_87.asp (accessed 8 April 2005).

37 Chinese Defence Today website, Type 87 35-mm Grenade Launcher webpage, at http://www.sinodefence.com/army/crewserved/mg_35.asp (accessed 8 April 2005).

38 Chinese Defence Today website, QJY-88 5.8-mm Heavy Machine-gun webpage, at http://www.sinodefence.com/army/crewserved/mg_58.asp (accessed 8 April 2005).

39 Christopher Foss, "China markets Type W99 mortar," *Jane's Defence Weekly*, 11 April 2001, p. 13.

40 Chinese Defence Today website, YW-381, 120-mm Self-Propelled Motar-Howitzer [*sic*] webpage, at http://www.sinodefence.com/army/artillery/tubeartillery/mor_120a.asp (accessed 8 April 2005).

41 *The Military Balance, 2004–2005*, p. 170.

42 "PRC Military Magazine Publishes Pictorial of Airborne Vehicles in Jan Exercise – MULTIMEDIA," in FBIS Shanghai *Guoji Zhanwang*, in Chinese, 1 March 2004, pp. 36–41.

7 HOW DOES THE PLA TRAIN?

1 For a review of PLA training exercises in the early and mid-1990s, see Dennis J. Blasko, Philip T. Klapakis, and John Corbett, Jr., "Training Tomorrow's PLA – A Mixed Bag of Tricks," *The China Quarterly*, June 1996, pp. 488–524. For updates to this study describing exercises up to 2001, see David Shambaugh, *Modernizing China's Military*, Los Angeles; University of California Press, 2002, pp. 94–107, and Susan M. Puska, "Rough But Ready Force Projection: An Assessment of Recent PLA Training," in Andrew Scobell and Larry M. Wortzel (eds), *China's Growing Military Power: Perspectives on Security, Ballistic Missiles, and Conventional Capabilities*, Carlisle: Strategic Studies Institute, 2002, pp. 223–50. Determining the size of PLA exercises by reading the Chinese media is fraught with difficulties. Often the press describes exercises conducted by a group army or division, when in fact they are describing exercises conducted by *elements* of that unit and not the entire unit at one time and place. In other cases, multiple units may be in the field conducting exercises at the same time, but are not operating in coordination with each other under the command of a single headquarters in a truly joint manner. Chinese press reports provide varying amounts of detail and can be extraordinarily vague about important aspects of the exercises. At the same time they can contain much colorful, but irrelevant, content. It is also common to have the same exercise reported in multiple sources at different times, with some sources providing more detailed descriptions than others. The Chinese press sometimes picks up overseas reporting on PLA exercises and then repackages it in similar stories that contain information that otherwise would not be included in domestic articles. Needless to say, Chinese and Hong Kong press reports are important means for the Chinese leadership and Communist Party to send messages to various audiences, both domestic and international, in times of escalating crisis. The propaganda value of Chinese reports, therefore, must be acknowledged and considered in the process of analysis. While specifics may be sketchy, incomplete, and less than timely, it is nevertheless possible to understand general trends and important training topics by monitoring the Chinese press. See Chapter 9 for more qualifications about taking the Chinese media too literally and the limitations on the kind of judgments that can be made from these sources.

2 See "Newsletter Describes Mammoth Military Exercise, Jiang's Presence," in FBIS Beijing, *Xinhua* Hong Kong Service, in Chinese, 0801 GMT, 13 October 2000, which describes an October 2000 exercise as "the largest joint military exercise the Chinese armed forces would stage with the latest technology ever since the nation's extensive competition in military skills in 1964." This exercise took place in four widely separated

areas of China – the Yanshan Mountains, Bohai Sea, Inner Mongolia, and northeast China – and included "more than 10,000 troops from all services and arms of different military regions." This number of troops suggests that less than an entire army division participated in the exercise.

3 The size of the PLA exercises in the fall of 1995 and spring of 1996 was exaggerated in many contemporaneous foreign reports. While the exercises included participation by all services of the PLA, the number of troops involved in amphibious operations would best be described as small-scale, perhaps no more than regimental size for the actual landing operations. See Blasko, Klapakis, and Corbett, "Training Tomorrow's PLA – A Mixed Bag of Tricks," pp. 519–24, for a description of the exercises based on analysis of Chinese television coverage.

4 Responsibilities for training at various command levels is derived from "Article on Handling Four Major Relationships in Implementing New PLA Military Training Program," in FBIS Beijing, *Jiefangjun Bao* (Internet version-WWW), in Chinese, 4 June 2002, p. 6.

5 "Article on Handling Four Major Relationships In Implementing New PLA Military Training Program."

6 For one example, see "Putting scientific research results to test in close-to-real-combat exercise," *PLA Daily* online, 14 October 2004.

7 "Article on Handling Four Major Relationships In Implementing New PLA Military Training Program," describes evaluation system.

8 "Lanzhou Military Region Air Defense Units Conduct 3-month Live-fire Exercises," in FBIS Beijing, *Jiefangjun Bao* (Internet version-WWW), in Chinese, 19 September 2002, p. 2.

9 The *PLA Daily* online website at http://english.chinamil.com.cn/ (accessed 8 April 2005) has a "Military Training" page that caches several months of English language articles concerning all aspects of PLA training. It is an excellent quick reference to view reports of routine training activity in the force. Many articles on training can be found on the Chinese language *Jiefangjun Bao* website at http://www.chinamil.com.cn/ (accessed 8 April 2005) or the *Xinhua* webpage compiling Chinese military stories at http://www.xinhuanet.com/mil/zg-l.htm (accessed 8 April 2005).

10 The *new* "three attacks [or strikes], three defenses" replaced the *traditional* "three attacks, three defenses," which were defined as "striking at tanks, aircraft, and airborne landings and defending against atomic, chemical, and biological weapons," around the year 2000. See "Drill Said to Show Further Improvement in PLA's Ability to Win Future War," in FBIS Beijing, *Xinhua* Hong Kong Service, in Chinese, 0832 GMT 16 October 2000. The threats included in the traditional "three attacks, three defenses" represented a land invasion of China, most likely from the former Soviet Union.

11 "PRC Deputy Chief of General Staff Stresses Improved Qualities of Reserve Units," in FBIS Beijing, *Guofang*, in Chinese, 15 March 2003, pp. 4–7, and "Defense Paper on New Missions of Urban Militia in Future High-tech Operations," in FBIS Beijing, *Zhongguo Guofang Bao* (Internet version-WWW), in Chinese, 13 January 2003, p. 3.

12 "Article Urges Relaunch of Training in Defense Against Atomic, Chemical, Air Raids," in FBIS Beijing, *Jiefangjun Bao* (Internet version-WWW), in Chinese, 18 June 2002, p. 6.

13 The official position of the Chinese government is that China does not possess chemical or biological weapons and supports the complete destruction of chemical and biological weapons.

14 Identification of Military Region combined arms training centers is found in *Directory of PRC Military Personalities, October 2004.*

15 For example, see "PRC Magazine Profiles Real Troop Confrontation Drills, Interviews Base Commander," in FBIS Beijing, *Junshi Wenzhai*, in Chinese, 5 September 2004, pp. 8–11, and "PLA Weapons, Tactics on Display in Exercise 'Iron Fist-2004,'" in FBIS

Beijing, *Zhongguo Qingnian Bao* (Internet version-WWW), in Chinese, 26 September 2004.

16 "PRC Magazine Profiles Real Troop Confrontation Drills, Interviews Base Commander."

17 See for example, "Article on Pushing Integrated Military Training," in FBIS Beijing, *Jiefangjun Bao* (Internet version-WWW), 14 September 2004, and "Conference on PLA general armaments construction convenes in Beijing," *PLA Daily* online, 30 August 2004.

18 Blasko, Klapakis and Corbett, "Training Tomorrow's PLA – A Mixed Bag of Tricks," p. 496.

19 *Jiefangjun Bao*, 12 April 2000.

20 These force structure and training developments are discussed in Dennis J. Blasko, "People's Liberation Army Ground Forces: Moving into the 21st Century," in *Chinese Military Update*, Volume 1, Number 2, Royal United Services Institute for Defence and Security Studies, July 2003, and "PLA Ground Forces: Moving Toward a Smaller, More Rapidly Deployable, Modern Combined Arms Force," in James C. Mulvenon and Andrew N.D. Yang (eds), *The People's Liberation Army as Organization Reference Volume v1.0*, Santa Monica: RAND, 2002.

21 "PLA to simulate landings, attacks," *Xinhua*, 6 August 2002.

22 "PLA to conduct maneuver at Dongshan Is. this month," *People's Daily* online, 8 July 2004, and "China's Dongshan Island Military Exercises to Aim at Air Superiority Over Taiwan," in FBIS Beijing, *Renmin Wang*, (Internet version-WWW), in Chinese, 3 July 2004. The *People's Daily* online article is in English, but is shorter and contains less detail than is found in the earlier Chinese version of the report translated by FBIS. Additional information is found in "PLA to hold drill in Fujian: report," *PLA Daily* online, 13 July 2004, and "Three purposes of military maneuver at Dongshan Island," *People's Daily* online, 19 July 2004.

23 "China's Dongshan Island Military Exercises to Aim at Air Superiority Over Taiwan."

24 *Zhanshi Bao* (Guangzhou Military Region newspaper), 18 October 2001.

25 Material set off by quotation marks in these three bullets is from "China's Dongshan Island Military Exercises to Aim at Air Superiority Over Taiwan."

26 "Three purposes of military maneuver at Dongshan Island."

27 "China's Dongshan Island Military Exercises to Aim at Air Superiority Over Taiwan."

28 The author reviewed hundreds of articles and excerpts of articles from the Chinese media to compile the information for the years 2001 to 2004. Most articles do not contain complete identification of units involved in training exercises and some articles may duplicate or expand on information contained in other reports. Some exercises are likely to go unreported. Therefore, this list is only an approximation of the actual level of amphibious training conducted.

29 Lyle Goldstein and William Murray, "China Emerges as a Maritime Power," *Jane's Intelligence Review*, October 2004. The number of amphibious ships in this article strongly suggests that the US Department of Defense's estimate in its 2000 "Annual Report on the Military Power of the People's Republic of China" that the "PLAN's amphibious fleet [with nearly 50 amphibious landing ships] provides sealift to transport approximately one infantry division [10,000–12,000 men and equipment]" is no longer accurate. Subsequent DOD reports through 2004 did not change that estimate. Thom Shanker and David E. Sanger, "U.S. Lawmakers Warn Europe on Arms Sales to China," *New York Times*, 2 March 2005, reports construction of "23 new amphibious assault ships that could ferry tanks, armored vehicles and troops" since 2001; this report did not, however, give the total number of amphibious ships before the building spree began, nor did it give the total size of the force in 2005. The 23 new amphibious assault ships most likely includes ships and craft of all sizes, only some of which are the larger LSTs and LSMs mentioned by Goldstein and Murray.

31 For a few examples, see "Tibet holds anti-terrorist maneuvers," *People's Daily*, 13 September 2004; "Drill tests Sino-Pakistani forces," *China Daily/Xinhua*, 7 August 2004; "Coalition-2003: a successful joint anti-terrorism maneuver," *PLA Daily* online, 14 August 2003.

32 *Ningxia Daily*, 13 August 2004.

33 "PRC Special Operations Forces Conduct Infiltration Training," in FBIS Beijing, *Jiefangjun Bao* (Internet version-WWW), in Chinese, 9 June 2002, p. 1, and "Jiefangjun Bao Report on Nanjing MR Special Forces' Airborne Drill," in FBIS Beijing, *Jiefangjun Bao* (Internet version-WWW), in Chinese, 3 June 2002, p. 2.

34 For example, see "An Eagle of Tianshan Mountain," *PLA Daily* online, 15 July 2004.

35 Estonian Military Sporting Society, International Long-Range Reconnaissance Patrol Competition "ERNA Raid 2003", Republic of Estonia, found at http://www.teres.fi/erna/2003/ohjeet/Invitation_to_Erna-2003.pdf (accessed 8 April 2005).

36 Tension between conventional officers and special forces officers is not uncommon in other militaries. The "special" status and independence granted to SOF units can be a cause of friction, especially when resources are limited.

37 Many reports and photos document the expanded roles of the helicopter force; see, for example, "Shenyang Helicopter Regiment Trains to Perform Various Operational Missions," in FBIS Beijing, *Jiefangjun Bao* (Internet version-WWW), in Chinese, 16 September 2002, p. 1. In the summer of 2002, the Chinese media had a series of articles on the commander of the 38th Group Army helicopter regiment, Sun Fengyang, praising his leadership and the unit's capabilities.

38 See Dennis J. Blasko, "Chinese Airborne Forces: Changing Times, Changing Missions," in *Chinese Military Update*, Volume 2, Number 1, Royal United Services Institute for Defence and Security Studies, June 2004.

39 Blasko, Klapakis, and Corbett, "Training Tomorrow's PLA – A Mixed Bag of Tricks," p. 517, footnote 33.

40 *Jiefangjun Bao*, 27 March 2001.

41 "An airborne unit succeeds in air dropping drill," *PLA Daily* online, 25 November 2003.

42 "Assault maneuver with live ammunition and heavy equipment successfully held by airborne unit," *PLA Daily* online, 14 July 2004.

43 "PLA Airborne Heavy Equipment Forms Combat Capability," in FBIS Beijing, *Jiefangjun Bao* (Internet version-WWW), in Chinese, 14 July 2004, p. 1.

44 "Heavy Equipment Drop Made 'Breakthrough,'" in FBIS Beijing, *Kongjun Bao*, in Chinese, 20 July 2004, p. 1.

45 International Institute for Strategic Studies, *The Military Balance, 2004–2005*, London: Oxford University Press, 2004, p. 172. The Tu-154M aircraft in the PLAAF would not likely be used for parachute operations. Likewise, Chinese civilian aircraft impressed for military service would seem to be unlikely candidates for airborne operations because of the special rigging and equipment necessary for airdrop. Civilian aircraft would more likely be used in second and third waves for airlanding operations once an airfield had been secured.

46 "China Looking Into Procuring Large Batch of IL-76s, IL-78s," in FBIS Moscow, *Agentstvo Voyennykh Novostey*, WWW-text, in English, 1454 GMT, 6 January 2004.

47 Calculations found in Blasko, "Chinese Airborne Forces: Changing Times, Changing Missions."

48 "Georgy Shpak Supports Sharing Experience Between Russian, Chinese Paratroopers," in FBIS Moscow, *ITAR-TASS*, 8 December 2000.

49 As a US Army attaché in Beijing I had the opportunity to observe and escort numerous senior military officers to PLA small-scale military demonstrations. I did not, however, observe large-scale or unscripted training events, such as those which were opened to

foreigners starting in 2003. Shpak's comments on individual training were echoed by many foreign officers who saw other PLA units up close.

50 A very few examples include "Honing tenacious fighting spirit in inclement weather," *PLA Daily* online, 25 February 2005; "No frostbite occurs in a 12-day-long camp and field training," *PLA Daily* online, 31 January 2005; "Busy in midwinter training," *PLA Daily* online, 28 January 2005; "Training in snow," *PLA Daily* online, 15 December 2004; "Building up will-power of troops under harsh weather conditions," *PLA Daily* online, 16 November 2004; "Division in Xinjiang tempers troops in Karakorum and Kunlun Mountains," *PLA Daily* online, 9 August 2004.

51 For example, see "A drivers' training center built for frontier units in Xinjiang," *PLA Daily* online, 18 February 2005.

52 For example, see "China's military pledges strong backing in opposing 'Taiwan independence,'" in *People's Daily* online, 7 March 2005.

53 "Doctor is provided for every new recruit company in Fujian Provincial Military Command," *PLA Daily* online, 4 February 2004; "Brigade provides psychological consultants for new soldiers," *PLA Daily* online, 10 December 2003; and "Psychological test software used on a trial basis in recruitment," *PLA Daily* online, 10 November 2003.

54 "Ideological and political work at training ground boosts troops' morale," *People's Daily* online, 29 January 2004; "Turning study enthusiasm into driving force in military training," *People's Daily* online, 19 January 2004.

55 "PRC: Military Transformation With Chinese Characteristics Underway," in FBIS Beijing, *Zhongguo Qingnian Bao* (Internet version-WWW), in Chinese, 11 April 2004.

56 "Jiefangjun Bao: How Jiang Zemin Has Developed Deng Xiaoping's Military Thought," in FBIS Beijing, *Jiefangjun Bao* (Internet version-WWW), in Chinese, 26 August 2004, p. 6.

57 "PRC: Li Jinai Stresses Importance of Informatization in Weaponry Support," in FBIS Beijing, *Xinhua* Domestic Service, in Chinese, 1218 GMT, 29 August 2004.

58 "Legal guarantee for standardizing national defense mobilization of civil transportation," *PLA Daily* online, 10 October 2003, and "New law allows military to commandeer civilian vehicles," *PLA Daily* online, 10 October 2003.

59 "Legal Framework of Anti-Secession Law, Two Other Laws May Be Introduced by End of Year," in FBIS Hong Kong, *Ta Kung Pao* (Internet version-WWW), in Chinese, 2 March 2005.

60 "Group army enhances field support efficiency in frigid mountainous area," *PLA Daily* online, 14 August 2003; "Unit of Beijing MAC reforms its logistics service," *PLA Daily* online, 3 November 2003.

61 "Explore new way of intensive logistics support," *PLA Daily* online, 25 November 2004; "Caring about soldiers' 'everyday food,'" *PLA Daily* online, 31 October 2003; "Chinese Armed Forces Improve Food, Housing, Clothing, and Transportation," in FBIS Beijing, *Xinhua* Domestic Service, in Chinese, 0246 GMT, 24 July 2002.

62 "New logistics support items for plateau troops (III)," *PLA Daily* online, 17 September 2004; "'Convenient dishes' enter field camping site," *PLA Daily* online, 17 September 2004; and "Self-heating field ration for frontier patrol troops developed," *PLA Daily* online, 13 September 2004.

63 "New Field POL equipment developed by POL Research Institute of PLA General Logistics Department," *PLA Daily* online, 22 September 2004; "Airdrop exercise of fuel supply launched in Xinjiang MAC," *PLA Daily* online, 25 September 2003.

64 For example, "All-in-one joint logistics support system set in motion in Jinan MAC," *PLA Daily* online, 2 July 2004.

65 "New logistics support items for plateau troops (II)," *PLA Daily* online, 16 September 2004, and "An airborne unit succeeds in air dropping drill," *PLA Daily* online, 25 November 2003.

66 "All-in-one joint logistics support system set in motion in Jinan MAC," *PLA Daily*

online, 2 July 2004, and "PLA Logistics Make Outstanding Progress," in FBIS Beijing, *Jiefangjun Bao*, (Internet version-WWW), in English, 30 December 2003.

67 "'Significant Improvements' Made in PLA Armament," in FBIS Beijing, *Jiefangjun Bao* WWW-text, in English, 31 December 2003; "A group army: armament support capacity improved in coordinated exercise," *PLA Daily* online, 2 July 2003; "JFJB Commentator on Studying, Implementing PLA Rules on Armament Repair Work," in FBIS Beijing, *Jiefangjun Bao* (Internet version-WWW), in Chinese, 26 June 2002, p. 1.

68 "JFJB Article Discusses Need To Train Specialists To Operate Modern Weaponry," in FBIS Beijing, *Jiefangjun Bao* (Internet version-WWW), in Chinese, 10 May 2002, p. 2.

69 "Let specialized elements undergo intensive and rigid training," *PLA Daily* online, 19 August 2004.

70 "PRC: Over 1,000 Reserve Troops Leave Fuyang, Anhui for Sea Training Off Zhejiang," in FBIS Hefei, *Anhui Ribao* (Internet version-WWW), in Chinese, 6 July 2004; "First float bridge over Huaihe River by Bengbu militia and reserve forces," *PLA Daily* online, 25 May 2004.

71 The integration of militia units into PLA rear area defense planning can be found in *Houqin Jijuan Changyong Wenshu Xiezuo Shili* (*Examples of Writing Common Documents for Logistic Organs*), Yellow River Publishing House, 2001, p. 279.

72 "Beijing MR Holds First Drill With Reservists Joining Active Servicemen," in FBIS Beijing, *Xinhua* Domestic Service, in Chinese, 0611 GMT, 2 September 2002.

73 "China shows military muscle in weekend drill," *People's Daily* online, 27 July 2004.

74 The PLA has allowed foreigners to observe small, scripted training demonstrations at its "showcase" units for many decades. While better than no access at all, such demonstrations had limited utility in evaluating actual PLA capabilities. Though most demonstrations were put on by units "open to foreigners," other units could sometimes be seen by observers from countries which enjoyed particularly good relations with China. Even with the opening of larger exercises to foreign observers in 2003, access still depends to some degree on the state of political relations between the Chinese government and the governments of other countries.

75 A listing of PLA multilateral exercises is found in "China launches military exercise," *Xinhua*, 25 September 2004, and updated in the *China's National Defense in 2004*, Appendix V, and in Beijing, *Zhongguo Guofang Bao* (Internet version-WWW), in Chinese, 28 December 2004.

76 In a small irony, the 2004 Chinese Defense White Paper mistakenly gives the date of this exercise as October 2003. In fact, Northern Sword 0308, as its name implies, was well reported as it occurred in August of that year. See "Foreign Military Personnel Watch PRC Military Exercise in Inner Mongolia," in FBIS Beijing, *Xinhua* Domestic Service, in Chinese, 1359 GMT, 25 August 2003.

77 See the *Xinhua* website for a summary of articles and photographs of this exercise at http://news.xinhuanet.com/mil/2004-09/25/content_2016094.htm (accessed 8 April 2005).

78 "ARF Delegation Views Chinese Special Forces Anti-Kidnapping/Anti-Hi-jacking Exercise," *Xinhua* online, 7 November 2004, at http://news.xinhuanet.com/mil/2004-11/07/content_2186478.htm (accessed 8 April 2005).

8 WHAT IS THE ROLE OF THE PLA IN CHINESE SOCIETY?

1 This chapter draws on my chapter, "Servant of Two Masters: The People's Liberation Army, the People, and the Party," in Nan Li (ed.), *Chinese Civil–Military Relations: The Transformation of the People's Liberation Army*, Routledge: forthcoming.

2 "RMRB Commentator on Promoting Military–Civilian Unity," in FBIS Beijing, *Renmin Ribao* (Internet version-WWW), in Chinese, 10 January 2004, p. 6. The 2004 White

Paper on National Defense includes an entire chapter on "The Armed Forces and the People."

3 "RMRB Commentator on Promoting Military–Civilian Unity."

4 "PRC Municipality Gives More Demobilized Soldiers Cash Instead of Jobs," in FBIS, *Hubei Ribao*, in Chinese, 0000 GMT, 2 March 2005.

5 The PLA often publishes (or displays at exhibits) statistics of the number of man-days and vehicles dedicated to construction tasks. Unfortunately, the vast majority of such statistics are vague and unverifiable. Without vouching for the accuracy of any specific statistic, one can say that the PLA is actively involved in projects that support economic construction, but the exact percentage of the force applied to these efforts is uncertain. For example, in 2001 General Fu Quanyou told a militia work conference that an average of nearly six million militia personnel "have been mobilized each year to participate in the construction of key projects and to carry out urgent, difficult, dangerous, and heavy tasks." See, "China: CMC's Fu Quanyou Addresses National Urban Militia Work Conference in Wuhan," in FBIS Wuhan, *Hubei Ribao*, in Chinese, 15 December 2001, A1, A2.

6 *China's National Defense in 2004*, "The Armed Forces and the People." It is interesting to note that this directive applies to PLA units, not necessarily members of headquarters staffs, schools, or non-operational components of the PLA. Nevertheless, these other organizations also support civil projects.

7 See "Military traffic and transport construction gains great achievements," *PLA Daily* online, 12 October 2004, which states: "A military–civil joint military traffic and transportation system is basically in place. Traffic and transportation enterprises and military supply systems at all levels have set up leading bodies for military traffic and transportation. In combination with the features of each industry and the reality of their work, all units have succeeded in identifying many new ways and measures to ensure the effective performance of military traffic and transportation."

8 "100 military hospitals achieve notable success in aiding western region hospitals," *PLA Daily* online, 11 August 2004.

9 *China's National Defense in 2004*, "The Armed Forces and the People."

10 Joseph Fewsmith, "China's Response to SARS," Summer 2003; Thomas Christensen, "PRC Foreign Relations after the National People's Congress: Iraq, North Korea, SARS, and Taiwan," Summer 2003; and James Mulvenon, "The Crucible of Tragedy: SARS, the Ming 361 Accident, and Chinese Party–Army Relations," Fall 2003. These articles are found in the Hoover Institution's "China Leadership Monitor" available on the Internet at http://www.chinaleadershipmonitor.org/pastissues.html (accessed 4 April 2005).

11 *China's National Defense in 2004*, "The Armed Forces and the People."

12 Through the process of defense conversion, which began in the 1980s, many military-use airfields, ports, real estate properties, and other facilities were turned over to local governments or otherwise converted to commercial or dual use (by both military and civilian units). The *civilian-managed* defense industries (which are *not* under PLA control) also have participated in this process by transferring facilities and technologies to civilian production. As part of the defense conversion bargain, military assets and technologies were "spun off" to civilian entities in order to promote economic construction. Additionally, many, but not all, civilian assets and technologies have been "spun on" to the military and defense industries in order to help in their modernization efforts.

13 "Chinese military forces to build 280 sewage plants this year," *PLA Daily* online, 15 July 2004, and "PLA makes headway in ecological protection," *PLA Daily* online, 13 October 2004.

14 "Highlights: Chinese PLA Leaders' Activities, PLA Regulations, Military Media," China–FBIS Report, in Chinese, 1 October 2004, "Jiang Zemin Signs Decree To Promulgate Newly Amended PLA Regulations on Environmental Protection."

15 Thanks to Susan M. Puska for this observation.

16 "PLA makes headway in ecological protection," *PLA Daily* online, 13 October 2004.

17 "PRC: Zhang Lichang Attends Tianjin Militia Meeting on 'Eight-Task' Program," in FBIS Tianjin, *Tianjin Ribao* (Internet version-WWW), in Chinese, 6 November 2003.

18 *China's National Defense in 2000*, "Armed Forces Building."

19 *China's National Defense in 2004*, "The Armed Forces and the People."

20 "PRC: Army Sets Up Special Flood-Fighting Units," in FBIS Beijing, *Xinhua*, in English, 1349 GMT, 11 June 2002.

21 "All-Army Conference on Building Flood-Fighting Units Held in Hubei, 14–16 May," in FBIS Wuhan, *Hubei Ribao* (Internet version-WWW), in Chinese, 17 May 2002.

22 *China's National Defense in 2004*, "The Armed Forces and the People."

23 "Rescue, Disaster Relief Included in Military Training," *Xinhuanet* online, 13 March 2002.

24 "The first simulated training ground for flood fighting built in Shenyang MAC," in *PLA Daily* online, 13 July 2004.

25 "Field support integration explored for flood fighting and rescue," *PLA Daily* online, 17 September 2004.

26 For example, see Larry Wortzel, "Beijing struggles to 'ride the tiger of liberalization,'" *Jane's Intelligence Review*, January 2001, p. 30.

27 US Department of State, "Country Reports on Human Rights Practices – 2004," Released by the Bureau of Democracy, Human Rights, and Labor, 28 February 2005, found at http://www.state.gov/g/drl/rls/hrrpt/2004/41640.htm (accessed 4 April 2005). This exact language was found in previous years' reports. In 2004, the sentence "Civilian authorities generally maintained effective control of the security forces" was added. This addition supports the conclusion that the *civilian leadership*, not the military, is responsible for domestic security.

28 US Department of State, "Country Reports on Human Rights Practices," found at http://www.state.gov/g/drl/rls/hrrpt/ (accessed 5 April 2005). Reports on China available on the Internet prepared by Human Rights Watch for 2000, 2001, 2002, and 2003 and Amnesty International for 2002, 2003, and 2004 also make *no mention* of PLA involvement in domestic security operations.

29 For foreign and Chinese observers who are not familiar with the differences between the PLA and PAP, it is understandable to confuse the two organizations. However, trained observers can quickly and easily distinguish between the uniforms and insignia worn by the two separate and distinct forces.

30 "China to enhance anti-riot police force," *People's Daily* online, 27 January 2001, which reports that the Ministry of Public Security ordered China's key cities "anti-riot squads of no less than 300 members for municipalities or 200 for capital of provinces."

31 Philip P. Pan, "China detains Buddhist leader, Americans ejected from temple site," *Washington Post* online, 19 August 2004.

32 Philip P. Pan, "Farmers' Rising anger erupts in China village: land seizures, stagnation fuel unrest," *Washington Post* online, 7 August 2004. A more recent article about incidents in the mid-1990s, Joseph Kahn, "China crushes peasant protest, turning 3 friends into enemies," *New York Times* online, 13 October 13, 2004, also mentions only the use of police to control riots, and *not* the PLA.

33 See John Pomfret, "Chinese miners battle police, soldiers in three-day riot over job cuts," *Washington Post*, 6 April 2000. This incident is cited in Larry Wortzel, "Beijing struggles to 'ride the tiger of liberalization,'" and "Challenges as China's Communist Leaders Ride the Tiger of Liberalization," Heritage Lecture no. 669, 13 June 2000, found at http://www.heritage.org/Research/AsiaandthePacific/pgfld-1043653 (accessed 15 June 2003), and Arthur Waldron, "The Rumblings of an Avalanche Threaten China," *International Herald Tribune*, 7 April 2000.

34 See *Directory of PRC Military Personalities*, August 1997, p. 222, and *Directory of*

PRC Military Personalities, October 1999, p. 66, for before and after identification of the PLA unit transformed to the PAP.

35 "Monthly Summary of Contributions," 28 February 2005, webpage at http://www.un.org/Depts/dpko/dpko/contributors/2005/February2005_1.pdf (accessed 5 April 2005), and "UN Mission's Summary detailed by Country," at http://www.un.org/Depts/dpko/dpko/contributors/2005/February2005_3.pdf (accessed 5 April 2005). National contributions and rankings are updated monthly on the UN website.

36 "Ranking of Military and Civilian Police Contributions to UN Operations," 28 February 2005, at http://www.un.org/Depts/dpko/dpko/contributors/2005/February2005_2.pdf (accessed 5 April 2005).

37 *China's National Defense in 2002*, "International Security Cooperation."

38 "Chinese blue berets ready for UN peace-keeping mission," *People's Daily* online, 25 January 2003.

39 "Logistics support for peacekeeping force published," *PLA Daily* online, 24 November 2004.

40 "UN Mission's Summary detailed by Country," 28 February 2005.

41 "Five capabilities of Chinese peacekeepers," *PLA Daily* online, undated, found at http://english.pladaily.com.cn/special/e-peace/txt/26.htm (accessed 5 April 2005), and "Chinese peacekeeping troops ready to set for the DRC," at http://english.pladaily.com.cn/special/e-peace/txt/17.htm (accessed 5 April 2005).

42 "Peacekeeping force to the D. R. Congo finishes 2nd shift," *Xinhuanet* online, 22 August 2004.

43 "UN awards peace medals to Chinese peacekeeping troops in Liberia," *PLA Daily* online, 15 September 2004.

44 "Reserve force servicemen go to Africa on peace-keeping mission," in *PLA Daily* online, 1 March 2004.

45 "China to send anti-riot peacekeepers for Haiti," *People's Daily* online, 5 June 2004; "Chinese peacekeepers prepare for Haiti mission," *China Daily* online, 7 June 2004; "Elite police prepare for Haiti tour," *Shanghai Daily* online, 4 September 2004; and "Chinese peacekeeping force leaving for Haiti," *People's Daily* online, 18 September 2004.

46 Imprecise or inaccurate reporting about this deployment was made by the *Washington Times* (Bill Gertz, "China will send troops to Haiti, U.S. expects political pressure," 6 September 2004), AP (George Gedda, "Chinese police expected to join U.N. force in Haiti," 27 September 2004), and the *Washington Post* (Edward Cody, "China readies riot force for peacekeeping in Haiti," 30 September 2004), and then picked up and repeated by other sources, including the *Chinese* media.

47 "China to build Asia's largest UN police training center," *Xinhuanet* online, 20 August 2002.

48 At the time of writing, despite much debate, the European Union has not lifted Tiananmen sanctions, while the United States remains steadfast in its opposition to any relaxation of sanctions on arms sales to the PLA.

9 CONCLUSIONS AND THE GHOSTS OF TIANANMEN

1 There are many examples of the PLA senior leadership's recognition of the long-term nature of transformation and reform. For example, in 2003 CMC members Guo Boxiong and Xu Caihou said "the PLA is capable of achieving modernization in armament in 20 years." See "PRC Journal Says Jiang Zemin to Push for 'Chinese-Style' Military Reform," in FBIS Beijing, *Zhongguo Xinwen Zhoukan*, in Chinese, 17 March 2003, p. 17. In that same article, a PLA armament expert stated, "the toughest task in the future would be leading the reconstruction of the army's internal structure and command system."

2 *China's National Defense in 2004*, "Revolution in Military Affairs with Chinese Characteristics." This personnel quality improvement plan was outlined by Jiang Zemin in June 2003; see "Talents: key to army building," *PLA Daily* online, 6 June 2003.

3 The elevation of the Taiwan scenario in prominence and priority in development to naval, air, and missile forces was noted by many foreign analysts prior to 1999. Good examples can be found in Hans Binnendijk and Ronald N. Montaperto (eds), *Strategic Trends in China*, Washington, D.C.: National Defense University Press, 1998; Mark A. Stokes, *China's Strategic Modernization: Implications for U.S. National Security*, Carlisle: Strategic Studies Institute, 1999; and James C. Mulvenon and Richard H. Yang, (eds), *The People's Liberation Army in the Information Age*, Santa Monica: RAND, 1999.

4 *China's National Defense in 2004*, "National Defense Policy."

5 *China's National Defense in 2004*, "Revolution in Military Affairs with Chinese Characteristics."

6 See for example, "PRC Military Journal Examines Conventional Deterrence," in FBIS Beijing, *Zhongguo Junshi Kexue*, in Chinese, 30 September 2001, pp. 88–93. Allen S. Whiting, *The Chinese Calculus of Deterrence: India and Indochina*, Ann Arbor: University of Michigan Press, 1975, is a classic study and remains applicable in the twenty-first century.

7 These factors can be summarized by the abbreviation taught to junior officers and military cadets as METT-T (mission, enemy, terrain and weather, troops and support available, time available) for performing mission analysis. Implicit in this formulation is the will of both friendly and enemy troops to fight and resist.

8 US Department of Defense, "Annual Report on the Military Power of the People's Republic of China," July 2003, p. 49.

9 Numbers of tank units in 1997 comes from International Institute for Strategic Studies, *The Military Balance, 1996/97*, London: Oxford University Press, 1996, p. 179. Numbers of armored units in 2004 is compiled from Tables 4.1–4.7.

10 Number of mechanized units derived from the *Directory of PRC Military Personalities*, June 1998.

11 Conclusions about PLA capabilities certainly cannot be made based only on prototypes or models of new equipment developed by the Chinese defense industries and displayed at international arms exhibitions or published in journals.

12 *Zhanyou Bao* (Beijing Military Region newspaper), 3 October 2000.

13 In the summer and fall of 2003 there were several reports of the formation of a 16th Airborne Army to be added to the 15th Airborne Army. Most reports appeared to focus on parachute insertion capabilities like the 15th's. However, by doctrine airmobile operations are considered airborne operations and little discussion at the time was given to the formation of an airmobile unit. I know of no new information to indicate the establishment of an airmobile unit, but given its applicability to a Taiwan scenario creation of such a capability would be well within the range of possibilities for future PLA developments.

14 The debate over lifting the arms embargo was equally motivated by differences over whether the west should assist China's military modernization by allowing it increased access to technology and weapons.

15 See Andrew J. Nathan and Perry Link (eds), *The Tiananmen Papers*, New York: PublicAffairs, 2001. Compiler of *The Tiananmen Papers*, Zhang Liang (a pseudonym), states: "[R]eversal of the verdict on June Fourth is another historical inevitability, as well as the wish of most of the Chinese people. June Fourth weighs on the spirit of every Chinese patriot . . ." (p. xii).

16 Thanks to Susan M. Puska for insight into the opinion of some younger Chinese.

17 Jiang Yanyong's letter is available on several Internet websites. This quote was taken from http://www.chinasupport.net/topbuzz72.htm (accessed 1 April 2005).

18 Philip P. Pan, "Chinese pressure dissident physician, hero of SARS crisis detained since June 1," *Washington Post*, 5 July 2004.
19 Joseph Kahn, "China frees surgeon who exposed SARS coverup," *New York Times*, 20 July 2004.
20 "PRC Leaders Bid Farewell to Zhao Ziyang's Remains; His Mistakes, Contributions Noted," in FBIS Beijing, *Xinhua* Domestic Service, in Chinese, 0324 GMT, 29 January 2005.
21 The story of the watches presented to soldiers who participated in action in Beijing in 1989 is from my chapter, "Always Faithful: The PLA from 1949 to 1989," in David A. Graff and Robin Higham (eds), *A Military History of China*, Boulder: Westview Press, 2002, p. 265.

SELECT BIBLIOGRAPHY

Allen, K., Pollack, J., and Krumel, G., *China's Air Force Enters the 21st Century*, Santa Monica: RAND, 1995.

Allen, K. and McVadon, E., *China's Foreign Military Relations*, Washington, D.C.: The Henry L. Stimson Center, 1999.

Binnendijk, H. and Montaperto, R. (eds), *Strategic Trends in China*, Washington, D.C.: National Defense University Press, 1998.

Bullard, M., *China's Political–Military Evolution: The Party and the Military in the PRC, 1960–1984*, Boulder: Westview Press, 1985.

Bullard, M., *Strait Talk: Avoiding Nuclear War Between the US and China Over Taiwan*, Monterey: Monterey Institute of International Studies, 2004 (e-book), at http://cns.miis.edu/straittalk/01%20Opening%20page%20strait_talk.htm (accessed 4 April 2005).

Burkitt, L., Scobell, A., and Wortzel, L. (eds), *The Lessons of History: The Chinese People's Liberation Army at 75*, Carlisle, Pa.: Strategic Studies Institute, 2003.

China Quarterly, No. 146, Special Issue: *China's Military in Transition*, June 1996.

Cheung, T., *China's Entrepreneurial Army*, Oxford: Oxford University Press, 2001.

Cole, B., *The Great Wall at Sea: China's Navy Enters the Twenty-First Century*, Annapolis: United States Naval Institute, 2001.

Finkelstein, D., *China Reconsiders Its National Security: "The Great Peace and Development Debate of 1999,"* Alexandria: The CNA Corporation, 2000.

Finkelstein, D. and Unangst, J., *Engaging DoD: Chinese Perspectives on Miltary Relations with the United States*, Alexandria: The CNA Corporation, 1999.

Gill, B., "China and the Revolution in Military Affairs: Assessing Economic and Socio-Cultural Factors," in *China and the Revolution in Military Affairs*, Carlisle, Pa.: Strategic Studies Institute, 1996.

Gill, B. and Mulvenon, J., "The Chinese Strategic Rocket Forces: Transition to Credible Deterrence," Paper presented to the National Intelligence Council Conference, 5 November 1999.

Godwin, P. (ed.), *The Chinese Defense Establishment: Continuity and Change in the 1980s*, Boulder: Westview Press, 1983.

Godwin, P., *Development of the Chinese Armed Forces*, Maxwell: Air University Press, 1988.

Godwin, P., *China's Defense Modernization: Aspirations and Capabilities*, Alexandria: The CNA Corporation, 2001.

Graff, D. and Higham, R. (eds), *A Military History of China*, Boulder: Westview Press, 2002.

Gunness, K., *Swimming in a New Sea: Civil–Military Issues in Today's China*, Alexandria: The CNA Corporation, 2004.

Handel, M., *Sun Tzu & Clausewitz Compared*, Carlisle, Pa.: Strategic Studies Institute, 1991.

Henley, L., "China's Capacity for Achieving a Revolution in Military Affairs," in *China and the Revolution in Military Affairs*, Carlisle, Pa.: Strategic Studies Institute, 1996.

Jencks, H., *From Muskets to Missiles: Politics and Professionalism in the Chinese Army, 1945–1981*, Boulder: Westview Press, 1982.

Joffe, E., *Party and Army: Professionalism and Political Control in the Chinese Officer Corps, 1949–1964*, Harvard University: East Asian Research Center, 1965.

Joffe, E., *The Chinese Army After Mao*, Cambridge, Mass.: Harvard University Press, 1987.

Johnston, A., *Cultural Realism: Strategic Culture and Grand Strategy in Chinese History*, Princeton: Princeton University Press, 1995.

Ju, Y., *Understanding China: Center Stage of the Fourth Power*, Albany: State University of New York Press, 1996.

Lane, D., Weisenbloom, M., and Liu, D. (eds), *Chinese Military Modernization*, Washington, D.C.: American Enterprise Institute Press, 1996.

Lilley, J. and Downs, C. (eds), *Crisis in the Taiwan Strait*, Washington, D.C.: American Enterprise Institute and National Defense University Press, 1997.

Lilley, J. and Shambaugh, D. (eds), *China's Military Faces the Future*, Armonk: M.E. Sharpe, 1999.

Mulvenon, J., *Professionalization of the Senior Chinese Officer Corps: Trends and Implications*, Santa Monica: RAND, 1997.

Mulvenon, J., *Soldiers of Fortune: The Rise and Fall of the Chinese Military-Business Complex: 1978–1998*, Armonk: M.E. Sharp, 2000.

Mulvenon, J. and Yang, A. (eds), *Seeking Truth From Facts*, Santa Monica: RAND, 2001.

Mulvenon, J. and Yang, A. (eds), *The People's Liberation Army as Organization Reference Volume v1.0*, Santa Monica: RAND, 2002.

Mulvenon, J. and Yang, A. (eds), *A Poverty of Riches: New Challenges and Opportunities in PLA Research*, Santa Monica: RAND, 2003.

Mulvenon, J. and Yang, R. (eds), *The People's Liberation Army in the Information Age*, Santa Monica: RAND, 1999.

Nathan, A. and Link, P. (eds), *The Tiananmen Papers*, New York: PublicAffairs, 2001.

Nathan, A. and Ross, R., *The Great Wall and the Empty Fortress: China's Search for Security*, New York: W.W. Norton & Company, 1997.

Pillsbury, M. (ed.), *Chinese Views of Future Warfare*, Washington, D.C.: National Defense University Press, 1997.

Pillsbury, M., *CHINA Debates the Future Security Environment*, Washington, D.C.: National Defense University Press, 2000.

Puska, S. (ed.), *People's Liberation Army After Next*, Carlisle, Pa.: Strategic Studies Institute, 2000.

Romberg, A., *Rein In at the Brink of the Precipice: American Policy Toward Taiwan and U.S.–PRC Relations*, Washington, D.C.: Henry L. Stimson Center, 2003.

Ryan, M., Finkelstein, D., and McDevitt, M. (eds), *Chinese Warfighting: The PLA Experience Since 1949*, Armonk: M.E. Sharpe, 2003.

Scobell, A., *China and Strategic Culture*, Carlisle, Pa.: Strategic Studies Institute, 2002.

Scobell, A. (ed.), *The Costs of Conflict: The Impact on China of a Future War*, Carlisle, Pa.: Strategic Studies Institute. 2001.

Scobell, A. and Wortzel, L. (eds), *China's Growing Military Power: Perspectives on Security, Ballistic Missiles, and Conventional Capabilities*, Carlisle, Pa.: Strategic Studies Institute, 2002.

Scobell, A. and Wortzel, L. (eds), *Civil–Military Change in China: Elites, Institutes, and Ideas After the 16th Party Congress*, Carlisle, Pa.: Strategic Studies Institute, 2004.

Segal, G., *Defending China*, Oxford: Oxford University Press, 1985.

Shambaugh, D., *Modernizing China's Military*, Los Angeles: University of California Press, 2002.

Spence, J., *The Search for Modern China*, New York: W.W. Norton & Company, 1990.

Stokes, M., *China's Strategic Modernization: Implications for U.S. National Security*, Carlisle, Pa.: Strategic Studies Institute, 1999.

Suettinger, R., *Beyond Tiananmen: The Politics of U.S.–China Relations 1989–2000*, Washington, D.C.: Brookings Institution Press, 2003.

Sun Haichen, *The Wiles of War: 36 Military Strategies from Ancient China*, Beijing: Foreign Languages Press, 1993.

Sun Tzu, *The Art of War*, translated by Samuel B. Griffith, London: Oxford University Press, 1963.

Swaine, M., *The Military & Political Succession in China*, Santa Monica: RAND, 1992.

Swaine, M., *The Role of the Chinese Military in National Security Policymaking*, Santa Monica: RAND, 1998.

Wang Honqing and Zhang Xingye (eds), *On Military Campaigns*, Beijing: National Defense University Press, May 2000.

Whiting, A., *The Chinese Calculus of Deterrence: India and Indochina*, Ann Arbor: University of Michigan Press, 1975.

Whitson, W. and Huang, C., *The Chinese High Command: A History of Communist Military Politics, 1927–71*, New York: Praeger Publishers, 1973.

Wortzel, L. (ed.), *The Chinese Armed Forces in the 21st Century*, Carlisle, Pa.: Strategic Studies Institute, 1999.

Note: RAND documents can be found at http://www.rand.org/publications/electronic/interpol.html (accessed 3 April 2005); Strategic Studies Institute documents can be found at http://www.carlisle.army.mil/ssi/pubs/list.cfm?topic=asia (accessed 3 April 2005).

INDEX